CONTROL YOUR DREAMS

CONTROL

How Lucid Dreaming Can Help You Uncover
Your Hidden Desires, Confront Your

YOUR

Hidden Fears, and Explore the Frontiers
of Human Consciousness

DREAMS

by Jayne Gackenbach
and Jane Bosveld

1817

Harper & Row, Publishers, New York
Grand Rapids, Philadelphia, St. Louis, San Francisco
London, Singapore, Sydney, Tokyo, Toronto

FIRST EDITION

Library of Congress Cataloging-in-Publication Data

Gackenbach, Jayne, 1946-
    Control your dreams: how lucid dreaming can help you uncover your hidden desires, confront your hidden fears, and explore the frontiers of human consciousness/by Jayne Gackenbach and Jane Bosveld.—1st ed.
        p.   cm.
    Includes index.
    ISBN 0-06-015933-2
    1. Dreams.   2. Success.   I. Bosveld, Jane.   II. Title.
BF1091.G28   1989
154.6'—dc20   89-45040

89   90   91   92   93   DT/HC   10   9   8   7   6   5   4   3   2   1

To Our Parents

Contents

Part Two: Biology and Consciousness

Foreword

Jayne Gackenbach and Jane Bosveld have done all of us who are interested in our inner lives a great service in writing this book. Modern sleep research has shown that we spend about 20 percent of our sleep in the dream state, or about an hour and a half for an eight-hour sleeper. If you could dramatically improve the quality of that dream life, it would be like increasing the life expectancy of your *conscious* life by 10 percent. That's quite an improvement! What is this improvement?

From the perspective of the waking state, most dreams are, to put it bluntly, stupid. We are not mentally clear in them. We don't recognize the reality of our situation, namely that we are dreaming, not in the ordinary physical world, and we don't have our full waking skills and powers of observation, memory, reason, volition, etc. Dreams can sometimes be unpleasant or boring, but we usually cannot do anything about frustrating dream situations we could handle easily in our waking state. True, you may be able to learn things about yourself from *retrospectively* analyzing dreams in your later waking state, but the dream experience itself is too often dull, frustrating, and pointless in comparison with waking consciousness.

In 1913 a Dutch physician, Frederik Van Eeden, shared an amazing discovery with the world: you could *awaken* in your dreams! Instead of dreaming being a rather passive and dim-witted event, you could not only appreciate your dreams more but actively turn them into adventures to your liking, ranging from flying over the most beautiful countrysides to conjuring up an absolutely real-seeming discussion with your favorite philosopher or deceased friend. The quality of your consciousness would be *lucid*, clear, much more like the waking consciousness you are experiencing right now than typical dreaming consciousness. Even though your mind felt clear and you knew you were actually dreaming, the dream world around you would remain perfectly real to your senses.

Of course multitudes of people have independently discovered the existence of lucid dreaming for themselves by spontaneously having a lucid dream. Such people tend to have only isolated personal knowledge, however, and do not reap the benefits and broadening that come from sharing knowledge with others. The major historical exception to this is Tibetan Buddhism, where a detailed knowledge of developing and using lucid dreams has existed for centuries, but this knowledge (covered in this book) was inaccessible to us until recently. Frederik Van Eeden was one of the first Westerners to "publicly" discover lucid dreaming by sharing his knowledge through publication.

Many of us think the existence of lucid dreaming is indeed exciting and important, but the world didn't pay much attention in 1913. The *Proceedings of the Society for Psychical Research,* in which Van Eeden's article appeared, reached an audience of only a few hundred intellectuals who left few signs of reacting to the article.

In many ways the world wasn't ready to appreciate Van Eeden.

Most people regarded dreams as unworthy of serious attention. They were some sort of mental aberration resulting from disturbances of otherwise sound sleep, caused by what I once called the "pickled walnut" theory of dreaming; if you ate something as weird as pickled walnuts before retiring, your upset stomach would cause you to dream. The few intellectuals of the time who were interested in dreaming were caught up in Freud's theories that dreams were actually meaningful representations of negative unconscious processes; you might analyze them, but you didn't fool with them lest they not act as a "safety valve" to relieve troublesome instinctual pressures. Besides, the world was too enchanted with the progress of the physical sciences to be very interested in mental curiosities: as science helped us solve the problems of poverty and illness, all other problems would disappear.

By the 1960s we were beginning to discover that material progress and wealth weren't enough, even for those of us fortunate enough to have them. *Meaning* is the most important element in a happy life, a sense of understanding the nature of reality and its purpose, and your place in the scheme of things. While freedom from gross poverty and physical suffering is certainly desirable, simply acquiring more and more material goods didn't bring much happiness.

The 1960s brought us Eastern religions, biofeedback, sensory deprivation, meditation techniques, psychedelic drugs, and acid rock as reactions to the rampant materialism of our culture. Many of us wanted deeper experiences of life; we wanted to find deep values. Some, including me,[1] believed that various altered states of consciousness were rich places to seek them, for in an altered state we could temporarily see things from a different perspective and think and evaluate with different logics and emotions instead of endlessly recycling the same old waking-state perspective that seemed so lacking.

Many altered states are difficult or somewhat dangerous to achieve and explore, but there is one available to everyone: dreams. We now know, as detailed in this book, that everyone spends about 20 percent of their sleep time in a physiological state highly associated with dreaming, whether they remember their dreams or not. *If* we could learn to work with the altered state of dreaming, *if* we could sometimes make dreaming lucid, what possibilities might open for us?

I was one of the few people in the 1960s who knew of and appreciated Van Eeden. As a child I had suffered from occasional nightmares. I discovered lucid dreaming on my own as a way to cure my nightmares, so I knew its reality and its practical value. I was able to help rescue Van Eeden's discovery from oblivion by reprinting his article in my 1969 *Altered States of Consciousness*[2] anthology.

In the same book I also reprinted an article by psychologist Kilton Stewart, reporting that a whole tribe of Malaysian people, the Senoi, practiced lucid dreaming regularly and, apparently as a result, led very happy and mentally healthy lives. Contemporary research[3] has suggested that Stewart, at the disadvantage of working through translators, significantly exaggerated Senoi prowess in lucid dreaming, but the basic idea was both true and inspiring: by taking a more active, lucid role in your dreams, you can lead a more adventurous night life and psychologically grow by exploring this altered state. The *Altered States* book was a bestseller for a scientific book and spread the idea of lucidity widely.

While many people were inspired and tried, with varying degrees of success, to become lucid in their dreams, many others, especially in the scientific community, remained skeptical. How could the sleeping brain produce a fully awake consciousness that existed in the dream world? Perhaps lucid dreams were not real at all, or were just moments of vivid imagination (as if we understand imagination enough to casually devalue it!) during brief awakenings in the night?

The work of two independent research teams described in this book, however, Alan Worsley and Keith Hearne in England and Stephen LaBerge in California, clearly established that lucid dreams occur in the same physiological state as ordinary dreaming. The lucid dreamer is clearly physiologically asleep and dreaming, even if her consciousness is awake.

That's interesting to know, but what difference does it make to developing your own ability to dream lucidly?

We are a predominantly materialistic society that rather blindly worships science, and Big Science today is almost exclusively *physical* science. There is a strong attitude among both scientists and lay people that what is *real* is what is physical, chemical, electrical, physiological. This attitude permeates our culture and has important negative consequences for our psychological lives, as I've discussed elsewhere.[4]

With respect to dreams, they have been dismissed as unimportant, *merely* subjective, for a long time. The 1950s discovery that dreams occur in a specific physiological state—stage 1 brain waves and rapid eye movements—had a great "political" effect: dreams became "real" in the scientific community and it was legitimate to study them. Instead of hardly any scientists studying dreams (to the possible detriment of their careers), many scientists began to study them and adequate research support was available. Similarly, the discovery that lucid dreaming occurs in a physiological state made lucid dreaming "real" for many scientists and legitimized its study. This has resulted in many studies of various aspects of lucid dreams that might not otherwise have occurred: what are they like, what kind of people have them, how effective are various techniques for inducing them, etc.

Personally I think it's silly that mental events have to be "physiologized" to legitimize their study, but since the knowledge gained from those studies is useful to all of us, it's fine that it has happened. It is also poor science to insist on physiologizing;[5] it poses a major obstacle to understanding and developing our psychological and spiritual lives.

Gackenbach and Bosveld have written a fascinating book to share our current knowledge of lucid dreaming. It is particularly useful in being solidly based on the latest scientific knowledge, as well as clearly written. The authors also have a wide perspective. This book does not just list dry scientific facts about lucid dreaming; it puts them in the perspective of what lucid dreaming can mean to the individual and to society in both psychological and spiritual terms. The result is fascinating. Pleasant dreams!

Charles T. Tart

University of California
Davis, California

and

Institute of Noetic Sciences
Sausalito, California

REFERENCES

1.   Tart, C. Science and the sources of value. In *Phoenix: New Directions in the Study of Man*, 1979, 3, 25–29.
2.   Tart, C. (Ed.) *Altered States of Consciousness: A Book of Readings*. New York: John Wiley & Sons, 1969.
3.   Domhoff, W. *The Mystique of Dreams: A Search for Utopia through Senoi Dream Theory*. Berkeley, California: University of California Press, 1985.
4.   Tart, C. *Open Mind, Discriminating Mind: Reflections on Human Possibilities*. San Francisco: Harper & Row, 1989.
5.   Tart, C. States of consciousness and state-specific sciences. *Science*, 1972, *176*, 1203–1210.

Acknowledgments

This is the last piece of writing to be done on this book, so I'm not absolutely sure whether to acknowledge and thank the people who are responsible for it or curse them. But hey, at this point, it seems like the same thing. According to the stories I've been told —and this is the least researched information in the book—the idea for the project came from Harper & Row editor Craig Nelson, who during lunch with literary agent Barbara Lowenstein said, "I think it's time for another book on dreams." Barbara, who can recognize a book contract at a hundred paces, agreed. As soon as she got back to her office, she called Dick Teresi, an editor at *Omni,* and said, "Who did that lucid dreaming story you ran?" Dick, whose steel-trap mind suddenly developed a hole, said, "Call Jane." I was not the editor who thought up the idea of running a lucid dreaming experiment—Pamela Weintraub was— but I certainly wasn't going to tell Barbara that. A few weeks later, I was at the annual meeting of the Association for the Study of Dreams and ran into Jayne Gackenbach, who had collaborated on the *Omni* project. She asked me what I was doing at the conference, was *Omni* planning to do more on dreams? I told her, yeah, that we were always looking for another good dream story, but that I was also there gathering information for a book. She looked at me and said that she, too, was working on a book on dreams. It was opportunistic love at first sight. We spoke on the phone later and were off and running.

Once we got going, it was remarkably smooth sailing, thanks largely to the support of friends, modems, veterinarians, and coeditors at *Omni*. Speaking of the latter, not all top editors like the idea of their editors working on outside projects, so it was my good luck that Patrice Adcroft, *Omni*'s editor, gave her support. Thanks, Patti, and may all your dreams—and everybody else's— be lucid.

JANE BOSVELD

Twelve years ago along the James River outside of Richmond, Virginia, I began to experience an unusual dream state called lucid dreaming. The dreams were probably a reaction to the illness and subsequent death of a friend of mine, an eighty-five-year-old woman who until her death lived in a log cabin close to the land that she had loved and nurtured for more than fifty years. Professionally I was at the point in my doctoral training where I was expected to pick a dissertation topic. It occurred to me that these rarely studied dreams would be interesting to investigate. With the financial and moral support of the Association for Research and Enlightenment, in nearby Virginia Beach, Virginia, I embarked on a career of investigating consciousness in sleep. After receiving my doctoral degree from Virginia Commonwealth University with a dissertation on dream lucidity, my investigations took me briefly to the hills of western Pennsylvania at Clarion State College and to the rolling plains of Iowa. There, at the University of Northern Iowa, I spent nine years researching lucid dreaming and, with the help of colleagues at Maharishi International University in Fairfield, Iowa, other forms of consciousness in sleep. This book was written with the support of both the University of Northern Iowa and the University of Alberta, where I spent my sabbatical year.

The colleagues and friends who have guided and advised me in these dozen years of research and theorizing about consciousness in sleep are too numerous to mention. Nonetheless I want to be sure to acknowledge a few who have contributed both directly and indirectly to my work on lucid dreaming: Kathy Belicki, Fariba Bogzaran, Erik Craig, Bob Cranson, Joe Dane, Gayle Delaney, Robert Dentan, Rita Dwyer, Patricia Garfield, Albert Gilgen, George Gillespie, Gordon Globus, Milt Kramer, Stan Krippner, Don Kuiken, Judith Malamud, Scott Sparrow, Vera Sullivan, Charles Tart, Paul Tholey, Mary Tuttle, Bob Van de Castle, and Alan Worsley. I'd like to thank these individuals, as well as others unnamed, for their guidance and assistance. There are four close colleagues whose friendship in the form of professional advice as well as personal support has been most influential in developing my ideas about consciousness in sleep. They are Skip Alexander, Stephen LaBerge, Alan Moffitt, and most especially Harry Hunt, without whom this book would not exist.

Finally, to my family and friends who have put up with my single-minded obsession with consciousness in sleep—thank you for your tolerance and support. But especially I acknowledge the love, tolerance, advice, and general support of my husband and colleague, Thomas Snyder. He has been both intellectually and emotionally there for me from the beginning of my work in our log cabin in Virginia, through the many years in Iowa, and now in Canada.

JAYNE GACKENBACH

What's in a Dream?

This book is about a special type of dream, a dream in which you realize that you are dreaming, not after you awaken and think to yourself, "Oh, that was a dream," but one in which you say to yourself while in the dream, "Oh, I'm *dreaming*!" These dreams are called lucid dreams, and though not everyone has had one, most people can learn to have one. We will tell you how.

This book is also about why you may want to have one. It details how lucid dreaming can enhance your psychological well-being and perhaps influence your health. It is an exploration of how lucid dreams challenge our notions of what is real and what is illusion, and about what it means, after all, to be conscious.

This book is about the evolution of the human mind as revealed in the scientific study of the lucid dream.

PART ONE

THE JOURNEY BEGINS

Chapter 1

Conversations in the Night

THE MEANING AND POWER OF DREAMS

_Perhaps there are other worlds more
real than the waking world._
—MARCEL PROUST

Awake we define the landscapes of our lives. We decide what ideas to embrace, whose hand to hold, what to name the cat. We choose to notice stock market fluctuations or the passing of constellations through seasonal skies. Our genetic inheritance and the happenstance of our surroundings intertwine, creating continually what we believe to be ourselves. But the cartography of waking consciousness is only part of who we are. Another world exists in the three pounds of matter that form our minds. We close our eyes and drift into it each night, letting go of what we know out of biological necessity. And many of us rarely pay attention to what transpires there, as inattentive to our dreams as a bored postal worker separating letters into zip codes.

If that were to change, if we were to look more closely at our dreamworlds, we might discover terrain as varied and compelling as any we have known while awake. And once honed, our night vision could reveal the architecture of futuristic cities, the voice of a friend long dead, the attics of homes we once knew and have buried out of reach of waking memory. We might glimpse the spaceships of an alien culture, smell the sweet familiar scent of ripe corn, or spend an evening listening to the pulse of drumbeats around a tribal fire. The roads of our dreamworlds run through both space and time, linking what we have known with what we have imagined, illuminating the movement of our lives in a rich brocade of metaphor.

Our dreams can release us from reality. A group of survivors of Hitler's concentration camps reported having had few dreams of horror during their imprisonment. Instead, they told of happy dreams, about the good times they once had had or the joy that would again be theirs when they were freed from Auschwitz, Dachau, or Bergen–Belsen. But like political regimes, dreams can also entrap us: Some people suffer a lifetime of repetitive nightmares, so terrifying that sleep itself becomes an enemy.

We are born again each night in our dreams. Paradoxically, we may often disown them, unable to make sense of and therefore casting off the strange, illusive images of night. But that to some degree is a product of our culture. In many ancient societies the dream was believed to be a nocturnal counterpart to waking life, alive with secret knowledge and spiritual enlightenment. A great hunter might discover game in a dream and then use that knowledge to lead his tribe to nourishment. Many primal people continue this tradition. The Arapesh of New Guinea, the Tarahumara (Raramuri) of Mexico, the American Zuni, and tribes of the Great Plains still look to dreams for guidance.

In western European cultures, the value placed upon dreams has gone through many transformations. The ancient Greeks and Romans visited dream temples searching for voices of the gods to heal or instruct them. A literature of dream interpretations arose: To dream of drinking muddy water, laughing, or eating sweets was a sign of illness; to dream of weeping or being beaten or even having one's throat cut meant good luck. By the Middle Ages things had changed. Dreams were more often thought to be the work of the devil than of God. "Thou shalt not suffer a witch to live," the Bible demanded. It might also have included "or those who pay attention to their dreams."

As blind belief gave way to reason, dreams became the tools of philosophers who saw in them riddles of consciousness. "No one has any certainty apart from faith," wrote Pascal, "whether he wake or sleep." Descartes saw the same uncertainty between waking and dreaming. Writers, too, found another world in the dream. Emerson wrote that dreams "seem to suggest an abundance and fluency of thought not familiar to the waking experience. They pique us by independence of us, yet we know ourselves in this mad crowd, and owe to dreams a kind of divination and wisdom. My dreams are not me; they are not Nature; . . . they are both."

It was not until the nineteenth century that dreams were examined scientifically as entities in themselves. Early investigations into the neurobiology of the brain led to a host of theories about the origins and purposes of dreaming. Researchers used themselves as scientific subjects, recording their dreams and conducting experiments to see what might influence the content of night consciousness. Did nightmares follow spicy meals? Were dreams of falling caused by a foot dropped and dangling from the bed? The father of modern dream interpretation, Sigmund Freud, saw dreams as the unconscious mind unmasked. Analyze your dreams, he said, and you will discover the reasons for your distress, the buried voice of your soul. Freud's publication of *The Interpretation of Dreams* ushered in a new era of dream research that was to dominate thinking on sleep and dreams for nearly half a century. Gradually people accepted his idea that dreams were messages from the unconscious and that paying attention to them was the key to understanding the human mind.

The biology of dreaming, however, remained something of a mystery through the first half of this century. Scientists for the most part thought that the brain was dormant during sleep, that dreams were purely psychological in nature. Then, in 1953, an event occurred that proved otherwise. While doing sleep research in the laboratory of the noted sleep researcher Nathaniel Kleitman, an ambitious graduate student, Eugene Aserinsky, began studying the way children's eyes moved during sleep. It was a particularly tedious job that entailed counting the various eye movements of a number of youngsters. As is so often the case in scientific experiments, patience paid off in the end and Aserinsky found what appeared to be a quite regular pattern of eye movements in all the children. After running the same experiment on adults—this time using an electrical device to record the eye movements—he discovered that after about an hour and a half, the slow, regular eye movements of sleep suddenly changed into rapid and jerky ones. This burst of activity lasted for up to a half hour or more. Aserinsky and Kleitman began monitoring other physiological responses and found that during these periods of rapid eye movements (REM), heart and respiration rates rose and brain-wave patterns changed, suggesting that for some reason the nervous system had become aroused. It was the researchers' next finding that electrified the scientific community: Subjects who were awakened during the periods of rapid eye movements almost always reported vivid dreams. Years later, researchers discovered that if subjects were awakened during other stages of sleep, they also frequently reported thoughtlike sequences or dreamlets, but it was during REM sleep that the elaborate dramas we think of as dreams most regularly occurred.

Since Aserinsky and Kleitman's discovery, the study of the biological aspects of dreaming has dominated sleep and dream research. Humans, scientists have found, are not the only dreamers in the animal kingdom: all mammals, except one, experience rapid eye movement sleep and, if deprived of that sleep, make up for it the next night with longer REM cycles. The one mammal that doesn't experience REM sleep—the echidna, or spiny anteater, of Australia—happens to sport a prefrontal cortex proportionally larger than that of humans. One researcher theorizes that this primitive mammal's huge cortex, long believed to be the hallmark of highly intelligent animals, evolved to handle the processing of waking material and that other mammals developed the capacity to dream in order to process much of that information in "downtime," or nighttime, sleep.

Other research revealed that REM bursts originate in the brain stem, an area of the brain devoid of logical thought processes. This finding led Harvard Medical School psychiatrist J. Allan Hobson and colleague Robert W. McCarley to suggest that dreams have little to do with unconscious thought. Rather, they are random images that the sleeping mind makes sense of by incorporating into elaborate stories. In other words, dreams arise to structure unrelated mental images that are produced spontaneously by the brain. Nobel laureate Francis Crick and his colleague Graeme Mitchison have gone even further, suggesting that dreams are nothing more than the excess residue of waking life. The dreaming brain, according to their hypothesis, is akin to a garbage truck, first collecting and then dumping waking refuse. And like all junk, dreams are best forgotten.

Not surprisingly, Crick and Mitchison's theory received a less than positive response from many researchers. Psychiatrist Gordon Globus, author of *Dream Life, Wake Life*, for example, had this to say about it.

> I would be more inclined to take this polemic seriously if Crick and Mitchison gave us reason to think that they had ever honestly labored at the "clinical bench," open-mindedly studying their own dreams or the dreams of others. Their position that dreams are at heart mechanical, meaningless productions is based on predilection, unmitigated by contact with dream data. Clinicians are better informed, simply because of their extensive experience in working with actual dreams. And most everyone who seriously studies their own dreams . . . finds them personally meaningful.

Indeed, clinical research provides strong evidence that paying attention to dreams is important. Rosalind Cartwright, a *tour de force* in dream psychology, has demonstrated in numerous studies that dreams provide direct access to the key emotional issues of our lives. They help us to cope with depression and function as a "mechanism" for psychological healing. And Donald Kuiken, of the University of Alberta in Canada, has documented the impact that dream emotions have on waking thoughts and feelings.

Nevertheless, the physiological theories of dreaming such as Hobson and McCarley's have set a heavy task before the many dream researchers who believe that dreaming is more than the sum of its physiological parts. As Alan Moffitt, a developmental psychologist at Carleton University in Canada, points out, contemporary dream psychology must now define an "intellectual base" to justify the clinically and popularly accepted notion that working with dreams is good for you. Similarly, David Foulkes, one of today's leading dream theorists, argues that both psychoanalysis and the psychophysiological study of dreaming have failed to provide a satisfying explanation of dreaming. He proposes a "call to mental arms" to rescue the dream from the limitations of psychoanalysis and the bleak restrictions of a purely biological definition.

"Dreaming," he writes in *A Grammar of Dreams*, "must be seen as something more than anomalous perceiving. It is a human conceptual achievement of the first magnitude, and one of the core problems of cognitive psychology. Dreaming needs once again, as it was by Freud, to be recognized as a problem so central to the study of the mind that its resolution can help to reveal the fundamental structures of human thought."

Most contemporary dream scientists agree that dreaming needs to be incorporated into a larger theory of mind, that it must be understood as a complex symbolic activity that complements waking thought. Toward that goal, Globus has drawn on the recent information-processing theory of connectionism to explain why dreams are not only meaningful but also the most harmonious and orderly solution to our waking problems. The theory of connectionism proposes that our brains pass along information through a web of neurons, or neural networks, and that these networks determine how we respond to incoming information. When the millions of neurons and their connections are jiggled by stimuli—by words, sounds, or smells in the waking world, or by memories of those events during dreaming—they process the information, eventually "settling" to a place of harmony. While asleep that harmonious place is the dream.

This settling out of information can be likened to a game found in many indoor amusement parks in which children dive into a room filled with lightweight balls. As a child (the stimulus, or daily memory) hits the balls (the neurons), they scatter, popping up in the air. Each ball moves as it is hit by the balls surrounding it. In a few moments, all the balls and the child come to rest, each finding its secure niche. This niche may mean that the child's head is buried underneath the balls or that his or her body is covered with them. The system of balls and child settles out in a harmonious fashion. Harmony in this sense is not necessarily good (the child's head on top of the balls) or bad (the child's head beneath the balls); it is simply the place in which all the balls and the child come to rest. Certain constrictions do exist in this system such as the number of balls, the number of kids jumping into the balls, the buoyancy of the balls. Most kids find the experience of jumping into the balls fun, while some adults have commented that they found it scary. In all cases, though, the balls settle to the best "fit" just as waking experience and memories settle into dreams.

As the scientific dialogue concerning the function and meaning of dreams has evolved, the concept of consciousness in the apparent unconscious state of sleep has begun to dominate the field. In fact, Foulkes has recently gone so far as to state that "dreaming reveals not the unconscious but the conscious." Much of the excitement about consciousness in sleep is due to the examination of the unique dream experience that is the subject of this book—lucid dreaming. Simply put, a lucid dream is a dream in which, to greater or lesser degrees, you are aware, or conscious, that you are dreaming. Many, perhaps most, people have suddenly realized during a dream that they are dreaming, but the thought typically dissolves quickly, overpowered by the compelling imagery of the dream. Some individuals, however, "wake up" within the dream; they realize they are dreaming and at the same time can recall their waking lives. It is an experience rich with emotion, charged with the *wow* of a spectacular view rarely glimpsed, of an altered state of consciousness naturally induced. Depending on the nature of the experience, the lucid dreamer may be a passive observer or an active participant, perhaps directing the actions of the dream. "Lucidity enables the further development of intentional action within the dream state," explains Moffitt. "In effect, one can develop a new form of competence, a type of skill not available during the waking state."

Lucid dreaming calls into question our understanding of what it means to be awake. As Moffitt and his colleague Robert Hoffman write, "Cognitive psychology can no longer make the assumption that being awake has a clearly defined, unequivocal meaning."

To be awake within a dream is to feel oneself in a profoundly different reality, another world that bridges waking and sleeping consciousness. You are "in" the dream *and* "outside" of it all at once. Obviously, this duality can create both confusion and curiosity in people not familiar with lucid dreaming. For example, Steve Fox, the managing editor of *Omni* magazine, had his first adult lucid dream last year. "I was walking along the water at the beach in my hometown," he writes, "when suddenly I took off and began to fly above the water, with my hands stretched out in front of me like Superman. At this point, I realized that I was dreaming. I felt euphoric. After a few minutes, I started to wonder what position my body was in back in bed—specifically whether my arms were outstretched. My curiosity became more urgent until I decided to wake myself up to find out. Upon awakening, I discovered I had been sleeping on my stomach with my arms stretched out under the pillow."

Fox regretted letting his curiosity interrupt and end his lucid dream. But, like many novice lucid dreamers, he had to return to the waking state to ground himself. If and when he finds himself once again awake within a dream, he will be more familiar with the territory and perhaps be able to explore it further without retreating to waking consciousness. Indeed, lucid dreaming requires experience and daring to glean fully the knowledge that comes with this most unusual exploration of the imagination.

Historically, there have been a number of such explorations. In the nineteenth century, the Marquis d'Hervey de Saint-Denys, a French professor of Chinese literature, published the first serious work on dreams and dream control. From the age of thirteen Saint-Denys regularly recorded his dreams in both word and picture, amassing in just the first five years twenty-two volumes of material. A scientist at heart, Saint-Denys carried out many experiments in an effort to understand his nocturnal ruminations and how he might manipulate them. He developed the ability to turn lucid within dreams and found he was able to design an experiment while awake and carry it out after turning lucid in a dream. "While dreaming," he writes in his book *Dreams and How To Guide Them*, "I was often conscious of my true situation; I retained some impression of the preoccupations of the day before, and as a result had sufficient control of my ideas to guide their further development in whatever direction I chose."

He found that his dreams became more coherent as he exercised control of them. He rid them of unpleasant thoughts, tumultuous desires, and painful images. "The fear of disagreeable visions weakens as we perceive how foolish it is," he explains, "and the desire to see agreeable ones becomes more active as we develop a growing power to induce them of our own accord. Thus the desire becomes stronger than the fear; and, since the dominant idea is what produces the images, the agreeable dream triumphs."

He cites numerous dreams in which conscious control of the dream produces the images he desired. In one,

I dream I have discovered great magical secrets by means of which I can call up the shades of the dead and also transform men and things according to my desires and will. First, I call up two people who died several years ago, whose images now appear in faithful detail and with the utmost clarity. I wish to see an absent friend and immediately see him lying asleep on a sofa. I change a porcelain vase into a rock-crystal fountain, from which I desire a cooling drink—and this immediately flows out through a golden tap. Some years ago I lost a particular ring whose loss I felt deeply. The memory of it comes into my mind, and I should like to find it. I utter this wish, fixing my attention on a piece of coal that I pick up from the fireplace—and immediately the ring is in my fingers.

Although Saint-Denys's book is somewhat difficult to obtain today (an English translation does exist), it was not readily available even in his day. Freud failed to obtain a copy, much to his regret. But he heard sufficient detail about Saint-Denys's work to call him "the most energetic opponent of those who seek to depreciate psychical functioning in dreams." Although no evidence exists that Freud himself ever had a lucid dream, he took the word of others that it was indeed possible to be aware that one was dreaming. "There are some people," he wrote in *The Interpretation of Dreams*, "who are quite clearly aware during the night that they are asleep and dreaming and who thus seem to possess the faculty of consciously directing their dreams. If, for instance, a dreamer of this kind is dissatisfied with the turn taken by a dream, he can break it off without waking up and start it again in another direction—just as a popular dramatist may under pressure give his play a happier ending."

Still, Saint-Denys's studies failed to impress many of the leading sleep and dream researchers of the nineteenth and early twentieth centuries. Havelock Ellis denied that lucid dreams could actually be dreams, and French psychologist Alfred Maury, who by some accounts was the first person to conduct personal dream experiments, also doubted their existence, in part because he himself had never had one, a blind spot still frequently seen in contemporary dream researchers.

For other scientific explorers of the night, venturing comment upon such unusual realities as lucid dreaming was approached with caution. Early in this century, Dutch physician Frederik Willems Van Eeden decided that the best way to broach the subject was in a novel. The fictional form, he said, would allow him "to freely deal with delicate matters, and had also the advantage that it expressed rather unusual ideas in a less aggressive way." Eventually, though, Van Eeden grew braver and planned to produce a scientific work. No such book exists, but he did leave behind a

brilliant paper on the subject which he presented in 1913 to the
Society for Psychical Research, a British organization dedicated to
examining esoteric phenomena. In that paper, Van Eeden labels
the experience "lucid" dreaming and describes in detail his own
adventures with consciousness in dreams. "I obtained my first
glimpse of this lucidity during sleep in June, 1897," he explains.
"I dreamt that I was floating through a landscape with bare trees,
knowing that it was April, and I remarked that the perspective of
the branches and twigs changed quite naturally. Then I made the
reflection, during sleep, that my fancy would never be able to
invent or to make an image as intricate as the perspective movement of little twigs seen in floating by." With that realization,
Van Eeden turned lucid.

Compelled by the scientist's desire to explain, Van Eeden conducted numerous experiments to define the scope and nature of
lucid dreaming. The following is an example of his dream experiments:

> I drew with my finger, moistened by saliva, a wet cross on the palm
> of my left hand, with the intention of seeing whether it would still be
> there after waking up. Then I dreamt that I woke up and felt the wet
> cross on my left hand by applying the palm to my cheek. And then a
> long time afterwards I woke up really and knew at once that the hand
> of my physical body had been lying in a closed position undisturbed
> on my chest all the while.

Like many of today's lucid dreamers, Van Eeden was fascinated
with the sensations of his voice within the dream. "I use my voice
as loudly as I can," he explained, "and though I know quite well
that my physical body is lying in profound sleep, I can hardly
believe that this loud voice is inaudible in the waking world." But
though he sang, shouted, and pontificated loudly in any number
of lucid dreams, his wife, who shared his bed through all of
his experimenting, never once was awakened or if awake herself never heard him utter a word out loud. "In these lucid
dreams . . . ," Van Eeden says, "the sleeper remembers day-life
and his own condition, reaches a state of perfect awareness and is

able to direct his attention, and to attempt different acts of free volition. Yet the sleep, as I am confidently to state, is undisturbed, deep and refreshing."

Van Eeden and Saint-Denys were not alone in their interest in dream consciousness and its potential for control. French biologist Yves Delage conducted his own exploration of lucid dreaming, as did Englishwoman Mary Arnold-Forster, who learned to remember her dreams by instructing herself before falling asleep to take heed of what transpired, a technique that has since been used by many people interested in recalling their dreams. Arnold-Forster also learned to recognize the bizarre elements in dreams, an ability that served to trigger enough conscious awareness that she awakened and gained even more immediate access to the content of her dreams. For whatever reasons, though, her proficiency at dream control never allowed her a sustained experience of lucid dreaming.

A contemporary of Arnold-Forster, Englishman Hugh Calloway, who wrote under the name of Oliver Fox, delved much deeper into lucid dreaming. The description of his first experience with lucidity (at age sixteen) echoes the excitement expressed by many novice lucid dreamers. "Instantly, upon turning lucid," he writes, "the vividness of life increased a hundred-fold. Never had sea and sky and trees shone with such glamourous beauty; even the commonplace houses seem alive and mystically beautiful. Never had I felt so absolutely well, so clear-brained, so inexpressibly *free*! The sensation was exquisite beyond words; but it lasted only a few minutes and I awoke."

Unaware of Van Eeden's name for these dreams that occurred in an altered state of dream consciousness, Calloway called them "dreams of knowledge." Similarly, a number of years later Russian philosopher P. D. Ouspensky referred to lucid dreams as "half-dream states." He beautifully describes one such dream.

Besides myself there was in the room only a small black kitten. "I am dreaming," I say to myself. "How can I know whether I am really asleep or not? Suppose I try this way. Let this black kitten be transformed into a large white dog. In a waking state it is impossible and if it comes off it will mean that I am asleep." I say this to myself and immediately the black kitten becomes transformed into a large white dog. At the same time the opposite wall disappears, disclosing a mountain landscape with a river like a ribbon receding into the distance. "This is curious," I say to myself; "I did not order this landscape. Where did it come from?" Some faint recollection begins to stir in me, a recollection of having seen this landscape somewhere and of its being somehow connected with the white dog. But I feel that if I let myself go into it I shall forget the most important thing that I have to remember, namely, *that I am asleep and am conscious of myself.* . . .

A number of other scientists and philosophers wrote descriptions or papers about lucid dreaming, but it was the 1968 publication in England of Celia Green's classic book *Lucid Dreams* as well as psychologist Charles Tart's reprinting of Van Eeden's paper in his book *Altered States* in this country a year later that introduced a large reading public to the phenomenon. For many people, though, it was through the 1972 publication of Carlos Castaneda's *Journey to Ixtlan* that they first learned of lucid dreaming. In the book, the sorcerer Don Juan teaches Castaneda's main character how to lucid dream. "Become accessible to power; tackle your dreams," instructs Don Juan. Referring to the lucid dream state as "*dreaming*," Don Juan describes its importance. "In *dreaming* you have power; you can change things; you may find out countless concealed facts; you can control whatever you want." To harness this power, the sorcerer tells his pupil to look at his hands in his dreams; this will awaken consciousness within the dream. Or, explains Don Juan, "pick anything at all. But pick one thing in advance and find it in your dreams. I said your hands because they'll always be there. . . . When they begin to change shape you must move your sight away from them and pick something else, and then look at your hands again." Lucid dream researchers have since verified the effectiveness of this technique in inducing lucidity.

Adding to the popular interest in dreams was the best-selling book by Patricia Garfield called *Creative Dreaming*. In it she provided readers with an extensive description of lucid dreaming as well as other forms of dream control. For the first time, the general public had a guidebook to their dreams.

Surprisingly, the scientific study of lucid dreams lagged, for the most part, somewhat behind popular interest. It was not until the mid-1970s that researchers began to take a serious look at what this strange phenomenon was all about. The first milestone came when two groups of researchers, one in England, the other in the United States, independently discovered that lucid dreamers could communicate with the outside world by moving their eyes in a predetermined fashion while in the midst of a lucid dream. Both groups carried out their experiments in laboratories with their subjects hooked to machines that charted the stage of sleep the dreamer was in when he signaled. In each case, the dreamer was in REM sleep when he signaled. This surprising finding, which is detailed in Part Two, gave scientists their first entry into the private world of dreams and spawned a new era in the study of dreaming. It was now possible to identify when a subject in a dream laboratory was lucid dreaming and to chart the physiological changes associated with the state.

Paralleling the discovery of preset eye movements as a signal from the lucid dream state was a change in attitude among dream researchers. David Foulkes's "call to mental arms" was taken up by serious dream researchers. Sociological ingredients also spurred interest in lucidity. There now exists a "dreamwork" movement, in which individuals band together to study their dreams. To some degree the resurgence of interest in dreams was an outgrowth of the post-World War II baby boom generation. In the 1960s this generation rebelled against what they saw as the rampant materialism of twentieth-century America. They cast off the shackles of organized Christianity and turned to Eastern religions in their search for spiritual meaning. During the seventies, interest in Buddhism, Hinduism, Taoism, mystical Christianity, and Sufism filled bookshops with new translations of religious and philosophical texts. Courses in Chinese and Indian philosophy were filled to capacity, and meditation groups sprang up across the country. The desire for meaning on a very personal level had reinstated itself. Today, as the parents of this generation pass away, as death becomes a reality that each individual must make peace with, the interest in the spiritual continues. What happens after death? Does the soul survive? Does it reincarnate? The surge of interest in dreams and lucid dreaming in particular may to some degree reflect the need to answer these questions. But the fascination with dreams also reflects our desire to explore and understand ourselves as beings whose lives do not end when we turn off the lights and close our eyes. We are curious about the shadows of our souls that peak out at us in dreams. We want to see them more clearly.

SHADOW PLAY

As with most highly charged or unusual experiences, lucid dreams are rarely forgotten. What is it about lucid dreaming that creates such an indelible effect? Is there something intrinsic in the experience that makes it stick in the mind? Because most of us have not experienced the thrill of a full-blown lucid dream, one in which our awareness that we're dreaming permeates an entire dream or allows us to direct the contents of it, we must turn to the testimony of others for the answer. Psychotherapist Kenneth Kelzer writes in his autobiographical book about lucid dreaming called *The Sun and the Shadow* that "there is a definite 'energy shift,' a 'rise in consciousness,' a feeling of 'expansion' or 'awakening' accompanied by a strong mental clarity" in lucid dreams.

Other lucid dreamers talk about the thrill of observing their own dreams as if they were making a movie, of creating a fantasy and watching it unfold all at the same time. In a 1985 conference on lucidity held at the University of Virginia, a panel of veteran lucid dreamers reported on their dream histories. Most of the panelists' lucid dreams tallied in the hundreds, often first appearing in childhood and then coming in clusters at various times in their lives. For all the participants lucid dreaming had become an intrinsic part of their lives. They felt enriched, perhaps enlightened, by the clarity and emotionally charged atmosphere of lucid dreams; they had also reclaimed a good portion of their lives (one-third of a human life is spent sleeping).

Lucid dreaming often evolves, beginning with short bursts of awareness that can come to dominate the dream. Those who cultivate lucidity often play with it, learning new skills and testing the limits of the state. "I learned to fly very fast and very high," explains Daryl E. Hewitt of San Francisco, "to pass through walls, including steel, and to burn holes through them with laser from my fingertips, to study the lucid dream environment in exquisite close-up detail, explore other planets, and especially to alter the dream environment at will, as in making things appear, disappear, and change shape and color."

But Hewitt noticed that after about five years of "such truly memorable experiences," he began to run out of things to do in his lucid dreams. Like many a lucid dreamer before him, he decided to conduct some experiments to see if he could improve the quality of his dreams. "On a half-dozen occasions I dreamed and managed to be undistracted by dream imagery long enough to practice deep, rhythmic breathing," he explains. "In each case awareness seemed to expand into an egg-shaped sphere which encompassed my dream body, with a corresponding dramatic intensification of consciousness. As this happened, colors flowed like pools of neon light in my inner vision, as they sometimes do in meditation and before falling asleep."

By willing within the lucid dream to engage in an activity strikingly similar to waking meditation, Hewitt reached a new level of lucidity, which he calls ecstatic lucid dreams. These dreams deliver him to a deeper level of consciousness best described as joyful or blissful. The parallels to the experiences of people who practice meditation while awake cannot be overlooked. Indeed, at virtually every level of analysis, there are strong links between lucid dreaming and meditation, links that may shed considerable light on the nature of human consciousness. The content of both experiences, for instance, can be quite similar, as are the personalities of meditators and lucid dreamers. The physiological changes that occcur in both meditative states and lucid dreaming also resemble one another. And, perhaps most important, the practice of meditation has been shown to increase the frequency of lucid dreams. In addition, both meditators and lucid dreamers can control the nature and content of their experience. The question is, why would someone choose to control their meditation or their dreams?

SO YOU WANT TO CONTROL YOUR DREAMS . . . WHY?

Books about dreams are filled with suggestions about how to influence the content of your dreams. Some people have been able to dream about flying simply by telling themselves before falling asleep that they want to fly in a dream. But control is not unlimited or always predictable. One of the authors of this book prompted herself before falling asleep to fly in her dreams and wound up on the outside of a rocket, holding on for dear life, as it blasted off. Not exactly the sort of flying she had in mind. Similarly, if the bogeyman is chasing you in a dream, you may be able to exert some control over what happens in the situation, but he may still come after you, whether or not you try to will him away. The important questions to ask are *why* do you want to do away with him and *should* you act on that desire?

Control is a concept entrenched in American society. From financial independence to freedom of religion, we want to be able to determine for ourselves what our lives will be like. This extends even to our dreams. If there is a way to control what we dream about, then why not learn to and perhaps get more of a handle on those odd experiences we have at night? Indeed, it is a compelling subject and one, if magazine sales are any indication, that people are fascinated by. The April 1987 issue of *Omni* magazine, for instance, was snatched up by hundreds of thousands of readers across the country. The cover read "How to Control Your Dreams." Other magazines, including *Psychology Today*, have scored successes with stories about dream control.

But control in psychological terms is not necessarily positive. It is often better to let go of our emotions than to keep them under tight reins. Dreams are by and large outside of our conscious control, revealing aspects of ourselves that we may not notice in our waking lives. We may be perplexed about what a dream means, but our questions may enlighten us: "Why did I have that dream? What does it mean? Why does it still bother me?" As Kuiken has said, "Dreams provide hints of a personal reality typically unknown—a personal reality which contrasts with everyday self-perception."

Our desire for dream control in some respects may be an unacknowledged effort to rid ourselves of disturbing emotions or behavior, but it may also be an expression of our desire to understand what we are at heart. We know that somewhere within our dreams, there may be hidden aspects of our deeper selves. As Globus puts it, "There is a mysterious dimension to our lives when we open up to it. . . ."

By learning to have lucid dreams we are enlarging our experience of the mysterious. When we actively enter our nocturnal imaginations, we create another definition of ourselves as creative beings. It's an endeavor not everyone will care to undertake, but for those who do, this book will provide a map and a scientific description of what you might encounter along the way.

Chapter 2

Inducing the Light

A GUIDE TO LEARNING HOW TO LUCID DREAM

Oneironauts, intrepid explorers of the dreamworld, have been hunting for a reliable and easy way to induce lucid dreaming for years. Early methods included scenting pillows with lilac, musk, or some other perfume to see which might arouse the sleeping brain, awakening it enough to obtain lucidity, but not too much to interfere with sleep. Investigators have had themselves hypnotized or awakened sporadically during the night to prod a lucid dream loose from the system. Others have suggested to themselves before falling asleep that they will have a lucid dream.

But finding a formula guaranteed to inspire the lucid muse has been more like hunting for the Holy Grail than mixing up a mental cocktail. What works for one person may not work for another. Nevertheless, researchers have remained undaunted by this surprisingly difficult task and have evolved a number of reliable, though certainly not universal, induction techniques. They are imperfect maps to a shadowy world, and as with terrestrial cartography, some maps are more elucidating than others. We hope our guide will lead you successfully to the lucid dream. Decidedly holistic in approach, it combines the work of a number of investigators and is designed to help you place all your dreams in context as well as to introduce you to the subject matter of this book.

BEGINNER'S MIND

Nan-in, a Japanese [Zen] master . . . received a university professor who came to enquire about Zen. Nan-in served tea. He poured his visitor's cup full, and then kept on pouring. The professor watched the overflow until he could no longer restrain himself. "It is overfull. No more will go in!" "Like this cup," Nan-in said, "you are full of your own opinions and speculations. How can I show you Zen unless you first empty your cup?"

—Paul Reps, *Zen Flesh, Zen Bones*

If, as we believe, lucid dreaming is strongly related to meditation, it should come as no surprise that by practicing meditation you may be able to induce lucid dreams. Studies of the dreams of meditators have supported the anecdotal evidence that meditators experience a significantly higher incidence of lucid dreams.

Gregory (Scott) Sparrow, author of the classic work *Lucid Dreaming: Dawning of the Clear Light,* was one of the first to note the connection between meditation annd lucid dreaming. "When lucidity began to arise with increasing regularity . . . I soon noticed that it emerged predictably after a deep or fulfilling meditation," he explains. "It became clear that when my devotional life was intense, lucid dreaming would arise as a concomitant. This relationship became more pronounced when I began meditating for fifteen or twenty minutes during the early morning hours (between two and five in the morning). As I would return to sleep, dreams of amazing clarity as well as brief periods of lucidity would occasionally ensue."

Since Sparrow's observation, other researchers have systematically examined what role meditation may play in inducing lucid dreaming. Psychologist Henry Reed, the first to conduct such a study, found that lucidity was more likely to occur on days when a subject had meditated than on days when he or she had not. Other researchers have also found this connection. In a number of studies with those who practice transcendental meditation (TM), Gackenbach and colleagues at Maharishi International University (MIU) have found that meditators consistently report more lucid dreams than control subjects.

Shamanic ceremonies, in which drumming and chanting are used to create a state similar to meditation, also increase the frequency of lucid dreams. For instance, Fariba Bogzaran, a psychology graduate student, discovered that when she entered a shamanic state through chanting or listening to drumbeats before falling asleep, she increased the number of lucid dreams from six or seven a month to about seventeen.

A word of caution about the techniques: Sparrow discovered that if he practiced meditation in the predawn hours for "attunement," lucid dreams consistently followed, but if he meditated in order to induce a lucid dream, he would fail to have one. "My dreams admonished me severely for such confounded motives!" he says. "I am slowly learning to tread gently."

Sparrow's lesson is echoed by Gyaltrul Rinpoche, a Tibetan Buddhist monk. In a discourse on the "Tibetan Yoga of the Dream State," Gyaltrul stresses that when attempting to gain consciousness in sleep, one must have motives that are transpersonal in nature. One should meditate, the monk explains, using Buddhist terminology, "for the sake of wanting to benefit all sentient beings in order to bring them temporary and permanent happiness." In other words, meditation should be virtuous, not self-promoting, in nature.

Although most of the studies in which meditation has been associated with lucidity have used TM meditators, it seems likely that what is true for TM will also be true of other meditation techniques. Indeed, all meditations strive for atonement, for the emptying of the "cup" and an expansion of awareness. Each varies in its approach and style. Some, for instance, present you with stories or koans to meditate upon; others instruct you to concentrate on your own breathing, letting all thoughts pass through your mind freely. Many books can help you get started, but it is no accident that all serious meditation schools stress the importance of a master or guide to help you in your endeavors. Unexpected feelings and emotions are sometimes aroused during meditation; a more experienced meditator can help you understand them.

DREAM WORK 101

Although some meditators claim that in general they do not remember their dreams nor care to, regarding them as yet another form of "illusion," studies have found that most meditators recall more dreams than the averge nonmeditator. But what about people who lack sufficient discipline or desire to meditate on a regular basis? How can they learn to induce a lucid dream? Both Gackenbach and psychologist Harry Hunt of Brock University in Canada have found that simply by remembering your dreams, you increase the likelihood of experiencing a lucid dream. In fact, in some cases high dream recallers have as many lucid dreams as meditators. Although the practice of meditation tends to improve one's dream recall, other ways have been shown to be effective in helping people remember their dreams. The secret seems to lie in the value one places on the dream itself. Not surprisingly, lucid dreamers are in touch with their sleeping minds. They not only recall their dreams but also are more likely than others to keep a dream journal, an indication that they value their dreams.

We all know that if we wish to remember something because it's important to us, we do so with greater success than if we try to remember something we don't particularly care about. It is difficult to remember dreams in part because we live in a society in which there is little regard for the dream. A good first step toward dream recall is associating with those who share your interest in dreams. A surprisingly easy candidate is your child. If given half a chance kids love to talk about their dreams, and setting up a time for dream telling is a good way to encourage both your child and yourself to remember dreams. (This also serves to encourage more openness and may make it easier for you and your child to discuss other private experiences.)

Also helpful are dream groups. These generally informal groups hold weekly meetings in which they share dreams and help one another to understand and "incubate" (encourage) the progression of certain themes or emotions being worked out in dreams. Psychologist Montague Ullman is one of the pioneers of dream groups. If you were to attend one of his groups, he would have you recount a dream without giving any sort of explanation of what you think the dream might mean. Then the other members of the group talk about your dream, what it makes them think of, how they associate meaning to it. After this you would enter into the discussion. Finally, you would choose which lines of thinking about your dream were most important. Ullman stresses this last step. After all, he says, the dreamer owns the dream, not the group or, for that matter, the therapist.

You need not share your dreams to remember them, however. One of the most prominent dream workers to experiment with various techniques for encouraging dream recall is Patricia Garfield. "If you regard your dreams as important and take time to recall them," she writes in her popular book *Creative Dreaming*, "they will come to you more easily and more often."

Here are a few hints from Garfield and other dream researchers who have learned to call forth dream memories.

- Prepare for the dream: Tell yourself before falling asleep that you want to and will remember your dreams. Keep a notebook and pen (perhaps one equipped with batteries and a small light) near your pillow or try telling them to a tape recorder.

- When you awaken after a dream, keep quiet, perhaps closing your eyes again to return to the dream in order to remember it. Let your mind wander.

- Upon awakening naturally (without an alarm or radio) let

your thoughts wander. Because you probably have awakened just after a REM cycle when dreams are most likely to have occurred, doing this will often recapture a dream. If you must awaken to an alarm and find that you aren't remembering any dreams, set the alarm back a half hour. This might awaken you from a different part of your sleep cycle.

• If you find yourself being distracted by external happenings —your three-year-old wants to talk—or by internal thoughts about what you have to do when you get out of bed, try setting aside a morning for dream recall when you're less likely to be disturbed.

• Keep your eyes closed while trying to recall dreams and rehearse the dreams in your mind's eye before opening your eyes. Outside images will disrupt those of your dreams.

• If none of the above steps helps you recall a dream, you can try setting an alarm in the middle of the night or ask a friend to awaken you at a specific time. Such unusual arousals may enable you to remember a dream.

Once you've been successful at recording some dreams, it's best to engage in a little analysis to become familiar with your dream symbols and what they represent in your waking life. Like meditation, psychotherapy is a form of self-observation that may help to integrate your feelings and actions and connect you with your dreams. When you analyze your dreams, you are also analyzing yourself.

Ullman and dream therapist Gayle Delaney have each written in-depth accounts on analyzing your dreams. They both emphasize asking questions as a way of getting at the heart and soul of your dreams. Try asking yourself the questions Delaney recommends in her dream analysis:

• When you reexperience the feelings you had in the dream, what do they remind you of in your current life?

• Do you have any ideas already in mind about the meaning of this dream?

• Describe the opening setting of the dream.

• Does it remind you of anything?

- Who is X, Y, and Z? (Describe the characters in the dream and your associations to them.)
- Is there some part of you that is like X, Y, and/or Z? (Even if your dream character is someone you despise, you may see some of his/her characteristics in yourself.)
- What is your waking relationship with X, Y, and Z?
- What are the major objects in the dream, and what are they used for or how do they work?
- What do the objects in your dream remind you of, and why are they important (or not important) to you?
- What are the major events or actions in the dream, and what do they remind you of in your waking life?

Although analysis alone won't necessarily lead you to a lucid dream, it creates a solid framework of self-reflection on which to move forward. Once you have examined the contents of your dreams and what they seem to mean, you will probably notice that certain objects or symbols reappear from time to time. You can then choose one of those symbols as a focal point for inducing lucidity. Say, for instance, that you frequently dream of a talking parrot. By saying to yourself during the day or before you fall asleep at night that the next time you see the parrot you will recognize you are dreaming, you may be able to trigger lucidity. As Jill Gregory, a dream worker from Novato, California, points out, "If you become familiar with the symbols and themes in your dreams, you will be more likely to recognize their significance in your waking life and recognize them as dream symbols while still asleep."

This sort of gentle conscious encouragement is a form of auto-suggestion and has been used with success by many people to produce lucid dreams. Another type of autosuggestion is to tell yourself before falling asleep that you want to dream about a particular theme or that you want to have a lucid dream. Garfield, for example, induced lucidity by simply telling herself before going to sleep, "Tonight, I will have a lucid dream."

Sparrow is somewhat wary of this technique by itself, stressing the importance of an appropriate cognitive strategy. "To the extent that one has continued to repress the awareness of unresolved, possibly painful pre-personal memories and issues (and that probably fits most of us to varying extents), the statement, 'I want to become lucid,' implies a paradox," he explains. "It seems to say: I am willing to become aware of what I've been unwilling to become aware of. How can we know ahead of time what we will suddenly perceive through our wide-open dream eyes? How can we know if we're ready for it?"

Sparrow illustrates the point by relating the experience of one of his clients who had been forced to take a day off work to recover from a disturbing lucid dream. In the dream, the woman "found an old flattened doll beneath a pile of rubbish, picked it up, and prelucidity thought, 'If I was this doll, I know what I'd like.' She began hugging and stroking the doll, and it came to life," he explains. "As it dawned on her that she was dreaming, she nonetheless felt deeply disturbed to realize that this 'doll' was indeed alive in some sense. One can appreciate the significance of her finding out that [the] abused child (very abused) was still alive (in her), but it was a fact that went against her ego definition. Wonderful facts can be devastating from the standpoint of a well-fortified ego. Knowing this woman, I feel that she was fortunate to have been in therapy when such 'good' news became conscious to her."

The point is clear: Do not force a state of mind that you may not be ready for. Work with all of your dreams and the personal issues they raise. If an image disturbs you, try to figure out why. If a dream frightens you, talk about it with a friend. Most of us have not been taught to work with the dark side of ourselves, which sometimes surfaces in dreams, and it is important to approach our dreams with that knowledge clearly in hand.

Seeking to have lucid dreams outside of a program of "self-work," whether in the form of meditation, dream work, or psychotherapy, is not recommended. Although it's possible to cultivate a talent for lucidity without some sort of larger context, the result will often be hollow and empty. Lucid dreaming should not be looked upon as some sort of merit badge, or as a sign of spiritual superiority. Those who are truly on a spiritual path recognize that authentic personal growth is a holistic affair that encompasses all aspects of an individual's life. In fact, a sure sign of people whose egos are bigger than their spiritual understanding is the touting of special abilities such as lucid dreaming or mystical encounters. Don't be fooled by false Buddhas.

THE IMPORTANCE OF BEING CRITICAL

Once you have begun to recall your dreams and to work with them as aspects of yourself, you may still find that you rarely have a lucid dream. Numerous techniques exist that may prove instrumental in helping you get past this point. A number of researchers, foremost among them German psychologist Paul Tholey, emphasize the importance of developing a critical attitude about what is real. For instance, some people have successfully induced lucid dreams by drawing a C (for consciousness) on the palm of one hand. Each time they notice the C, they ask themselves, "What is real?" or, "Is this a dream?" After looking about them and testing the nature of the place in which they find themselves, they conclude that they are not dreaming, that what they are now experiencing is the waking world. By asking themselves this many times during the day, they are more likely to ask themselves the same questions while dreaming. And with any luck, they will realize then that they are dreaming.

Tholey says that it's important to ask these questions as frequently as possible, especially in situations that in some sense remind you of a dream. It also helps to ask the question as close to the onset of sleep as possible. "If," Tholey explains, "a subject develops while awake a critical-reflective attitude toward his momentary state of consciousness by asking himself if he is dreaming or not, then this attitude can be transferred to the dream state."

Traditional Tibetan texts also recommend daily questioning in order to induce lucidity at night, but they approach it differently. Rather than asking yourself is this real or is this a dream, the

Tibetans suggest that you affirm to yourself while awake that everything you are perceiving is a dream. As George Gillespie of the Department of Oriental Studies at the University of Pennsylvania explains, "During the day, the yogin should maintain the realization that all things are of the substance of dreams. He [she] should think, 'This is a dream.' " Or as Gyaltrul Rinpoche puts it, "You have to actually remind yourself that it is all an illusion. Reminding yourself throughout the day as often as you can remember that this is an illusion."

Once again we need to add a word of caution here. Asking, "Is this a dream?" or telling yourself, "This is a dream," may carry significant psychological weight, especially for individuals who have trouble distinguishing between fantasy and reality. A biologist from Oregon, for instance, stopped his lucid dreaming experiments altogether, because, he says, "I was beginning to become confused as to various states of mind—sleep, awake, dream consciousness."

Developing critical reflection is not the only path on the road to lucid dream induction. Some researchers recommend enhancing perceptual awareness instead. Lucidity can be characterized as a state of enhanced inward attentiveness and as such may be brought about by cultivating an active yet receptive attitude: You observe your dream self while at the same time accepting whatever dream imagery comes along. As we explained early in this chapter, one way of doing this is through autosuggestion (suggesting to yourself before falling asleep and after each awakening from sleep that you want to have a lucid dream). Garfield and Stephen LaBerge, a dream researcher at Stanford University, both reported success using this technique, but LaBerge found that his lucid dreams tapered off after a while. He began trying variations and eventually evolved a technique known as MILD (mnemonic technique for the voluntary induction of lucid dreams). With this method, you are instructed to tell yourself to awaken early in the morning (some people are much more successful at this than others) and then run through any dream you may remember in your imagination. After doing so, you should get out of bed and engage in ten to fifteen minutes of an activity that demands your full waking attention, perhaps reading a book or writing out a shopping list. Then you are to return to bed and say to yourself as you're drifting off to sleep, "Next time I'm dreaming I want to remember that I'm dreaming." While doing this, you should visualize your body lying asleep in bed and, at the same time, see yourself in the dream you just rehearsed, recognizing that it is a dream. This technique will help facilitate lucidity when you fall back asleep.

Sparrow has also experimented with a similar technique in which he found that subjects who relived, or replayed, a dream as if they were lucid had greater success in inducing a lucid dream than those who did not do so. You can try this method yourself by relaxing with your eyes shut, perhaps before falling asleep, and visualizing a past dream, observing each action while noting that it is a dream action.

A more complex technique, but one that may have better results than MILD, comes from Tholey, who evolved his induction recipe after almost thirty years of research and clinical work with West Germans.

THOLEY'S METHOD

1. Ask yourself, "Am I dreaming or not?" at least five to ten times a day.
2. At the same time, try to imagine intensely that you are in a dream, that everything you perceive, including your own body, is merely a dream.
3. While asking yourself, "Am I dreaming or not?" you should concentrate not only on contemporary occurrences, but also on events that have already taken place. Do you notice something unusual, or suffer from lapses of memory?
4. You should ask yourself the critical question as a rule in all situations characteristic for dreams, that is, whenever something surprising or improbable occurs, or whenever you experience powerful emotions.
5. If you have a reoccurring dream event or subject—frequent feelings of fear, for instance, or appearances of a dog—you

should ask yourself the question whenever you find yourself in a
threatening situation or see a dog in the daytime.

6. If you often have dream experiences that never or very rarely
occur in a waking state, such as floating in the air or flying, then
you should, while awake, try to imagine that you are having
such an experience, telling yourself all the while that you are
dreaming.

7. If you have difficulty recalling your nonlucid dreams, you
should employ methods to improve your memory of them. In
most cases, though, practice in obtaining the critical-reflective
frame of mind will improve your dream recall.

8. Before drifting off to sleep, don't try to will lucidity by force of
thought; simply tell yourself you are going to be aware or conscious in your dream. This method is especially effective when
you have just awakened in the early morning and feel as though
you are falling back asleep.

9. You should resolve to carry out a particular action while
dreaming. Any simple action is sufficient.

To facilitate steps eight and nine, Tholey suggests ways of re-
taining waking consciousness while falling off to sleep and
through the hypnogogic imagery of early sleep. These include the
following:

- The image technique. Concentrate only on visual images
while falling asleep.

- The body technique. Concentrate entirely on your body
while falling asleep. Notice your breathing, the way your leg muscles relax, the heaviness of your arms.

- The image-body technique. Concentrate on both imagery
and your body.

- The ego-point technique. Imagine that you are only a
"point" from which you perceive and think in the dream world.

- The image-ego-point technique. In addition to the ego-point,
also concentrate upon imagery.

Although Tholey's method is more comprehensive then
LaBerge's MILD, it is also complicated and time-consuming. It

may, however, be far more effective. Two French scientists who worked with Tholey's technique found that even those participants who dropped out of their study often obtained good results.

"YOU ARE GETTING VERY SLEEPY" ☆ Hypnosis

Psychologist Joseph Dane of the University of Virginia was able to induce lucid dreams in a number of women who had never before experienced lucidity by using hypnosis. And unlike many other lucid-dream experiments, he was successful at inducing lucidity in the sleep lab. "Tonight," he told each woman after having hypnotized her, "you're going to turn off the automatic pilot in your dreams and fly with awareness. Tonight, as you dream, you will somehow manage to recognize that you're dreaming while you're dreaming. Something will happen in your dreams to trigger your awareness, and you will remember that you are dreaming."

By selecting subjects with no history of lucid dreaming, Dane controlled, to some extent, individual propensities; by selecting all women, he stacked the deck. As we explain in chapter 9 (page 162), women seem to be neurologically predisposed to lucid dream. In his study, Dane hypnotized each woman and gave strong verbal encouragement to have a lucid dream. Each woman was also requested under hypnosis to have a dream about the meaning of hypnosis. With half of the women, Dane went further and used posthypnotic suggestion to encourage the women to find a personal dream symbol that could assist in bringing about a lucid dream. Dane writes of the process: "One subject's dream about hypnosis was of playing with her dog. During this dream, the subject very much wanted to pick up and throw a ball for her dog. However, she was totally unable to do this until the dog barked at her. From her own account, it was as if she were unable to act until the dog had given her permission to do so. As she put it, 'It was just such a relief when he told me I could pick it up and throw it.' The subject readily agreed that this dream was a possible reminder from her unconscious that although we may 'play' with the unconscious and believe that we are in control and 'humoring' it, it is often the unconscious which actually dictates what we can and cannot do. On this basis, the subject's dog was chosen as her personal symbol."

The lucid dreams of the women who used a personal dream symbol were longer and regarded by the dreamer as more involving than those of the other women. "The qualitative level of their experience," says Dane, "was well beyond what would normally be expected in laboratory experiments."

Because only a small percentage of the population is capable of entering a deep hypnotic state, this form of lucid dream induction is limited. Other more accessible forms of trance, however, also seem to work. Hildegard Klippstein, a hypnotherapist from West Germany, employs a light trance to induce lucidity in her clients. "By working in trance," she explains, "the patient can experience at least two levels of reality at the same time." By interacting with the therapist while in a trance and maintaining awareness of that state, an individual mimics and therefore practices the duality of consciousness typical of lucid dreaming.

Klippstein's method can be illustrated with this dream from her client Gerd. Gerd had failed his university entrance qualifying exam and instead began training as an engineer. He would have to take an intermediate exam to continue his training and was certain he would fail again. After beginning therapy he had this dream:

> I'm traveling in the first railroad car of the train. On an embankment there is a switch to a side-track. The train drives on this side-track at a very high speed and can't be stopped. It knocks down the buffer-stop, and finally some of the railroad cars are hanging down the embankment. I manage to get out of the first car uninjured, even though it was hanging only a few feet off the ground.

The dream seemed to indicate that Gerd was preparing to fail his test. Klippstein put Gerd in a light trance and began working with him on the dream as though it had been a lucid dream. "Before getting out of the train," Klippstein explains, "I asked

Gerd to look to the other side of the car. He saw the emergency brake and had the idea to pull it. Then he went to the locomotive engine and convinced the engineer to drive the train back to the other track. Then he threw the switch, and the train could drive on in another direction."

Gerd had two lucid dreams which mirrored what he had learned during trance and also got the highest score of anyone on his intermediate level test. Such light trance techniques, Klippstein argues, work effectively to induce lucidity.

For both hypnotic and other forms of trance, one needs to enlist the aid of an experienced therapist in order to induce lucid dreams. But it does appear to be a productive and reliable path for those willing and able to give it a try.

THE MASK OF LIGHT ✰

So far we've been exploring the inner routes to dream lucidity, the battery of mental promptings, and exercises that have been shown to produce lucid dreaming. But researchers have also been experimenting with external or environmental cues. These have generally taken the form of an auditory stimulus: A recording of a voice, for example, saying, "This is a dream," may be timed to play, generally at ninety-minute intervals, throughout the night. The sound of the voice, which roughly coincides with periods of REM sleep, is supposed to seep into the sleeping mind and partially awaken it. Unfortunately, a vocal stimulus often awakens the dreamer, interrupting dream time rather than producing a lucid dream.

Tactile stimuli have also been somewhat erratically successful. Water sprinkled on the face or mild electric shocks to the arms have produced lucid dreams in some subjects. But the former requires the aid of a friend who can recognize rapid eye movements and sprinkle the water on your face; and the latter, which was developed by Keith Hearne, the first scientist to chart a lucid dream in a sleep laboratory, hasn't been shown to be particularly successful.

A relatively reliable external lucidity prompt that does not require the assistance of another person has only recently been developed. It is a light mask designed by LaBerge and his colleagues
at Stanford University. It looks like something the Lone Ranger
might wear—a sleek, black eye mask that fits tight around the
head. But unlike the Kimosabe's, LaBerge's mask is worn during
sleep and begins flashing red lights when it detects especially frequent eye movements. The light is then incorporated into any
dream that may be going on, and with the right training, the
dreamer learns to recognize the light as a signal that he or she is
dreaming.

In laboratory research LaBerge found 55 percent of frequent
lucid dreamers (one per month) had at least one signal-verified
lucid dream using the mask. So if you are a frequent lucid
dreamer, the mask may aid you on a night when you particularly
want to have a lucid dream. But because only one in five people
spontaneously has lucid dreams once or more a month, it is un-
clear how effective the mask will be in inducing them in the general public.

In another study, LaBerge found that mental preparation in
combination with the mask yielded far better results than the
mask alone. But again there were problems. First, less than one-
fourth of his subjects (virtually all previous lucid dreamers) were
successful in using the mask with the mental preparation. Second,
LaBerge was surprised by the high percentage of dreams in which
his subjects didn't recognize the light as a signal to turn lucid. The
incorporations were generally unusual enough that one would
expect people to recognize them as bizarre. The sun would begin
flashing, or a light would start to flicker, or a huge orange mandala would appear. One subject dreamed of showing the mask to
a friend and suddenly it began to flash. In fact, the mental gymnastics people went through not to recognize the incorporations
were remarkable. One subject, for example, took off the mask
halfway through the night and then fell back to sleep. In his dream
he thought, "If I was still wearing that stupid mask I'd know I
was dreaming."

A recent study by Stephen Burton and colleagues at the University of Mississippi may shed some light on the resistance reported by LaBerge's subjects. In trying to train people who suffer from sleep apnea, a condition in which people breathe erratically during sleep, the investigators conditioned them while awake to take a breath whenever they heard a particular tone. The researchers then played the tone repeatedly while the subjects slept, hoping the tone would induce irregular breathing. Problematically, the subjects were less likely to breathe when the tone was sounded during a REM period than when it was played during non-REM sleep. It was as if the dreaming mind resisted the external prompting. Similarly, the light mask may be viewed as intrusive, and even if dreamers acknowledge the light, they may still not realize they are dreaming. The system during dreaming seems to be constructed in a way that inhibits any gross external attempts to influence it. In the final analysis, then, and not surprisingly, internal preparation, such as meditation and the development of a critical attitude, may be far more efficacious than external methods in inviting consciousness into the nocturnal mind.

Chapter 3

Looking Inside the Dream

SONGS, SEX, AND THE THRILL OF FLYING

On Christmas day in 1911 Dutch physician Frederik Van Eeden recorded the following dream:

It began with flying and floating. I felt wonderfully light and strong. I saw immense and beautiful prospects—first a town, then country landscapes, fantastic and brightly colored. Then I saw my brother sitting—the same who died in 1906—and I went up to him saying: "Now we are dreaming, both of us." He answered: "No, I am not!" And then I remembered that he was dead. We had a long conversation about the conditions of existence after death, and I inquired especially after the awareness, the clear, bright insight. But that he could not answer; he seemed to lack it. Then the lucid dream was interrupted by an ordinary dream in which I saw a lady standing on a bridge, who told me she had heard me talk in my sleep. And I supposed that my voice had been audible during the lucid dream. Then a second period of lucidity followed in which I saw Professor van't Hoff, the famous Dutch chemist, whom I had known as a student, standing in a sort of college-room, surrounded by a number of learned people. I went up to him, knowing very well that he was dead, and continued my inquiry about our condition after death. It was a long, quiet conversation, in which I was perfectly aware of the situation. I asked first why we, lacking our organs of sense, could arrive at any certainty that the person to whom we were talking was really that person and not a subjective illusion. Then van't Hoff said: "Just as in common life; by a general impression." "Yet," I said, "in common life there is stability of observations and there is consolidation by repeated observation."

"Here also," said van't Hoff, "and the sensation of certainty is the same." . . . The whole atmosphere of the dream was happy, bright, elevated, and the persons around van't Hoff seemed sympathetic, though I did not know them. . . . After that I had several ordinary dreams and I awoke quite refreshed, knowing that my voice had not been audible in the waking world.

Van Eeden's description illustrates a few of the complexities of the dream world, the movement from one dream to another, the shifting of consciousness from typical dreaming to lucidity and back again. Indeed, consciousness, both waking and sleeping, runs along a continuum that encompasses many different levels of mind.

It is in the most specific form—individual dreams—that the diversity of the dream world can best be observed. Here one finds the shadowy faces, the winding roads, the hieroglyphic scribbles, the architecture of our dream scripts. Discerning what goes on in our minds while we sleep has long been a sticky problem for researchers. Some individuals have excellent dream recall, being able to relate almost every detail of a complicated dream. But others find that their dreams slip away from them as soon as they awaken. One way of collecting information about dreams is to place subjects in a sleep lab and awaken them during each REM period. Researchers know that dreaming almost always occurs— though not exclusively—during REM, and that when asked what they were thinking upon being awakened from this period of sleep, subjects will report dream material. Another technique for obtaining information about dreams is to ask people to keep diaries in which they record as much as they can remember about their dreams.

In the 1950s, psychologist Calvin S. Hall was the first to systematically look at what people dream about. He and other researchers, most particularly Robert Van de Castle of the University of Virginia, developed several scales for analyzing the manifest content of individual dreams. Manifest content is composed of the obvious facts in a dream: where the dream is set, how many characters are in it, the sex of those characters, the actions that take place. Latent content, on the other hand, concerns the underlying structures and perhaps meaning of the dream.

After analyzing thousands of dreams, Hall and Van de Castle uncovered some fascinating information about what dreams are made of. A good number of our dreams, they found, are set indoors, most often in houses. In fact, one out of almost every three dreams takes place in some sort of dwelling. In our dream houses the living room is the most popular setting, followed in order by the bedroom, the kitchen, the stairway, and the basement.

We also seem to move around a lot in our dreams. Most frequently we ride in cars, but airplanes and boats also carry us to our destinations. Sometimes we are driving the car or flying the plane; other times we are passengers, important distinctions according to Hall. "As a passenger," he explains, "the dreamer is playing the part of a passive person who is dependent upon others. As the driver, he [or she] expresses a self-image of independence and mastery."

Dreams are most often populated with at least two other characters besides the dreamer. When we are children and teenagers, our mother and father are often in our dreams. This changes after one has grown and has a significant other or others. Then spouses and children replace parents as major characters. The other people who enter our dreams, says Hall, are those "with whom we are emotionally involved. The emotion may be one of love, fear, or anger, or a mixture of these feelings. We do not dream about people with whom we have achieved a stable and satisfying relationship." Interestingly, we can find out who is dreaming about us by looking at the people in our own dreams. The people we dream about, Hall believes, will probably also be dreaming of us.

Men dream more often about other men than they do about women; women dream nearly equally about both sexes. As surprising as this may seem it fits in with the theory that one dreams most often about unstable relationships. "For men," explains Hall, "relations with other men are more unsettled than relations with women. Women on the other hand, have about an equal amount of emotional conflict with members of both sexes." As for the strangers in our dreams (they appear in about four out of every ten dreams), Hall believes they represent the unknown, the ambiguous and the uncertain.

Talking, sitting, watching, and other "passive" activities account for about a quarter of all dream activities. In fact, says Hall, "what strikes one most about dreams is the absence of strenuous activities." We also prefer to engage in pleasurable activities rather than the humdrum business of waking life. Our dreams are full of dancing and the playing of games. It seems odd, then, that Hall's research also found a preponderance of emotionally unpleasant dreams. Feelings of anger and fear are twice as common as feelings of joy and happiness. Here again, perhaps, we find the unresolved events and feelings of waking life expressing themselves at night.

Hall was looking at the content of dreams in general and did not distinguish between lucid and nonlucid dreams. But how does the landscape of lucid dreaming compare with that of ordinary dreaming? Does the added awareness that one is dreaming change the nature and/or content of the dream? Gackenbach began probing these questions in 1976, using dream reports from a variety of people including students at the University of Northern Iowa. Her subjects were not experienced lucid dreamers; they understood what a lucid dream was and reported having had one at least once, but they had never tried to induce lucidity or practice it. Indeed, Gackenbach's subjects were quite typical dreamers, the perfect pool through which to glimpse the nature of lucid dreams as they arise naturally and spontaneously.

There were problems in trying to understand what lucid dreams were like and how they differed from ordinary ones. For one thing, lucid dreams tend to be more easily remembered than other dreams. Because of this, one of the factors Gackenbach needed to separate out in her studies was dream recall: She had to systematically analyze dream content, taking into account how much or how little of the dream was remembered. Otherwise, it would be impossible to know if the differences found in the content of lucid and nonlucid dreams were due merely to better recall or something particular to lucid dreaming.

In addition, Gackenbach discovered that much of what seems to characterize lucid dreams wasn't relayed by reading a dreamer's report of the dream. Independent judges, who read through the dream reports and scored them, often attributed quite different emotions to the dream than the dreamer did. For example, this lucid dream was related by one of Gackenbach's subjects, a college student from a small town in Iowa:

> There is a huge swimming pool, and my best friend and I are standing by the edge. A festival is going on and the marching band is there. The pool has a ledge a few inches above the water all around it. Two friends from high school are swimming across the pool. I'm surprised because one, I knew, was a very good swimmer, but I didn't think the other could swim at all. My friend and I decide to jump onto the ledge to talk to the guys and to pick up a child's toy. We're on the ledge and the marching band comes up on us. They're marching around the ledge. We can't climb up the wall so we join the band. Instruments are handed to us and we play with them. I'm smiling, grinning, because I feel silly and also because it's sort of fun. While we are marching I move my eyes [she was practicing signalling with her eyes for an upcoming stay in Gackenbach's sleep lab]. When the band reaches the other side of the pool we fall back. A girl I graduated with says she'll hold our instruments while we swim across, but I say "No thanks. We can both hold them." And I jump into the water.

After reading this dream, an independent judge reported that it contained feelings of apprehension, confusion, and mild happiness. The student, on the other hand, indicated that she felt no negative or unpleasant feelings in the dream at all. And the positive feelings, she said, were so strong that she could still feel them when she recalled the dream. This "eye of the beholder" discrepancy in evaluation turned up often in Gackenbach's research, leading her to postulate that perhaps the greater awareness within the lucid dream affects the value the dreamer places on the dream, which is not apparent from written dream reports. In fact, the judges noticed far fewer differences between lucid and nonlucid dreams than did the dreamers themselves. The subjective experience of a lucid dream, subjects reported, was very different from that of an ordinary dream.

Lucid dreamers generally report strong feelings, both positive and negative, while judges report fewer happy feelings in student and adult lucid dreams than in their nonlucid ones. No differences were found for other feelings such as anger, confusion, or apprehension. The great emotionality of lucid dreams has also been reported by many veteran lucid dreamers. Scott Sparrow, a psychotherapist who was one of the first to write extensively about his lucid dreams, for instance, recounts this dream which he says changed his life:

> It seems that I have come home from school. I become aware that I'm dreaming as I stand outside a small building which has large black double doors on its eastern side. I approach them to enter. As soon as I open them, a brilliant white light hits me in the face. Immediately I am filled with intense feelings of love.

Sparrow's friend and fellow psychotherapist Kenneth Kelzer reports a similar emotional reaction to a lucid dream that he calls "The Gift of the Magi." In the dream after traveling as one of the magi, Kelzer reaches the Christ child and says:

> I reach into my bag to offer my gift to the child. With tentativeness, and sobbing continuously, with a flood of tears streaming down my cheeks, I ask "Will you accept pure gold?" The child with a delicate little smile radiates in silence.

Although these dreams were intensely emotional, an independent judge reading the descriptions would not realize the impact the dreams have had on the dreamers. Both Sparrow and Kelzer say the dreams changed their lives. Of course, not all lucid dreams are so stimulating. They vary, like ordinary dreams, in their emotional content. Celia Green, one of the pioneer investigators in lucidity, points out that the "emotional quality of lucid dreams ranges from a fairly neutral acceptance of the experience to varying degrees of excitement, liberation, expansiveness, experimental zeal, surprise at the various features of the dream, and possible appreciation of its beauty."

As gardens of emotional diversity, lucid dreams carry the dreamer into new terrain. We not only feel more strongly about lucid dreams, we also hear more sounds, sing more songs, and listen more than we do in nonlucid dreams. Curiously, though, dreamers can rarely remember the exact words spoken in their dreams whether or not they are lucid. They can express in general terms what was talked about, but are rarely able to quote exactly from the dream. Likewise, reading in a lucid dream is somewhat difficult. In 1938, Harold von Mores-Messmer explained this unexpected difficulty in a German academic journal:

> I read without difficulty. Then I try to read individual words backwards. The row of letters seems to extend itself; there are many more than would make up the word in actuality. When I have read several words backwards and forwards, something strange happens. Several of them no longer consist of the letters which make them up, but instead form figures which have a distant resemblance to hieroglyphics. Soon I see only these signs; each has the significance of a word or a syllable; individual letters have disappeared completely. I know what each figure means, my eyes glide along them in the usual left to right direction, and I read whole sentences without any difficulty. Unfortunately, I had no time to look at the figures more closely, for it became dark around me, and I continued to sleep and forget that I was dreaming.

One of the ways lucid dreamers can test to see if they are dreaming is to read within the dream. If you were to reread this paragraph now, you would see the same words as you read the first time. If you were dreaming you probably wouldn't. There appears to be an absence of verbal continuity in the dream state. Some researchers hypothesize that this may be true because of the relatively visual rather than verbal nature of dreaming.

Another sensory experience that appears to change when one enters the lucid state is vision. Most individuals remember a rich visual quality in their early lucid dreams. This gradually fades as one habituates to lucidity. However, it may reemerge in long-term lucid dreamers, particularly in dream pursuits of a transpersonal or spiritual nature. Depicting these changes in visual atmosphere is difficult: Finding the right words to describe the variations in light, for example, requires a vocabulary that many of us do not have.

Baptist minister and veteran lucid dreamer George Gillespie, who has examined the changes in light in his own lucid dreams, reports that light moves from ordinary dream light (which has the same visual quality as ordinary dreams) through unique experiences of light, like disks or patterns of light such as "versions of lattices, lines, dots and colors constantly changing" to the "fullness of light." The last, he says, can be overwhelming in its brilliance and transpersonal in feeling. Sometimes, he says, "I feel that God is present in the light." This sensing of the divine in the light of lucid dreams is not unusual among lucid dreamers seeking spiritual experiences. Indeed, the feeling of "God in the light" is one of the more stark experiences available in both lucid dreams and meditation and consequently lends support to the theory that lucidity is a form of meditation.

SEXUALITY, FLYING, AND BALANCE

Scientists have shown that if you are running in a lucid dream there will be an increase in the muscle tension in some of the muscles in your legs that are used when you are awake and running. Although this may also be true in nonlucid dreams, it is much more difficult to chart since the scientist can't be sure that the dreamer is dreaming until he or she wakes up. (In lucid dreams, as explained in chapter 8 (page 145), the dreamer can carry out a planned action, say running, and signal with a preset number of eye movements that he or she is running. The change in electrical activity of the muscles at that moment can be charted and compared with the activity before and after.) Similarly, lucid dreamers can also experience physical orgasms. Here's one such dream from a client of Kenneth Kelzer's. It's called "The Giant Blue Penis":

> I see an image of a world map. The continents are painted in color on a glasslike surface with a light in back of the glass. The whole map is translucent, in an oblong shape. I realize that it is not a current world map; some of the land masses seem different or somewhat distorted. I gaze steadily at this image, coming very close as I examine it carefully. Now I realize I am dreaming. Suddenly, I am feeling extremely sexual. I know that I have to seek sexual satisfaction before I can do anything else. I am fully lucid, floating on my back in an amorphous sky. Then a great blue penis appears! It is about three feet long and one foot thick. It comes "out of the blue" with no body attached to it. I take it inside of me and shortly come to a tremendous orgasm. I experience a tremendous rush and flood of feelings going through my whole body. The power of all the feelings that surge through me is intensified beyond real life and beyond all belief. I realize I have never had such a powerful orgasm before. The immensity of the sexual feelings are so great that I awaken.

Despite reports of this nature, Gackenbach's data show no more sexuality in lucid dreams than in nonlucid ones. This was true not only of the college students she monitored, but also of a group of adults who were well educated, middle class, and highly interested in their dreams. Her findings come as no surprise to Tholey, who argues that consciousness during sleep actually prohibits what may seem to the dreamer to be inappropriate sexual expression. He cites the lucid dream of a man trying to take off his underpants in preparation for dreamed sex with a young girl. Each time he removed the pants, he discovered another pair— always of a different color—underneath. He simply couldn't get naked.

Clinicians suggest that sexual encounters can appear in the lucid dreams of people who frequently turn lucid when there is the expectation of the healthy enjoyment of sex. Though sexual lucid dreams are usually highly pleasurable, they are surpassed in frequency, if not enjoyment, by another activity—dream flying.

Freud believed that dreams of flying were symbolic of sexual longing; other theorists have suggested that they are an expression of freedom. Although dream flying is a frightening affair for a few people, it seems to be primarily a fun and sometimes thrilling event for most of us.

Psychologist Havelock Ellis suggested that flying in dreams occurred because there was no stimulation coming from the feet, a sign that they were not on the ground. As odd as that may sound, there may be a physiological cause for flying in dreams. Some theorize that such dreams help the brain make sense of conflicting sensory information: When one is awake the kinesthetic, or bodily, sensations are constantly being processed by the brain in a continual feedback loop. Similarly, the body's vestibular system (the inner workings of the inner ear that help maintain balance) react to outside stimulations. In fact, many cultures try to create mystical states of consciousness by inducing dizziness, which discombobulates the vestibular system. During sleep, sensory input is restricted—the brain knows in one sense that the body is lying down and inert. But it is getting conflicting signals as the dream body engages in various activities. Indeed, psychologist Harry Hunt theorizes that the REM state destabilizes balance, interferes with perception, and leads either to "striking disorganizations of visual/kinesthetic imagination [strange body distortions and nightmares] or to its special development [lucid dreams]." Whether we experience nightmares or lucid dreams may in part be linked to the health of the vestibular system: People with healthy systems and strong emotional balance may produce lucid dreams or dreams archetypal in nature, while those with poor physical and emotional balance may find their dreams filled with morbid body distortions and nightmares.

Emotional, intellectual, and physical balance are all necessary components for lucidity. If the consciousness of the state is not repeatedly "balanced," the dreamer can either wake up or become mentally reabsorbed into dream activities and forget that he or she is dreaming. Interestingly, the intense emotional response many people have when they turn lucid—the feeling of "Wow!" at realizing they are dreaming—will often excite them so much that they awaken. Lucid dreamers often stress the importance of remaining emotionally detached or balanced in the dream. To maintain a high degree of lucidity, one must remain calm.

In a similar way, physical balance is essential, especially for an activity like flying. Gackenbach spent years perfecting dream flight in her own lucid dreams, learning the angle, speed, and tilt of flying. In doing so, she came face to face with just how hard it sometimes is even to get off the ground:

> I wanted to show Thomas, my husband, I could fly. I was hopping about at first, then I took off high in the air. I got to electrical wires and wanted to soar very high but I seemed to be held back. I was afraid I'd fall! I kept thinking, You can't fly when you're awake but you can when you are asleep. But then I reasoned, I want to be awake in my dreams, but then I can't fly. Upon awakening it occurred to me that I seemed to be getting awake and asleep confused, and it is making me a bit afraid to fly.

Kelzer says balance in lucid dreams is, in many respects, like learning to ride a bicycle. But, he notes, there is another aspect of learning to stay balanced in the lucid dream that is quite different. "It felt more like a state of inactivity, quite distinct from bicycling or any other kind of action of 'doing,'" he explains. "This aspect seemed more like the fullest cultivation of a feeling state, a feeling of deep receptivity, openness and allowance for these lucid energies to emerge and run their course."

Skilled lucid dreamers can remain lucid at times when they feel themselves about to awaken by training themselves to move their dream bodies, perhaps doing somersaults or spins within the dream, or other actions which activate the vestibular system. Interestingly, these aspects of lucidity—flying, balance, and movement—are the ones that survive the transition to higher states of consciousness. An example of how the "felt sense" of movement remains without the usual reference points that generally ground one during a dream comes from a long-term meditator:

> At times I experience this inner awareness when I am not dreaming. It begins with an awareness that I am *not* dreaming, and I know I am *not* awake. I become aware of a whirlpool of vast energy and sound —rising and falling—oscillating within itself. I experience it as a natural part of myself. I feel completeness, as though I had arrived home after a long and tiring journey. I feel a deep silence, even in the midst of all this motion, and at this point I have a strange awareness that the life I live here on earth is just a dream, and that this vast field of energy is who I really am. Through all of this I don't forget who I am as a person, or the fact that I know I am not dreaming.

DREAM CHARACTERS

Gackenbach has found that there tend to be fewer characters in lucid dreams than in ordinary dreams. As directors of their dreams, lucid dreamers seem to limit the roles others play and concentrate on themselves. Rarely do lucid dreamers create a partner to fly with them; instead they become caught up in the technique of flying and the unique perspective it offers them. Despite this tendency, Paul Tholey has found that lucid dreamers may sometimes pursue interactions with other dream characters, creating them if they do not naturally emerge, in order to confront if not resolve psychological difficulties.

Tholey, who teaches lucid dreaming to his students, has found that dream characters sometimes display abilities that the dreamer does not have waking access to. In one experiment, he asked nine student lucid dreamers to instruct their dream characters to perform a variety of tasks, such as solving simple arithmetic problems, writing something down, or rhyming and speaking in a foreign language. The subjects had no knowledge of one another's dream reports, but all had similar results. "Part of the dream figures," explains Tholey, "actually agreed to perform the tasks

and did so successfully. Their performance was poorest in arithmetic: None of them [the dream characters] could solve problems
with two-digit numbers." One particularly absurd example of this
comes from a dream in which a student quizzes a small boy:
" 'What is three times four?' 'Eleven,' the boy replies after a moment's hesitation. At this I laugh and say, 'You can't even do
simple sums. The answer is twelve!' A superior smile appears on
his face. 'But, I didn't solve your problem. I worked out what
seven plus four is, and the answer to that is eleven, isn't it?' "

With verbal tasks, however, the dream figures exhibited more
talent, in some cases performing better than the dreamer did while
awake. For example, when Tholey instructed his subjects to ask
their dream figures to say a specific word from a language which
was apparently unknown to the dreamer, several dream characters were able to do so. Here is an example:

> I meet a female acquaintance in the room. I ask her, as I had planned
> to, if she can tell me a foreign word I am unfamiliar with. She imme-
> diately says, "Orlog." The word "orlog" describes our relationship. I
> fail to understand her as the "orlog" is unfamiliar to me. When I later
> ask the woman what this word means, she denies having said it,
> arguing that she used the word "charme" [charm]. On explaining this
> she gives me a charming glance.

After awakening the subject looked up the word "orlog" and
found that it was a Dutch word that roughly translated means
quarrel.

It's as if, says Tholey, the dream characters had a consciousness
of their own. "They behave as if they possessed their own perceptual perspectives, cognitive abilities (memory and thought) and
even their own motivations," explains Tholey. And if a dream
figure is asked if it possesses a separate consciousness, it is likely
to reply something like this: "I am sure that I have a consciousness, but I doubt if you have one because you ask me such stupid
questions!" That we may possess distinct ego states separate from
the one we consciously perceive as our own has been postulated
by other psychologists and certainly exhibited in people with mul-

tiple personalities. Most of us, however, remain quite unaware of our clandestine egos except during dreams where they take on a distinct "physical" quality and show themselves as dream characters.

MEASURING THE BIZARRE

The most striking difference between lucid and nonlucid dreams occurs in the area of cognition. Given that there is a greater thoughtlike component in lucid dreaming, which is demonstrated by the awareness that one is dreaming, it follows that there may be other cognitive variations as well.

One of the areas in which cognitive differences appear is in the category of bizarreness. Lucid dreams do not necessarily contain more bizarre elements, such as two-headed ducks, chairs that melt, or even dream flying, but they do exhibit a developmental pattern of bizarreness that ordinary dreams do not. This pattern also parallels certain experiences in meditators.

According to Hunt's research, bizarreness is most often associated with the prelucid state in which, for instance, you might dream you have awakened only to actually awake and find that you had been dreaming. But often some bizarre element in a dream is what triggers full lucidity: One recognizes the odd element and realizes he or she must be dreaming. But the bizarreness tends to decrease after the novice has turned lucid, resulting in a lucid dream that is more realistic than ordinary dreams. At this point of development, lucid dreams aren't as likely to have characters popping into them with bright purple faces or rabbits that fly or any other strange creations that occur in prelucid states. Some bizarre elements may creep in, such as dream flight, but on the whole these early lucid dreams are relatively true to life.

As one becomes more adept at lucid dreaming—and this is especially true of the lucid dreams of advanced meditators—bizarre elements reappear. Hunt has found an increase in "geometric imagery and white light experiences, and more abstract imagistic effects such as those common with psychedelic drug use and in deep meditative states." Here is a lucid dream from a long-term meditator that involves several bizarre elements:

> A layer of "dough" which resembles pie crust forms an outer shell in the shape of the halo of a Buddha. In the beginning I identify with the dough, a thick and heavy mass of ego and emotions accumulated over endless periods of time. Then I peel off the dough and inside is my real self in the form of a tanka [a Tibetan Buddhist symbol] yet made out of transparent raditations from the chakras, geometric, powerful, and made of pure light. Gradually, I identify with the front chakras and it softens from its geometrically concentrated power into soft golden rays that seem to come from the heart chakras. At the same time I am the source of this light. I do my mantra and pray that I will be able to hold this state of mind for the sake of all beings.

In a study conducted with his student Barbara McLeod, Hunt collected 307 dreams from eighteen long-term meditators and scored them on scales of lucidity and bizarreness. After comparing the meditators' dreams to those of nonmeditators, the researchers concluded that they were far more unusual and much more archetypal and/or transpersonal in nature. Among the types of bizarreness found in the meditators' dreams were "mandala imagery, diffuse white light experiences, flying and floating, and encounters with mythological beings—all rarely seen in normative dream diaries." Hunt suggests that if lucid dreaming was primarily a mental waking up inside REM sleep, then confusing thoughts and bizarreness should disappear altogether. Clearly, they do not.

CONTROLLING INTEREST

Although it never occurs to some lucid dreamers, the conscious element found in lucid dreams makes it possible (in varying degrees) to control the content of the dream. In Gackenbach's work, she has consistently found that both dreamers and judges recognize that it is significantly easier to control the content of lucid dreams than it is of nonlucid ones. Indeed, the opportunity to perform experiments, create characters, confront danger, or fly is what first attracted many early dream investigators to lucidity. For Van Eeden or Saint-Denys, it was a scientific dream come true.

The anecdotal evidence for controlling lucid dreams abounds. One twenty-five-year-old computer operator, for instance, decided while dreaming to try to see God. "I closed my eyes [his dream eyes] and concentrated on the idea of God, repeating the word God over and over," he explains. "Then I had a vision of a long wooden table with food on it, something like a painting of a still life. I found I could control the perspective from which I viewed the table: close up or far away, up and down."

Although not a traditional vision of God, the man's dream changed his perspective and gave him new insight into his own conception of the divine. More impressive than this sort of individual experiment of lucid dream control are those that take place under controlled conditions in sleep labs. There dreamers have been able to carry out all sorts of prearranged experiments, including many physiologically oriented tests that shed light on the underlying biology of the lucid dream state. But it is in spontaneously arising lucid dreams that the range of control becomes evident. In this dream, New York–based writer Sandy Fritz managed to use lucidity to continue a frightening dream that might otherwise have awakened him:

I'm in a glen, heavy and green, and a waterfall is splashing there. I walk to an aircraft; it is waiting for me. At first I'm flying the aircraft. Then I realize I am the passenger, in the back seat, and the jet flies with its own life. There is no control and I am scared. Up it goes, and my shoulder straps are loose. We do a long, belly-up somersault in the air, and I'm falling. First thought: "Wake up." Second thought: "You're safe. It's a dream." Then we are pointed straight at the ground, tiny squares of landscape grow large as we speed downwards. A bank, a curve, and we are crashing through a waterfall that is suspended in the air. The violence and turbulence of this is deafening. Up again and upside down, I realize I have no shoulder harness now and am falling on my back at enormous speed. I'm very scared, but even more awed, and once again I remind myself of the dream reality. The jet and I crash through the waterfall with tremendous velocity, and this time it shatters, like a crystal chandelier, exploding into shards that are prisms. Now I am the aircraft and am completely lucid. I experiment with flight. For me, when I look to a far horizon, my speed increases. To slow down and go lower, I focus on landscape detail. After a while, I practice landing and taking off. To land, I focus on something tiny, this time on the wrinkles of bark on a tree, then touch down like a light Superman. I'm on the ground puzzling how best to take off again, and a suggestion arises to treat the air as a fluid. A deep-kneed jump up, followed by two breast stroke motions, raises me up to a height where I can adjust my focus and my speed. After a spell of this I feel completely happy with myself. I wake up with my heart pounding. The entire waking day, I could do nothing but marvel at my dream.

Fritz says that normally he does not direct his dreams. "I don't plot out a dream and fulfill it," he explains. "If I have burning questions or need some information or want to find out what's happening in the life of someone I love, I can to some extent manipulate my dreams, but it's difficult and generally takes repeated attempts. It's one thing to be alert in an alien information flow, and another thing to frame the direction that information flow takes while remaining alert enough to remember it."

Fritz's observation about the limits of dream control is echoed throughout the lucid dream literature. Although there is fairly general agreement that dream control is enhanced during lucid dreaming, most also agree that it is by no means absolute. Waking expectations play a role in the degree to which one is able to control the course of a dream. Gackenbach noticed that some of her subjects were surprised to hear that they might be able to control the content of their lucid dreams, remarking that it had never occurred to them to change the dream. But even when lucid dreamers try to change the content of a dream, they can run into difficulties. For instance, they may not always be able to make a threatening dream character go away or to enter into psychologically dangerous territory. Although not all psychologists agree, Tholey believes that an internal safety mechanism exists in the lucid state, as it does under hypnosis, that prevents the sleeper from going experientially beyond what he or she can psychologically handle.

Even prolific lucid dreamers have sometimes noticed the limitations of dream control. "At best," says Kelzer, "the lucid dreamer is able to take charge of his [or her] personal experience within the dream but is not actually able to control the dreamscape itself to any great extent." Hunt goes even further and suggests that some attempts at control can dampen the experience by turning the dream into a nocturnal laboratory in which to perform experiments. Only by pursuing lucidity as "something" in its own right do the expansive feelings of a peak experience occur. Hunt cites one of his own lucid dreams as an example of how deliberate attempts at control can lead to the loss of expansive feelings:

> I was walking along a favorite path in the woods, with a beautifully bound set of books under one arm, when I suddenly realized that I owned no such books and that I was in fact dreaming. The realization was accompanied by a special sense of presence and significance, which started to fade as I began to wonder what I should do next. I decided I would attempt to fly, but uncertain how to do that, I decided to edge out along a half-fallen tree leaning out from the hill and extending over a large lake (which had not existed on that spot since the last ice age) whence I would jump and then fly. As I edged out along the tree I became increasingly dizzy and realized that I was close to waking up. To avoid this I resolved to leap off immediately when far enough above the water. But as I was about to let go, I saw sharp rocks just beneath the surface. By now totally forgetting that these were only "dream rocks," I held on for dear life. As I awakened, completely disgusted with myself, I finally managed to let go, only to land in my bedroom.

In order to exercise any sort of control in a lucid dream one has to recall what one was supposed to do and then have enough control over the events of the dream to act on that decision. In an analysis of more than two hundred lucid dreams from her student sample, Gackenbach found that the more memory a subject had during the dream of his or her waking life, the more he or she felt in control. This is not surprising given the accounts of sophisticated lucid dreamers, but it does indicate that such felt control is a normal occurrence even in the dreams of the person who only occasionally turns lucid. Interestingly, the lucid dreams that were high in both control and waking memories were also rated as highly visual and colorful and filled with strong bodily sensations.

DREAM TYPES

Another way of analyzing different types of lucid experiences involves the way in which the dreams surface. Celia Green describes three distinct ways that lucid dreams are triggered: First, they can arise from feelings of fear or anxiety; second, they can occur because of some inconsistency that the dreamer notices; and third, they can be triggered by the dreamer's sense of dreamlike qualities. Gackenbach's analysis of naturally emerging lucid dreams in two student samples revealed that only 18 percent of lucid dreams are triggered by nightmares and only 11 to 19 percent were the result of the dreamer's recognizing some inconsistency in the dream. The bulk of her dream samples (48 to 67 percent) were triggered by the "dreamlike sense" (a largely unidentifiable "felt sense" that what one is experiencing is a dream). The nightmare-triggered lucid dreams, Gackenbach found, emerged after stressful experiences prior to sleep and tended to be high in negative emotions and low in dream control. Conversely, the dreamlike-initiated lucid dreams emerged after positive waking experiences and were perceived as more emotionally positive and higher in dream control. Lucid dreams that arose from the dreamer's recognition of an inconsistency were more varied.

Gackenbach's analysis also uncovered the first evidence that dream control may sometimes be detrimental to the dreamer. In nightmare-induced lucid dreams, control alleviated the negative emotions of the dreams only if the dreams were also low in waking memory. If the dreamers had strong waking memories, however, negative emotions were also high regardless of the amount of dream control. This suggests that when one is lucid as a result of a fearful dream situation and further has access to waking memory, it may be preferable to go with the dream as it unravels, rather than try to direct the content. If, however, one is lucid and does not recall much of waking life, then directing the flow may be adaptive. It appears that in higher levels of lucidity (where there are strong waking memories) dream control, as Hunt discovered, becomes detrimental, but in less practiced forms of lucidity, dream control may be helpful.

Inducing lucidity artificially may also adversely influence the quality of the lucid dream. For instance, after analyzing the content of one female subject's lucid dreams that had been induced with his light mask, Stephen LaBerge found that the dreams were rated positively along fewer dimensions than the woman's lucid dreams that arose spontaneously. Dream sex was also more common in the subject's light-induced lucid dreams than in spontaneous ones. Curiously, dream flying arose less frequently when the woman used the dream mask than it did when she did not use it. Dream flying is clearly a more radical departure from everyday living than dream sex, and therefore one can argue that it is more archetypical and represents a higher form of dream lucidity. This is substantiated by psychologist Deirdre Barrett's finding that dream flying does not typically precede lucidity, as prelucid bizarreness would imply, but follows after the dawning of consciousness. In addition, Gackenbach and colleagues analyzed the content of a group of long-term meditators and found only one reference to sex in the more than 150 reports. This same group reported 20 cases of dream flying. Because the relationship between lucidity and dream sex does not appear to be strong in either normative or meditating samples, its prevalence in lucid dreams that are prompted by the dream mask may be a result of employing an outside stimulant to force lucidity. This results in dream experiences that are not psychologically as evolved as those that arise naturally.

Chapter 4

Night Coach

THE CREATIVE LINK

One night William James dreamed that he had discovered the secret of the universe. He wrestled himself awake just long enough to scribble the wisdom on a notepad that he kept near his bed. After awakening the next morning, he grabbed the pad to rediscover the answer. This is what he read:

> *Higamus, hogamus,*
> *Women are monogamous;*
> *Hogamus, higamus,*
> *Men are polygamous!*

So much for the creative inspiration of dreams . . . well, maybe. Despite James's disappointing though certainly amusing perception, dreams have often been fertile ground for the growth of new ideas and artistic—and scientific—insight. Writers such as

Charles Dickens, Robert Louis Stevenson, and Charlotte Brontë found plots, characters, and settings in their dreams. Gothic novelist Ann Radcliffe would consume huge quantities of rich and indigestible food before going to sleep to stimulate horrible dreams. She then used the ghostly plots for her novels.

Musicians too have found material in dreams. The eighteenth-century violinist and composer Giuseppe Tartini dreamed one night that he gave his violin to the devil to see what kind of musician he was. The devil, Tartini relates, played such a beautiful solo that it surpassed anything Tartini had ever heard. When Tartini awoke the next morning, he jumped out of bed and grabbed his violin to try to recapture the devil's music. Although the "Devil's Sonata," as Tartini entitled the composition, was inferior to what had been played in the dream, it was considered to be Tartini's best work.

One of the most famous accounts of scientific inspiration in a dream comes from the founder of modern organic chemistry, the German chemist Friedrich August Kekulé. He reports that in the 1860s he discovered the formula for the benzene ring during a dream. "I turned the chair to the fireplace," he recounted, "and sank into a half sleep. The atoms flitted before my eyes . . . wriggling and turning like snakes. And see, what was that? One of the snakes seized its own tail, and the image whirled scornfully before my eyes. As though from a flash of lightning, I awoke. I occupied the rest of the night working out the consequences of the hypothesis."

The circular image of the snake suggested to Kekulé the hexagon shape of the benzene molecule.[1]

Stuart Holroyd, author of *Dream Worlds,* tells of another kind of scientific discovery revealed through a dream.

---

[1] According to an August 1988 *New York Times* article, Dr. John H. Wortiz, a professor of chemistry at Southern Illinois University, reports that Kekulé reported at least three different dreams in which he supposedly discovered the structure of the benzene ring. Wortiz suggests that in fact Kekulé may have made up the dreams in order to avoid sharing credit for the discovery of the benzene ring with foreign researchers. Wortiz is currently organizing a symposium to further investigate Kekulé's claims.

In 1893 archaeologists from the University of Pennsylvania excavated
the ancient Babylonian ruins of the temple of Bel at Nippur in what
is now Iraq. Dr. H. V. Hilprecht, professor of Assyrian at the university, was later given a detailed drawing of two fragments of agate
bearing inscriptions which members of the expedition wanted translated. After weeks of effort Dr. Hilprecht still had not succeeded in
deciphering the inscriptions. With some hesitation he conjectured that
the fragments had belonged to ancient Babylonian finger rings. Then
he had a remarkable dream in which, he said, "a tall, thin priest, of
the old pre-Christian Nippur, about forty years of age and clad in a
simple *abba*," appeared to him and led him into the treasure chamber
of the temple. This was a small low-ceilinged room without windows.
It contained a large wooden chest and some scraps of agate and lapis
lazuli scattered on the floor. The priest told him that the fragments
were not finger rings and gave him a detailed account of their history.
King Kurigalzu, said the priest, had once presented an inscribed votive
cylinder made of agate to the temple. Some time later, the priests had
received an order to make a pair of agate earrings for the statue of the
god Ninib. Because they had no other raw material for the earrings
they cut the cylinder into three parts, two of which they used for the
jewelry. The priest concluded by saying: "If you put the two together
you will have confirmation of my words. But the third ring you have
not found in the course of your excavations, and you will never find
it." Then he disappeared.

On waking, the professor told his wife about his strange dream.
When he examined the drawings, he was amazed to discover "all the
details of the dream precisely verified . . ." Later in the year he had an
opportunity to visit the museum in Constantinople (now Istanbul)
where the actual fragments were kept. Since no one had suspected
that the two pieces of agate were related, they were kept in different
parts of the museum. When Hilprecht put them together they fitted
perfectly, and the joined inscriptions made sense. His dream had given
him the right information.

We don't want to make this sound like "Ripley's Believe It or
Not." Indeed, most people go through their whole lives without
being aware of the creative inspiration in their dreams, but perhaps that's because they rarely listen to them. People who pay
attention to dreams know the creative punch they can throw
seemingly out of nowhere. In her chapter in *Conscious Mind,
Sleeping Brain*, Patricia Garfield discusses her work with a group

of advertising agency executives whom she was helping to "dream up" a new name for a product. The executives had already brain-stormed for names but without success. "They wanted something more. . . . Knowing how dreams are based upon emotional experience, I first endeavored to arouse the participants' feeling-loaded memories that could be associated with the product," Garfield writes. "Then I asked them to close their eyes and follow a guided fantasy meant to link their childhood experiences with an aspect of the product. Serene, smiling faces and furtive tears assured me that emotional wells had been reached." Garfield then instructed each businessman to dream about the product and visualize it. The next time the group met, even the men who did not usually remember their dreams reported dreams associated with the product. Potential product names were found in all of the men's dreams.

None of these examples of dream creativity should be surprising. Most current theories about the function of REM sleep suggest that it serves to integrate new information with old. It is an unedited creator that is forever weaving new stories without worrying whether the plot is realistic or the characters believable. Our dreams are new worlds spun by the muse that resides in each of us. While awake we may be so busy with making a living, tending the hearth, and rearing our children that we forget the part of us that creates. The mythmaker, the storyteller, appears only in our dreams. "Our dreams are first-hand creations, rather than put together from residues of waking life," writes psychiatrist Gordon Globus in his book *Dream Life, Wake Life.* "We have the capacity for infinite creativity; at least while dreaming, we partake of the power of immanent Spirit, the infinite Godhead that creates the cosmos."

Globus makes a distinction between creativity that gives rise to the sheer variety of "unique life-worlds" and "formative creativity," a deeper level of creative thought. "Usually," he writes, "we think of thought as empty, unfilled, abstract, so it is strange to conceive of thought as thinking up a world. Formative creativity is the power of Zeus."

Globus believes that in lucid dreams the creative element is most clearly demonstrated. "The lucid dreamer just thinks the dream world he or she wants to live in, and lo, that world concretely appears," he writes. In lucid dreams the worlds are created by deliberate thought. But what, one might ask, does that add awareness to the creative capacity of dreams?

THE CASE FOR CONSCIOUSNESS

Artist Fariba Bogzaran, a Persian currently living in San Francisco, uses lucid dreaming as the primary source for her artwork. Not only does she "see" her future works of art while lucid in sleep, but she also has made major changes in her style as a result of her lucid dreams. In fact, the most profound change in her art came in the following lucid dream:

> I stand by the door in a gallery, staring at a painting on the wall. It is my painting. . . . As I step forward to look at the detail of my work, I become aware that I am dreaming. . . . The painting, approximately six by seven feet in size, displays an image of a wall destroyed in the middle but with the four corners still intact. An imprint of a triangle and circle are inside it. Inside the circle, a figure of a nude man and woman stand.

When Bogzaran woke she felt compelled to execute the painting even though it was in a style that she had never used. Uncertainty drove her to rent a studio downtown away from the university so that her colleagues would not know what she was doing. "I couldn't identify with it," she explains. "I was even scared to show it to people, but finally I did." The response was positive and the painting was eventually accepted in a prestigious art show. But more important for Bogzaran was the "profound transformation of my painting style." It was as if "my unexplored, hidden, creative side was now able to merge with other important aspects of my life."

Bogzaran has learned to use lucid dreams for creative inspiration. In a typical dream she will walk into a gallery, museum, or studio in her dream, turn lucid, examine a completed painting or sculpture, and then later when awake attempt to create it. She has been more than satisfied with the results.

It is important to note that Bogzaran sees the finished painting in the dream before or after she turns lucid and that the painting is usually not a product of lucidity. Another artist, Shana-Elaine Brewer of Oak Ridge, Tennessee, also experiences creative inspiration that occurs "outside" lucidity. The following dream came to Brewer several days after she had been commissioned to design a stained glass window:

> Just after I had lain down in bed, the entire design flashed through my mind, and I got up to sketch it out quickly. The only problem I had was with a tree in the foreground, so I suggested to myself that I would dream of the tree and be able to remember what it looked like so I could sketch it after I woke up. In the dream, I saw myself in front of an easel, sketching on a large, white sheet of paper. I was drawing the tree, which was full of flowing horizontal lines; there were five or six main sections outlined in heavy black line. . . . The odd part was that as I sketched, the different sections of the tree somehow became colored in various shades of green, although I was not coloring them myself. I awoke, . . . sat down, and resketched the tree I had dreamed about; . . . when the sketch was finished, the client was nearly speechless, saying only, "I usually don't like anything the first time, but this is perfect."

While Brewer was consciously involved in the creation of the dream tree, an active force outside her dream consciousness was coloring the tree. The same was true when Bogzaran saw the painting completed before turning lucid: Her dreaming mind— before she became aware that she was dreaming—had produced the painting. If the creative process in dreams can operate successfully outside lucidity, what then is the advantage of being lucid?

On a superficial level the value of lucidity can be explained as the part of the dreaming mind that seeks a solution to a waking problem that the nonlucid dream mind answers: A part-time artist, for example, places an empty canvas beside his bed before going to sleep and then while lucid recalls that he needs inspiration to fill it. He looks at the dreamed canvas and it "magically fills with a picture." Once the desire has been answered, lucidity helps to ensure that we will remember it. Lucid dreams—including the minute details in them—are much more easily remembered than other dreams.

This conscious presentation of a problem in sleep and the enhanced recall of lucid dreams are also useful for any problem, not just an artistic one, that demands insight. For example, electronics maintenance technician and exhibit designer Bob Rosengren of Seattle, Washington, had the following lucid dream when he was having problems with the electronic design for a museum exhibit.

> I was working on a very tight timeline before the exhibit opened last December 26, and ran into a problem with a circuit design. I could not solve it, and time was running out. About a week before opening day, I had a lucid dream in which I was in my small town, in a waterfront restaurant with my dream associates. I told them my predicament, as they saw I was upset. They told me to just "slow things down," and made some references to certain things not being ready at the same time other things were. None of that made much sense to me, but the words kept popping up in my head that morning at work. On a hunch, I decided to search through the data books on a couple of the integrated circuits I was working on, and suddenly realized that in my design I had neglected to allow for a twenty-two-nanosecond "setup time." After including a small delay, my circuit design worked perfectly.

Another example of this sort of creativity in lucid dreams comes from Robert Pelland, Jr., of Holland, Ohio. He was "having trouble with ink adheasment (sic) on plastics" and explains how a lucid dream helped him with the problem. "I wanted so bad to solve the problem that later on when I went to sleep I dreamt of a person telling me to use electricity to treat plastic, but I thought it was just a crazy dream and didn't pay any more attention to it, so we went on using this harsh toxic chemical to treat the plastic, but it didn't work on everything. A year later I found that there is a way of using electricity to treat plastic."

Many creative solutions in lucid dreams seem to take this somewhat passive form in which the solution or inspiration actually occurs outside of lucidity. But there is something else that consciousness in sleep may give us, something that may shed considerable light on the nature of consciousness.

NO BOUNDARIES

> "What are boundaries, please?"
> "Imaginary lines on the earth, I suppose. How can you have boundaries if you fly?"
>
> —T. H. WHITE
> *THE ONCE AND FUTURE KING*

We all experience boundaries—the feeling that we are limited by particular responsibilities or patterns of behavior. We are bound by motherhood, childhood, by our role as lover, friend, or enemy. We often place boundaries between layers of our personal consciousness, delegating much of our awareness to the unconscious. As children we learn to establish boundaries between reality and fantasy. Less obvious are the boundaries we place between our minds and bodies. We don't think of "me" as located in our elbows; rather "me" is located somewhere deep within us. And perhaps we can go even further than this; perhaps we set up boundaries between "self" and "other" and between "self" and the objects of the "real" world.

Are these boundaries real and inescapable divisions? Transpersonal theorist Ken Wilber argues that all boundaries are illusory and artificial; we are both mother and child, lover and enemy. All boundaries, he states, are imaginary, including the divisions we think exist between ourselves and other forms of matter. There are no boundaries, he contends, between ourselves and the world. Echoing the statement from T. H. White's book, an astronaut explains the falseness of boundaries: "As you pass from sunlight into darkness and back again every hour and a half, you become startlingly aware how artificial are the thousands of boundaries we've created to separate and define. And for the first time in your life you feel in your gut the precious unity of the Earth and all the living things it supports."

The concept of boundaries and their relationship to consciousness is central to the creative potential of lucid dreams. When we know that we are dreaming it is not at all unusual to decide to break through traditional boundaries. Lucid dreamers can push their hands through walls, fly, and transform themselves into other creatures. Veteran lucid dreamer Alan Worsley reports that in forty-five attempts to penetrate "matter" in lucid dreams, he was successful forty-one times. Boundaries existed for Worsley when he needed them, when, for instance, he wanted to play the piano, walk up stairs, open a door, use tools, or snap his fingers, but when he desired, he could walk through brick walls or float above the treetops.[2]

Artist Bogzaran suspects that at least in some of her lucid dreams it is the absence of strict boundaries that allows unexpected creativity to fill her works. "While awake," she explains, "I feel in some sense limited by my body's boundaries, but while lucid and creating, the separateness no longer exists."

She illustrates her point with the following dream:

> I am in a studio making a sculpture. There are about seven different life-size sculptures that are not yet finished. The sculpture that I am making is a life-size Greek-motif male sculpture. As I am working on his hand, I say to myself, "How did I get to make this sculpture? I am not a sculptor." As soon as I say that, I become lucid. A rush of excitement rises up my spine. While I am holding onto the sculpture, it starts to move in my hand. The upper part of the sculpture, which I had sculpted, starts a graceful move and I start moving with it, dancing a harmonious dance. Then I woke up. I wrote in my journal that I felt one with my creation. It was both an external and an internal oneness.

Bogzaran speaks of an experiential flow between subject (dreamer) and object (dream sculpture). But other variations of

---

[2] A psychophysiological model for this unbounded aspect of lucidity is offered by Gordon Globus. He writes: "REM sleep appears to be associated with decreased neural inhibition. Since it is inhibition which raises the height of boundaries in connectionist networks, decreased inhibition would dissolve boundaries." You will see in Chapter 8 that lucid dreaming can be conceptualized as an enhanced REM state.

the unbounded quality of creative inspiration are illustrated in this dream of an artist in Texas, who writes:

> I was doing a painting for a friend. This particular one had arisen from a discussion about the various theories concerning the origin of the three major Egyptian pyramids. My style as an artist is photorealism. . . . I had always worked from photos in my studio. Well, we had decided this painting should represent the pyramids at a time when they were fairly new. Of course, there are not any existing photos of them in such condition, and I've never been to Egypt. So I was constructing the painting by looking at an aerial view of archeological and geological maps and talking to Egyptologists. I was having a great deal of trouble drawing the foreground in relation to the pyramids—I couldn't get the perspective right on the cliffs, the sphinx, and the temple of the sphinx. I had spent the entire day erasing, redoing, over and over and was about in tears over it. Well . . . that night I dreamt that I was floating in the air in just the position I needed before the pyramids. It was as though I had entered my painting and it was now a real place. There was no one else. I just observed the scene. Upon awakening the next day, I went directly to the painting and was able to successfully complete the area of the painting I was having so much trouble with. The scene was as clear in my mind as if I had been there. It was wonderful.

Using essentially the same technique, Constance Ransdell of Louisburg, North Carolina, was stuck on a tough electrical engineering problem—she couldn't figure out how to get a particular circuit to work. She had a lucid dream in which she solved her problem. "In the dream, the circuit took a form of streets within a city, and I was looking down on them from a high altitude. I actually flew over the connections needed to make the circuit work. When I awoke, I made the necessary changes and the circuit worked as desired."

In these examples the ordinary boundaries between the "self," body, and world that each individual struggled with while awake were dissolved in sleep. Their ability to image solutions while awake were inadequate to the task. Only when asleep and lucid could they become fully absorbed in the problems and the subsequent solutions. However, even in lucid dreams we more often than not create boundaries between the conscious dream ego and the creative source. This is humorously illustrated by the dream of a writer who directed herself during lucidity to work on her book:

> I gave no specific instructions. . . . [Nevertheless] I became two peo-ple: the Writing Me and the Real Me. It didn't seem odd, since we have many personalities and I think the Writing Me is different than the Real Me. The two of us were talking and the Writing Me was sitting at a desk. I remember it clearly; it was an old-fashioned Frank-lin desk, small, the wood scarred with years of use. The Writing Me was putting something on paper. . . . As the Writing Me wrote, the Real Me looked over her shoulder and began to read. I was intrigued with the plot that the Writing Me was putting down and remember commenting but also recognizing it. The Writing Me said, "Caroline, you'd better get this on paper yourself because it would work as a good plot." I argued, "I already wrote that."
> Writing Me: "But you wrote it on a small piece of paper, as is your habit, and you threw it out without using it."
> Real Me: "No, I'm sure I used it. I have it in the book."
> Writing Me: "I'm telling you you didn't! Please, wake up and put it down again."
> Real Me: "I know I used it!"
> Writing Me: "Caroline, would you please wake up and write this down and quit arguing?"
> This was the end of the dream. I woke up almost with a start and knew that I had to write. However, I did encounter a problem. I couldn't remember the plot. I did go through my scraps of miscella-neous notes, however. I knew if I came upon it I would recognize it right away. I never found it and am sure that I did, in fact, throw away the very thing I was instructed to write down.

It's important to note that, in some sense, even with its limita-tions, this unbounded quality of lucidity is greater than that found in nonlucid dreams. In an ordinary dream you think that you're awake, that what's happening is real, and therefore the ordinary boundaries remain intact. Perhaps they are not as rigid as in wak-ing life—strange things do happen after all in many nonlucid dreams—but the majority of boundaries remain in place. When the illusion of boundaries in nonlucid dreams fades, lucid dreams are sometimes triggered. This can occur when one finds oneself flying and recognizes, "I can't fly when awake, therefore I must be dreaming." Another example is a lucid dream Gackenbach had while working on this book:

> My children were in a large sea, fairly far out, but it was shallow. I walked out to join them, but when I turned toward the shore it was farther away than I'd imagined. I got a bit afraid and then the edges of reality began to blend together, like water running over a watercolor painting. It was all swilly looking. I was terrified and called out to my daughter to help me, but then I began to reason the situation through. I thought, This can't be; I must be dreaming. When I knew that I was in a dream the fear faded immediately, as did the dream setting and I considered what to do. A voice inside my head said, Fly. It was so persistent that I decided to do just that.

Only with lucidity does the full impact of the illusion of boundaries begin to strike us. We emphasize "begin" because even in lucid dreams we will often continue to function under the assumptions of the boundaries we carry forth from waking life. For Worsley this was illustrated by his ability while lucid to float a few inches above the ground, and his difficulty in flying more than five hundred feet above it. But it is possible to dissolve all boundaries while lucid; indeed, it is an essential aspect of moving into higher states of consciousness.

Feelings of unboundedness can cause difficulties. Psychiatrist and nightmare expert Ernest Hartmann found that people who suffer from frequent nightmares tend to have "thin" psychological boundaries. "The people with nightmares struck us as vulnerable," Hartmann writes. "They were clearly sensitive people in many senses of the word: They were easily hurt; they were empathic; in some cases they were unusually bothered by bright lights, loud noises. . . ."

Hartmann explains that their self boundaries could be considered thin in a number of ways.

> Their interpersonal boundaries were thin in that they tended to enter relationships very quickly, and very trustingly. Often the relationships had qualities of merging and stickiness; it was not easy for them to

extricate themselves. They had thin boundaries in the sense of sexual identity: None saw themselves as old-fashioned, totally masculine men or totally feminine women; they were more willing than most to see aspects of both sexes in themselves. And in their sexual preferences a large number were bisexual in their actions, or at least in their fantasy life. In terms of dreaming and the boundaries around their dreams, they were also unusual: Some described frequently waking from one dream into another dream. Even their basic sleep-wake boundaries were less thick and solid than for most. They described not being certain they were awake for quite a while in the morning, especially if they had had a vivid dream.

SO WHAT HAS ALL THIS GOT TO DO WITH WRESTLING?

The dissolution of boundaries is central to West German psychologist Paul Tholey's lucid dream work with athletes, including himself. Tholey won several important skateboarding championships a few years ago in West Germany and did so primarily not by training when awake, but by training in lucid dreams. "He's been able to put out his ego consciousness while doing the task because of his training in lucid dreams," explains Tholey's colleague Kaleb Utecht. In other words, while dreaming Tholey dissolves the established boundaries between the mind and body and himself and "other" in order to fully experience his sport. More important, Tholey carries over the lived dream form of his sport to actual waking performance.

Before we pursue Tholey's remarkable training program, let's look at a related and far more common athletic training technique: mental imaging. It is standard practice these days for most serious athletes to spend time imaging their game. If they play basketball, they may see themselves running through smoothly executed plays and tossing perfectly arched balls through the net. Swimmers may envision themselves expertly stroking their way to world record times. Jean-Claude Killy, one of the greatest Alpine skiers of all time, won a race without practicing on the course (an injury prevented him from doing so) by running through it in his mind. Richard M. Suinn, a psychologist at Colorado State University, explains how golfer Jack Nicklaus uses mental imagery: "He first visualizes the ball landing on the green and actually seeing the bounce, then he visualizes the arc of the ball in flight, and then his swing and the ball leaving the ground. His final step is to link these together in proper sequence: visualizing the swing, the ball's trajectory, and its landing and bouncing on the green." Similarly, Suinn reports, tennis champ Chris Evert, who is renowned for her consistent good play, "painstakingly rehearses the forthcoming match. She centers on anticipating her opponent's strategy and style and visualizes herself countering with her own attack. And, Bill Glass, a defensive end for the Cleveland Browns professional football team in the 1960s, learned to rehearse the quick-step across the line, throwing off the offensive tackle and charging the retreating quarterback, as if it were in a 'motion picture.' "

These mental imaging techniques are popular with athletes because they help improve performance. The National Research Council, an advisory branch of the National Academy of Sciences, recently released a statement supporting the usefulness of mental practice for tasks that have significant mental components, especially when the imaging is combined with physical practice. Suinn compares the "body-thinking" of mental imaging exercises to the "powerful illusions of certain dreams." Perhaps, he says, the major difference between dreams and mental imaging is that the latter is subject to conscious control. Enter the lucid dream.

Tholey originally traced some of the positive effects of lucid dreaming on athletic performance to the improvement of the sensory field. The crucial thing is to make sure that a dreamed tennis stroke, say, was executed on a tennis court, in the hot sun, with a crowd watching. He also found a relationship between improvement in athletic performance and the athlete's ability to shift his ego awareness to a particular situation. "This is especially relevant," Tholey says, "for those sports in which quick and risky reactions to changing situational conditions are prevalent." In a skateboard competition, for example, one cannot take time to think about how one's body should lean at a certain moment. There isn't time. With practice, one learns to lean at the right time. Tholey is arguing that the amount of actual practice time can be dramatically reduced by rehearsals that recreate the whole athletic environment during lucid dreaming.

Take the experience of a West German martial arts competitor. For years this man had been a student of karate, tae kwon do, and jujitsu. He decided that he would like to learn aikido, a discipline quite unlike the others. After studying for two years, he was still unable to learn aikido, largely because his previously learned movements refused to give way to the "softer" movements of aikido. Then he had the following dream, which he considers to be instrumental in finally making a breakthrough:

> On this particular evening, after still not succeeding in wearing down the attacker and taking him to the mat, I went to bed somewhat disheartened. While falling asleep, the situation ran through my mind time and again. While defending myself, the correct balancing movement collided with my inner impulse to execute a hard defensive block so that I repeatedly ended up unprotected and standing there like a question mark . . . a ridiculous and unworthy situation for the wearer of the black belt. During a dream that night, I fell down hard one time instead of rolling away. That day I had made up my mind to ask myself the critical question in this situation: "Am I awake or am I dreaming?" I was immediately lucid. Without thinking very long about it, I immediately went to my dojo, where I began an unsupervised training session on defense techniques with my dream partner. Time and time again, I went through the exercise in a loose and effortless way. It went better every time.

The man practiced in his lucid dreams for a week. When he once again began training, he says, "I amazed my instructor with an almost perfect defense. And even though we speeded up the tempo I didn't make any serious mistakes. From then on, I learned quickly and received my own training license after one year."

One skier wrote a letter to Tholey explaining his success in using lucid dreaming to help him master a particularly difficult skill called jetting.

> Jetting [the man wrote], with its strong shift of the center of gravity backwards, had always made me so afraid that I constantly fell and

came home covered with bruises. When I learned lucid dreaming I began to dream about skiing over moguls. I often used the hump to initiate flying in my dreams, but at some point I also began to lean back shortly before the hump, thereby taking my weight off the skies in order to change direction with my heels. That was a lot of fun, and after a few weeks it became clear to me during a lucid dream that my movements corresponded to jetting. When I went on a skiing vacation again the following winter and took a course, I mastered jetting in one week. I am absolutely convinced that it was connected to my lucid-dream exercises.

Tholey believes that in order for athletic performance to be enhanced through practice in the lucid dream, the dreamer must break through the ego's ordinary boundaries. A particularly successful example of this is an Olympic equestrian from South America whom Tholey trained with lucid dreaming to become "one with the horse." The rider achieved a state of perfect mutual empathy with the horse to the extent that he perceived the world through the eyes, ears, and nostrils of the horse. The rider was able to transfer his dream experiences to his actual riding.

In a lucid dream, I can form my figures to an extremely exact degree —whether in the sand of dressage competition or across the landscape of a cross-country course during military-style competition. I manage to do this in slow motion, giving the horse "assistance" at exactly the right moment in a particular movement phase. During lucid dreaming "I ride" the course through several times (three to nine times), exactly and completely. Based on this experience, my "body knowledge" is sufficient to get through the course automatically without conscious or deliberate effort.

Similarly, a sailboat pilot who was trying to learn to fly a sailplane explains how in lucid dreams he developed such a perfect unity with his sailplane that "his wings could feel the winds which are so important to the control of the aircraft." This, in turn, helped him fly the plane while awake.

In his lucid dream training, Tholey emphasizes a method that incorporates many of the same elements as waking imaging training. You can try them yourself.

• First, while awake, you should of course practice your sport. It's safe to say no amount of lucid dreaming alone will improve your game if you never practice at all.

• Second, watch expert athletes practice the sport. If you play tennis, watch players like Martina Navratilova, Boris Becker, or Steffi Graf closely, observing how they perform particular shots. Many videos are available that will enable you to study a certain move or style of play that you want to emulate. The important thing is to form a mental model of perfect performance in your mind.

• Third, when you turn lucid in a dream, replay that mental model. As with waking practice, be sure to internalize the performance. You are the outstanding tennis player or downhill skier. Also, be sure that your dream includes all the elements the actual sport would have. If you're practicing Alpine skiing, paint the dream scene with trees, snow, wind, mountains.

• Fourth—and this is the critical step according to Tholey— let your ego and body boundaries dissolve. You are the skier, the skis, the snow, the trees, the mountain, the wind. In a lucid dream about skating, dream psychologist Gayle Delaney describes this technique: "Because I know I'm dreaming, I can skate with wings on my blades . . . I can do anything. When I jump, I am weightless, and I fly as I turn in the air. When I spin, my balance is perfect. I feel a happiness that is one of the most profound I have ever known, and I am at one with the world. I feel all the forces of the harmony of the universe in my skating, and the intensity of my joy knows no bounds." It is this creative ability to become part of each facet of the activity in the dream that enables you to carry over the experience to waking performance

This unbounded state is easier to attain in the lucid dream because, as Globus points out, the lived world in the lucid dream is created anew by the intent of the dreamer. This does not mean that all motor behaviors and body boundaries are unlimited in the lucid dream. Worsley, for example, has explored the limits of breaking through physical boundaries while lucid. When he tried to stretch the length of his arm and both see and feel while lucid, he was unsuccessful in eight attempts. However, when he tried the task by willing his dream hand to crawl along a surface, he was successful in four out of seven attempts. "I discovered that I seemed to have two dream arms," says Worsley, "a visual arm and a haptic [one I could feel] arm. I could make the visual arm grow to a considerable length by willing my arm to stretch, but the haptic arm did not stretch with it unless I made special arrangements to keep it congruent with the visual arm. In order to do this, as my arm extended, I crawled my hand along a surface so that I could feel it doing something at the end of the arm, as well as see it."

In addition, Worsley observes that attempting certain movements while lucid may break through the physical boundary of sleep. When, for instance,

> I made a large movement of my leg while dreaming and sleep recording in the laboratory, I was lying face down. My legs were covered with a light quilt that was lying loose. Thus my lower legs were free to move by swinging upward from the knee. In the dream, which was lucid (signal verified), I was deliberately kicking backward with my right foot against a hard surface. Suddenly, I woke and found that my right lower leg was in the air. [The large movement was recorded on the polygraph and was followed in less than a second by characteristic signals that Worsley was waking up.] It seemed obvious to me that the kick in the dream had caused a large real movement of my physical leg.

Both the intent of the dreamer and the sleep environment may influence the outcome of such movements. Here is a lucid dream from research subject Bob Tucker that on the surface seems quite similar to Worsley's but with different outcomes.

> I was riding my bike to high school. . . . Then I saw a suitcase. Curious, I opened it and found some large bills wrapped in paper. I was deciding if it was right or wrong to steal it. I looked around and I saw nobody around so I started getting the large bills and some other items from the suitcase. Then I saw a large Indian. He wanted the money as well. He came at me. . . . I ducked and executed a perfect

side snap kick, and then I saw Mr. Kim, one of my old karate instructors. He just stood and watched. The large man took off his shirt revealing a muscular body. In anger he then ran at me. I had perfect timing again and perfectly executed an elevated front snap kick. He was lying on the ground and furious. I looked at my watch and noticed I was late for school. He came at me again with a wide right hook, which I blocked with my right arm, then drove a punch into his solar plexus. . . . Loudly he then said some slang words and finally left. I could not believe I fought so well. In other dreams my technique is good but slow. In this dream all the moves were premeditated and executed perfectly. I felt as if I was merely playing with this angered man.

Why did Worsley awaken when he kicked and Tucker did not? Clearly, individual differences determine to some extent the effect such movements have on the dreamer. Worsley was also in a sleep lab where it may take more effort and absorption to preserve sleep. Although both Tucker and Worsley knew they were dreaming, Tucker was totally absorbed in the dream world while Worsley was testing its limits and thus to some extent not entirely in it. And as other research has discovered, the more absorbed one is in the dream and the more vivid its imagery, the more likely one will be able to successfully apply the dreamed action when awake.

Being at one with the world around you, whether it be in a dream or in what we believe to be the "real" world, is crucial for excellence in sports. It is what the archer experiences in *Zen and the Art of Archery:* The Zen archer is so at one with the task, his lived world, that he can shoot bull's-eyes while blindfolded. Examples of this kind of unbounded state of mind can be found among many artists and athletes. University of Northern Iowa wrestling team psychologist David Whitsitt tells about the skills of sophomore Mark Schwab, a member of UNI's nationally ranked wrestling team. As a freshman, a year when most athletes don't even wrestle competitively, Schwab compiled more victories than any other wrestler in the history of UNI. Some people, Whitsitt comments, think Schwab was "born that way," but he thinks not. He explains the frustration of Schwab's coaches who normally shout instructions to their wrestlers while they are wrestling. But they can't get through to Schwab; he doesn't listen. It's as though his absorption is so complete that he simply doesn't hear them. And like a t'ai chi ch'uan master, Schwab wrestles with a flow to his movements, he wrestles as though there were no boundary between himself and his opponent.

Similarly, Tholey tells of a European junior boxing champion who managed to go "into" his opponents during a match after training within his lucid dreams. Tholey claims that at every second the boxer could predict what his opponent would do, in large part because he had practiced dissolving the boundaries between himself and his opponent while lucid.

"The sports equipment takes over the function of sensory and motor organs," explains Tholey. So, for example, a practiced skier feels the snow and the terrain with the skis, and rather than deliberately moving his body he moves the skis.

This single-minded absorption is similar to that found among meditators. Indeed, several researchers have found a positive relationship between the practice of meditation and sports performances for at least three groups of athletes: Olympic rowers, collegiate runners, and standing broad jumpers. This improvement in performance may in part be due to the positive effects of meditation, which has been shown to affect such things as muscle tension, reaction time, blood flow, and heart rate. In addition, meditation researcher A. J. Deikman reports that ego boundaries become more fluid in meditation, a state often sought by athletes and one found quite frequently in lucid dreams. This dissolution of ego boundaries is often spoken of in the meditative literature as occurring in moments of intense realization. This is strikingly illustrated by Michael Murphy and Steven Donovan in the book *The Physical and Psychological Effects of Meditation*. They relate an experience of Narendra, a disciple of the Indian saint Ramakrishna: "At the touch of the Master, Narendra felt overwhelmed and saw the walls of the room and everything around him whirling and vanishing. 'What are you doing to me?' he cried in terror. . . . He saw his own ego and the whole universe almost swallowed in a nameless void."

As we point out in chapter 9 (page 169), lucid dreamers (especially females) and TM meditators have been found to score high on measures of creativity. The dreams of meditators are more likely to be archetypical, vivid, bizarre, and recallable, a combination that may enhance creativity as well as self-awareness. As the great Indian sage Sri Aurobindo stated:

> As the inner consciousness grows . . . dream experiences increase in number, clearness, coherency, accuracy, and after some growth of experience . . . we can come to understand them and their significance to our inner life. We can by training become so conscious as to follow our own passage, usually veiled to our awareness and memory, through many realms and the process of the return to the waking state. At a certain pitch of this inner wakefulness this kind of sleep, a sleep of experience, can replace the ordinary subconscious slumber.

If creativity is at least in part a product of insight and recognition of unexpected relationships, a "sleep of experience" may serve to enhance our vision and help us to reclaim, as Murphy and Donovan have noted, "the full and external awareness that is our fundamental ground and source, in all of our experience."

Chapter 5

Phantoms in the Night

CONFRONTING YOUR DEMONS IN LUCID DREAMS

It was late Sunday night and Jill Day was having a nightmare. Before going to bed, she had watched a disturbing movie on TV about a serial murderer, and, recognizing her tendency to have dreams that are affected by such stories, she knew as she fell asleep that she had probably not seen the last of that emotionless killer. Perhaps because of that awareness, when the man from the movie suddenly appeared in her dream and threatened to kill her, she turned lucid. "I know this is a dream," she yelled at the man. "Now go away. Get out of here!" The image of the man dissolved, as did all other imagery, and she was left with a gray cloud of consciousness as she slowly drifed into the obscurity of dreamless sleep.

Banishing evil from a dream, jumping through a window and flying away from a heated argument. . . walking up to threatening dream characters and asking them what they want—such things are possible in lucid dreams. Conscious awareness within a dream enables one, in theory if not always in practice, to work with dream material therapeutically. The lucid dream is a relatively "safe" place to work through psychological problems. Indeed, the simple realization that what you are experiencing is a product of your imagination may offer some relief in a dream that is distressing. But working with your dreams while you're having them is not as simple as it sounds. In this chapter we'll explore lucid dream therapy, looking at both the advantages and dangers of using lucid dreams as an analyst's couch.

ON-LINE THERAPY

Lucid dreams enable you to work with dream material while you are experiencing it. You could, for instance, decide during a lucid dream to talk to a long-dead grandparent about a problem that may have existed between the two of you. Or you could choose to discuss the reason you are afraid of your brother *with* your brother while in the dream. Or you could decide to get back at him by clobbering him over the head with a flower pot or transforming him into a tree. To be actively involved with the dream experience while knowing that you are engaged in a self-created world introduces control into dreams. You can "will" yourself to confront difficult emotional issues and attempt to come to some understanding of why you feel the way you do. And you can do it in a safe setting where you maintain control.

Psychologist Joseph Dane calls working on emotional issues in lucid dreams "intrapersonal psychotherapy" and poses the question, "Which is the best therapist: waking or dreaming consciousness?" His answer to that question is both, "depending on which is healthier at the time." It is an answer, he explains, that forces the individual into the uncomfortable but necessary position of accepting responsibility for deciding what is "healthier" in any given instance. In other words, you become your own therapist. You recognize a problem in the lucid dream and attempt to resolve it, or at least to understand it. But as most people who have been in therapy know, identifying a problem is not as simple as it appears. You may quite innocently mislead yourself. So, for example, when you confront your brother in your dream and for the first time express your feelings honestly, you may feel some relief. But you may also be missing the deeper issue. Perhaps it is not your brother you're furious at, but some aspect of yourself that your brother represents. In many instances, you may be quite profoundly shut off from your true feelings, and though a waking therapist may not always be able to help, he or she will often serve as a guide to push you in the direction of emotional truth.

Psychologists, of course, have traditionally turned to dreams for information. They often provide insights into the nature of an individual's psyche. To be in a dream and conscious would seem to be an ideal setting for therapy, and for at least two psychologists it has been.

For the past decade, West German psychologists Paul Tholey and Norbort Sattler have been training students and patients to lucid dream. They have learned that most people can learn to lucid dream, and once having done so they can learn to deal effectively with unconscious conflicts. Tholey, who began studying lucid dreaming in 1959, first began investigating the therapeutic potential of lucid, or what he called klartraum (clear), dreams when he found both helpful and threatening figures appearing in his own lucid dreams. For example, after his father's death, Tholey often dreamed about him as a dangerous figure who insulted and threatened him.

When I became lucid, I would beat him in anger. He was then sometimes transformed into a more primitive creature, like an animal, or a mummy. Whenever I won, I was overcome by a feeling of triumph. Nevertheless my father continued to appear as a threatening figure in subsequent dreams. Then I had the following decisive dream. I became lucid while being chased by a tiger, and wanted to flee. I then pulled myself together, stood my ground, and asked, "Who are you?" The tiger was taken aback but was transformed into my father and answered, "I am your father and will now tell you what you are to do!"

In contrast to my earlier dreams, I did not attempt to beat him but tried to get involved in a dialogue with him. I told him that he could not order me around. I rejected his threats and insults. On the other hand, I had to admit that some of my father's criticism was justified, and I decided to change my behavior accordingly. At that moment, my father became friendly, and we shook hands. I asked him if he could help me, and he encouraged me to go my own way alone. My father then seemed to slip into my own body, and I remained alone in the dream.

This dream, Tholey reports, had a "liberating and encouraging" effect on his dreams and life. "My father never again appeared as a threatening dream figure," he says. "In the waking state, my unreasonable fear and inhibitions in my dealings with persons of authority disappeared."

Tholey has found that the lucid dream has several therapeutic advantages over nonlucid dreams. First, lucidity seems to create an environment in which the dream ego is less afraid of threatening dream figures or situations and is more willing to confront them. Second, the ability to manipulate dream content allows the dream ego to "get in touch with places, times, situations, or persons" that are important to the dreamer and that he or she desires to investigate. In addition, when conversing with other dream figures, the dreamer's ego is often capable of recognizing the complex dynamics that may be taking place between him or her and the dream figures. Most important, Tholey believes that if one can learn to handle the dream ego appropriately, it is possible to make positive changes in one's personality.

It is not lucid dreaming per se that allows self-healing and growth, but the action of the dream ego. Some of Tholey's students had trouble conjuring up threatening dream figures with which to interact. Others responded inappropriately when they did appear: Some dreamers became overly aggressive with hostile dream characters and killed them; others became totally submissive and allowed themselves to be killed. He offers the following advice to lucid dreamers who find themselves face-to-face with a fearful dream figure:

1. Do not attempt to flee from a threatening dream figure. Rather, confront him courageously. Look at him openly and ask him in a friendly way, "Who are you?" or "Who am I?"
2. If it is possible to address the dream figure, try to come to a reconciliation with him through a constructive dialogue. If agreement is impossible, try to frame the conflict as an open dispute. Refuse his insults or threats, but recognize his justified objections.
3. Do not surrender to an attack by a dream figure. Show your readiness to defend yourself by taking a defensive position and by staring the dream figure in the eyes. If a fight is unavoidable, attempt to conquer the dream enemy, but do not try to kill. Offer reconciliation to the conquered enemy.
4. Attempt to reconcile with the hostile dream figure in thought, words, and/or gestures.
5. If a reconciliation does not seem possible, separate yourself from the figure in thought, word, and/or bodily withdrawal.
6. After reconciliation, ask the dream figure if he can help you. Then mention specific problems in your waking or dream life with which you need help.

Some of these basic principles were originally recommended by anthropologist Kilton Stewart in his work with the Senoi of Malaysia, a relatively "primitive" tribe who Stewart contended worked extensively with their dreams. Although the Senoi's reliance on dreams as a guiding force in their lives has been written about extensively, later anthropological work suggests that there is more myth than reality in Stewart's ethnographic study.

Confronting and conquering fearsome dream characters or situations are common responses in lucid nightmares. Elaine Smith of Matewan, West Virginia, for example, used physical violence while lucid to handle the following nightmare:

> I was in a building with a group of people. The building was surrounded by zombies. I had a gun that misfired every time I tried to shoot a creature. They managed to break in and we were quickly surrounded. I knew that our escape depended on my gun working.

Suddenly, I realized that I was dreaming and that I could force the gun to work by willing it to do so. The gun began firing and we escaped.

An aggressive response to zombies or other nocturnal terrorists relieves the immediate stress of the nightmare, but guns are not required for a successful escape. Sharon Clauss of Redondo Beach, California, used verbal aggression to dispatch dream demons in the following lucid dream:

I am in a dark house. It seems to be sunset, and although it doesn't look like the house I grew up in, I seem to know that it is. There are objects flying from the walls and shelves, and I'm clutching my mom to protect her. We know that it is a ghost. We can't see it and we can't control its actions. I am worked up to the point that I refuse to believe this could be happening. I am so frightened by the unseen enemy that I begin to yell, "You can't hurt us. You have no strength, no strength!" The objects stop flying and there are a few banging sounds and then it quiets down. I have stopped holding my mom because I'm no longer afraid. I am angry. The house is dark and I think to myself, "I don't have to be in the dark, I want light," and the rooms are lit. It's as if the whole time I know I can control these things. It's mostly out of anger that I realize I'm dreaming. I just refuse to have these reoccurring nightmares of the ghosts, so I have settled this in my dreams by forcing myself to know it's not out of control.

Christine Baker of Brooklyn, New York, has used flying to turn a frightening lucid dream into a humorous one.

I am walking down an unidentified alley late at night. There are many fire escapes on the backs of the buildings which I am passing in the alley. I am being followed, but the knowledge does not disturb me very much. I feel more curiosity than fear. I finally look over my shoulder to see a man—but I can't see his face—wearing a fedora and trenchcoat and carrying a knife. When he realizes I've seen him, he begins to run after me. I still feel no real fear, however, because I am very much aware that this is a dream and I am in no real danger. I wait until he is perhaps twenty yards away from me, and then I take a running start and fly up to the nearest fire escape. My pursuer begins to climb up the fire escape after me, but I merely soar over to the next one, then the next one, laughing at his clumsy attempts to overtake me.

Baker says that beginning in childhood, she has consistently been able to cast off evil images while lucid, changing the course of a nightmare. "I have not had a nightmare which I was not able to control," she says.

As Tholey has said, you don't always need to confront an aggressive dream figure to "disarm" him. Patricia Garfield, author of several popular books on dreaming, explains that "by yielding, by providing no solid resistance, the intended victim can render an attacker helpless. He fails to get at a person who is so supple, so light, so quick, so 'like water,' that there is nothing to receive the brutal action. Exhausted, the attacker quits. We may not be brave enough or, depending on one's point of view, foolhardly enough to attempt such 'going with' a hostile figure while awake, but we are free to do so while asleep."

Even when we fail to manipulate a dream, we can still be left with a sense of mastery by learning to wake ourselves up. A woman on the West Coast relates one such lucid experience:

> I was in total darkness. I knew I was in my living room but there was no light at all. The only sound I could hear was the sound of my blood rushing in my ears. This sound filled the room and I was very afraid. Suddenly a man I recognized as Rutger Hauer (an actor who has portrayed the kind of villain that terrifies me) was standing in front of me. There was a light around him, a fuzzy light, but I could see him clearly. I said, "Time to bug out of this dream." He laughed at me and said, "Just because you know that you are dreaming does not mean you have the power to control it." I tried to "teleport" myself somewhere else and failed. He laughed again and I felt terrified! I told him, "I may not be able to change this dream, but I am strong enough to wake myself." I threw my head back and shouted, "Wake up *now!*" I awoke slightly disoriented but overall very excited.

Tholey's colleague Sattler teaches his clients that they can "always end a dream by fixation." If, for instance, you are locked in a room with a man who is threatening to slash your face with a knife, you will be able to wake up from the dream by staring directly at the knife or at a ring on the man's finger or at a light that may be on in the room. The essential thing is to stare at one object.

Working therapeutically with lucid dreams is quite different from merely controlling them. Control for the thrill of it can sometimes have disturbing consequences. A California man dreamed of being chased by a group of people who he believed was going to kill him. He found it hard to run away and was terrified. "I remember questioning if this was really happening to me," he explains, "and it was at this time that I realized that I was dreaming." Once lucid, he was no longer afraid and turned to face his attackers. "I raised my hand and pointed it at them as if to cast a spell on them," he recounts. "I thought of beautiful ladies and sex. One by one, they began to turn into beautiful ladies . . . but not fast enough, as some of the soldiers were almost upon me at this time. I dodged the few remaining soldiers by jumping over their heads and floating above them. Some of the soldiers ran away and the remaining soldiers turned into ladies. I began jumping on one of them and began raping her. Just as I was beginning to orgasm, I awoke."

Psychotherapist Scott Sparrow points out that although one can easily escape from or destroy a dream figure, the skill should not be thought of as an end in itself. "Such actions," he says, "often fit into a developmental continuum as intermediate accomplishments. As the therapist, I serve as one who encourages the dreamer not to get stuck in such intermediate stages, and to continue working toward dialogue, reconciliation, and integration."

In addition to getting stuck with a less than enlightening bag of tricks, some lucid dreamers may also get in the habit of turning nasty dreams into sweet ones. The consciousness in their dreams may begin to function as it does in waking life, complete with its unconscious defenses, such as denial or avoidance. As psychologist Gayle Delaney points out, the very appearance of dream consciousness contaminates the dream with the attitudes and ways of coping that one employs while awake. "The single most destructive advice is to encourage people to manipulate their dreams to have happy endings," Delaney says. "I encourage people to use lucidity to explore the dream rather than to control it." She believes that it is often better for people to wake up from a horrible nightmare than from a lucid dream that they have sugarcoated. The nightmare forces the dreamer to recognize, however superficially, that he or she is conflicted or in trouble.

In fact, lucidity itself may become a defense mechanism. "One can work at becoming more lucid at the expense of becoming more aware," explains Erik Craig, a Massachusetts-based existential psychotherapist. One may focus attention on lucidity "in order that the meaningfulness of one's dreams may be avoided." It is quite possible, Craig contends, for lucid dreams to become fetishes, "psychic objects for self-gratification or even self-congratulation." Lucidity can serve, he says, as "a narcissistic flight from one's fuller, though perhaps less appealing, possibilities."

In waking therapies, the pain caused by a nightmare can often stimulate associations and memories that serve to break down the patient's defenses and move him or her toward valuable insights. Craig's worry is that lucid dreamers may be avoiding the possibility of that insight when they change their dreams. He recounts a dream in which a high school student dreamed that her father was the captain of a ship. He was sitting on the bow of his ship apparently oblivious to a storm that raged about him and threatened to sink his ship. At this point the woman turned lucid: She realized that she could stop the storm and did so. This made both her and her father feel "great." By altering the dream, Craig believes that the woman sidestepped the deeper feelings of the dream, the painful feelings that gave rise to the nightmare, namely her distress over her waking father's alcoholism. The lucidity, says Craig, allowed her to "bolster her defenses against the awareness of this very painful and threatening event."

Learning to cope with our problems and not escape them is as much of a challenge in lucid dreams as it is in waking life. Not surprisingly, lucid dreamers will often employ the same defensive actions during a dream as they do while awake. That's one reason most clinicians argue that it's important to engage dream characters in conversation. By posing questions to the characters or to other aspects of the dream, you may be able to get in touch with and try to work through sensitive emotional issues. If the dialogue is productive, you may see the dream character change shape, become less fearsome, get smaller, disappear, or merge with your "self" in the dream. If you're not properly prepared for such dialogues, the responses your dream characters give you may not make sense. You may need to think carefully about what questions you ask, perhaps focusing on one aspect of the dream scene.

One of Delaney's clients, for instance, was a man with a history of dating attractive women who lacked depth and maturity. In a lucid dream, he came upon an empty house and asked the house why it was empty. A voice replied, "The house is empty because your life is empty." As sappy as the line was, it had a powerful effect, allowing the man to confront certain issues in therapy that he had been avoiding. He began discussing honestly why he feared intimacy, and he eventually was able to change his dating behavior and enter into a serious relationship with a mature, if less attractive, woman.

This sort of change is the goal of lucid dream therapy. Another example of insight gained through lucid dream therapy comes from one of Tholey's patients. For a period when he was thirty-eight the patient suffered from severe depression. Before going to sleep one night, he thought seriously about committing suicide. During a dream in which he turned lucid, the patient recounts, "I met a man who grinned diabolically and asked, 'Well, do you know the way to the Reaper [death] now?'" The dream disturbed the man to such an extent that he fell asleep the following night with the desire to obtain help in a further lucid dream.

In this dream he was skiing. He jumped in the dream so high that he turned lucid. After he finished skiing, he met a hooded man who was standing in front of a cave. As he came closer to the man, he noticed that a skull was looking at him. "In my shock," the man says, "I stabbed at Death with my ski stick, but

I only stabbed between bones." He then realized that aggressive behavior in a lucid dream was pointless, and he addressed the man. "Who are you?" he asked. The latter answered, "The plundering wolf!" The dreamer asked, "Can you help me?" Death invited him to go into the cave with him. At the far end of the cave, they came to a vault in which there was a tombstone. Death indicated a painted skeleton on the tombstone and said, "Look, this stands behind every man. But you are not dead, you are alive." He made it clear to the dreamer, in an impressive way, how unimportant his problems were in the face of death.

As beneficial as dialoguing with a dream character may be, Tholey believes the most effective technique is to get the lucid dreamer's "ego" to enter the body of another dream character. Tholey illustrates this with a lucid dream from a teenager who was having trouble with her boyfriend.

> I asked myself . . . why he didn't return my feelings and wanted to get an answer to this question in the dream. It was then that I became aware of my spirit, that is, that part of me I think of as my "self," detaching itself from my body and floating across to his body and entered into it. . . . It felt really strange; everything was so different and so much more restricted than in my body, and so unfamiliar. It was the kind of feeling you have when you have driven a Mercedes for years, know the car inside out, and then suddenly change it for an Austin Mini. . . . As time went on, however, I got used to being in his body. . . . I saw how he perceived me, the effect I had on him, and the feelings he had for me. I saw the conflict he was in. After all, he had, I suppose, become aware of my feelings for him, and he was very fond of me, but he did not want to go out with me as such. . . . I understood why he had been so reserved with me, and I realized that he would never return my feelings."

When Tholey suggests that dream figures have independent consciousnesses, that each one possesses personality traits and a set of behaviors in and of themselves, he does not mean to imply that they are somehow independent beings that exist outside the dreamer's own self. They are instead conflicting ideas and emotions coming from the dreamer.

Because of this, Tholey has gradually modified his approach to handling hostile dream figures. In the past, he instructed his patients on occasion to fight a dream character if necessary, but he now believes that one should never resort to aggression in an attempt to resolve a quarrel—instead, do anything to discuss the matter openly. "The appearance of a hostile, threatening dream figure may reflect, in symbolic form, an internal psychological conflict," he explains. "The threatening figure is often the personification of an 'off-split,' a 'repressed,' or an 'isolated' subsystem of the personality." By engaging this isolated part of oneself in conversation, one may establish some communication with it and begin the process of integration. If the lucid dreamer does battle with a hostile dream character, it may drive the figure into deeper isolation within the self.

DREAM BEHAVIORISM

Behaviorist psychology holds that it's possible to change an individual's behavior by reinforcing or rewarding the actions desired and punishing or negatively reinforcing undesirable actions. Understanding the reasons for one's action, behaviorists contend, is not necessary to change. Although most psychologists now view a pure behaviorist therapy with some skepticism, it can play a role in lucid dream therapy. Tholey has found that a patient can reap the benefits of a dreamed action without understanding why. One of his clients, a twenty-eight-year-old female student, for example, came to Tholey complaining of nightmares. She showed signs of anxiety and depression, a result perhaps of her failing relationship with her husband and her relationship with her dying father. Tholey discussed ways of dealing with the frightening characters that haunted her nightmares, and in a dream that followed these sessions, the woman had a lucid dream that in essential ways served to heal her pain. The dream went like this: The woman was in the house in which she had lived as a child, waiting for a group of people to arrive who intended to harm her. She remembered that this setting often occurred in her dreams, a thought that gave rise to lucidity. "Despite the fact that she was stuck with fear and wanted to flee," explains Tholey, "she overcame the fear and courageously stood her ground." Then people in long robes approached. As she looked at the first figure to come close—a gigantic man with a cold, blue face and glowing eyes—she followed Tholey's instructions and asked him, "What are you doing here? What do you want from me?"

The man looked at her sadly and helplessly as he said, "Why, you called us. You need us for your anxiety." At this, the man shrank to normal size. His face turned flesh colored and his eyes ceased to glow. Since this first lucid dream, the woman has not had any more nightmares and has felt less anxious in her waking life. But despite the effects, the woman was unable to interpret or make sense of the dream.

Tholey has several theories about how dreams may help to heal us even if we don't understand them. Perhaps, he suggests, dreams such as the one mentioned above represent the resolution of an unconscious conflict that need not become conscious in order to be resolved. The courage needed to confront a hostile dream figure may bolster the dreamer's ego in a way that affects his or her waking life. Or it may be that confronting our fears serves to desensitize us: Talking about nightmares in waking therapy, for instance, sometimes helps to process the unconscious fears that give rise to them.

This desensitization may be particularly useful in treating phobias. For example, Donna Crespo of White Plains, New York, used lucid dreaming to conquer her fear of bugs.

I used to be petrified of bugs: insects, spiders, nasty crawly things. It got to be a pain in the neck. I love camping, but who can take you seriously when you have to have someone else check your tent every night for bugs? Or a grown woman who's afraid of squashing a spider? It's ridiculous and embarrassing. So, one night I resolved that I was going to dream myself into a talk with bugs. I dreamt that I became very small, so small that cockroaches became ten feet tall. You would think that the very idea of a ten-foot cockroach would send me into hysterics, but I was in control of the dream and I wasn't afraid. So I had a conversation with this cockroach. And I looked at him close up. He really didn't look all that repulsive like bugs usually do when they blow up photos of them for *Smithsonian* or *National Geographic* magazines. We had a nice talk, and while I was at it, I dreamt myself into being a bug so I could see what it was like. I'm not saying that I scuttled around the floor, but I looked at this bug and saw him the way that other bugs must see him. It wasn't really scary anymore, just different. I could look at him and say, "Yeah, that's a cockroach," with as little emotion as I could say, "Yeah, that's a poodle." Then when I woke up I wasn't afraid of bugs anymore. I don't go around talking to them, but I could pick one up if I had to. I can handle them now, where before I couldn't even look at them.

Another lucid dreamer learned to temper his fear of heights. When he first began flying in his lucid dreams, the man explains, he ascended too quickly, which frightened him so much he woke up. He began experimenting with various heights in his dreams, learning gradually how to control how high he flew. "Now," he says, "when I'm awake and climbing or standing at a serious height, I don't feel nearly as frightened as before."

Psychologist Peter Fellows, who has used lucid dreaming with some of his patients, says that he never teaches "dream interpretation" as part of lucid dream therapy. He explains:

Time in a lucid dream is a precious commodity and I do not like to waste it. If, as I am dreaming, I become lucid at a point in the scenario where someone is sitting on my head, I do not begin to question him or her on the symbolic meaning of the experience. I act, and quickly. When symbolic dreams "work" for us, a waking life conflict is acted out in symbolic guise and resolved. Somehow, that resolution is translated back into real life with real effect. What lucidity enables us to do is to ensure that the dream conflict gets resolved and to reap the benefits in self-confidence that comes from doing so consciously. Interpreting the dream, knowing exactly what area of one's life the dream conflict is related to, is fine, but when the work is actually done, the result will be experienced whether or not the interpretation was correct.

This view is not unique to clinicians who deal with lucid dreams. Milton H. Erickson, a respected authority on hypnosis, uses hypnotic techniques that distract the conscious mind, leaving him free to talk to his clients' unconscious. He emphasizes that for hypnotic suggestions to work the conscious self does not need to remember what has been suggested to it—the changes will eventually arise "spontaneously" as a natural self-governing process.

Sattler agrees that intellectual insight is not essential to positive therapeutic outcomes. "You have to get in contact with all this old stuff," he says. "It's really the only way out . . . to live through something." In part this is true because while lucid you are working deep within the unconscious and then acting out the process in an alternative reality (the dream). When you wake up from the dream, you are then able to experience behavioral change without needing an in-depth understanding of what you have experienced.

LUCID BOUNDARIES

Obviously, lucid dreaming is not a panacea for life's problems. And it will never replace traditional psychotherapies. Indeed, working with lucidity may be most beneficial when it's used in conjunction with other therapy and perhaps when it is used in moderation. The whole issue of whether to control dreams or not is one of great concern among dream researchers. Complete control of dream content is probably not even possible. As Jungian analyst James Albert Hall has observed, "The waking ego is like a gatekeeper who can *permit* or deny entrance into the boundaries which he guards, but who is powerless to *command* the appearance or disappearance of a particular entrant (content), however much he might desire it."

Joseph Dane notes that Hall's analysis is also true in lucid dreaming and relates the following dream from one of his women patients as an example:

> Now I realize that I can control the dream sequence. I decide I want the rain to stop. It doesn't, and I wonder to myself why it's so important that it keep on raining, and what the rain could represent. I come to a platform where there are some people standing around. I go from

one to another asking them, "What time does the next train leave?"
But they all ignore me. It's as if I'm not even there. I begin to feel
angry and frustrated, but I stop myself and think, "The next one I
speak to won't be like this."

The next character the woman encounters not only gives her an
answer but also challenges her to further analyze the source of her
frustration and anger with the other dream characters. The character says, "Well, that depends on where you want to go." With
that comment, the dream ends. Although the dreamer may have
decided that the next dream character would not ignore her, the
answer she received seems to have revealed the reason for the
other characters' silence: Some part of the woman was telling her
that she was placing too much emphasis on "getting somewhere"
without first being clear where she was or where in fact it was she
wanted to go.

Dane suggests that deciding to control one's dreams is a bit like
"deciding" whether to control one's unconscious impulses in
waking life. The latter seems impossible, yet we attempt it every
day when we work on bad habits by saying, "I mustn't let myself
do that," as if some part of us could control, prevent, or give
permission for certain unconscious behavior. Similarly, dreams
can have their own agenda, and like everything else that arises
from the unconscious, that agenda may be positive or negative,
healthy or unhealthy. The difficulty is knowing ahead of time
which is which.

In the face of such uncertainty, says Dane, control becomes an
inappropriate goal. The issue is not whether or not to control the
content of a dream, but rather how to enhance cooperation between waking and dreaming consciousness in order to foster mutual respect between the two states of consciousness. Such
cooperation requires a sort of give and take between waking and
dreaming consciousness, just as there is give and take between
therapist and client. The focus in dream control should be on
learning how to control one's response to dream events, not on
controlling the creation of those events.

Psychotherapist Kenneth Kelzer cautions about the burnout

that can occur when dreamers use lucidity too often as a vehicle for self-growth. "What I am referring to," Kelzer explains, "is a mental state of exhaustion that comes from overdoing a good thing, from exposing oneself to too much mental-emotional intensity for too prolonged a period of time." To avoid this, Kelzer draws on his own experience, citing five things he has learned that help balance his lucid and waking experiences:

• He discusses his reflections about lucid dreaming with others, especially those who also have had lucid dreams.

• He compares the highly intense lucid dreams with those of lesser intensity.

• He doesn't worry if he hasn't had a lucid dream for a while. He accepts the fallow periods as time needed for integration.

• He doesn't force lucidity but allows it to come naturally.

• He engages in physical activity to give his mind time off from the exploration of the inner world.

In addition to following these five points, Kelzer recommends "the close tutelage of an experienced guide" when working with lucidity. As in meditation, discussing one's experiences with someone more familiar with the landscape can circumvent problems and help put things in perspective.

A guide will also be able to spot excesses. As Mark Barroso of Tampa, Florida, discovered, lucidity can be addictive. "Living in the dream world became preferable to reality," Barroso wrote in *Lucidity Letter*. "I would lie in bed, miss work, and wrap myself in a catatonic state in which to spin dreams, dreams, dreams. I would sleep in public places to use stimuli for my lucid dreams. . . . Basically, all I did was lucid dream and nothing else. With a life like that it could be hard to pay the rent. . . . I finally OD'd on lucid dreaming, and I stayed in bed for four or five days, only rising to drink and use the bathroom."

Lucid dreaming can also cause quasi-psychotic splits with reality. One can become confused over what is real and what has been dreamed. This is illustrated by Bruce Marcot of Portland, Oregon, who in 1976 was doing some very sophisticated lucid dreaming experiments. "I was able to become acutely aware of my body sleeping in bed," he explains. "I was asleep and dreaming, but conscious that I was dreaming, and conscious of my actual body in bed, which I willfully moved about. . . . I began to become confused as to when I was normally asleep, asleep in this lucid dream state, or awake. At one point, I was able to lie in bed, asleep in a lucid dream, with my [dream] eyes open and with full consciousness of moving my [dream] arms, legs, and face. It was only a step from there to sleepwalking in an aware, lucid dream state. What would distinguish these various states of mind if I was conscious and able to move? The various realities were beginning to eclipse one another. . . ." He decided to abandon the experiments before he became more confused.

One may also find that the expansion of consciousness that sometimes accompanies a lucid dream is more than he or she can handle. Here's an example from Vincent MacTiernan of New York. He is a sophisticated lucid dreamer who became so proficient that he attempted to solve math problems while asleep. In one lucid dream in which most of his attention was on solving a math problem he explains,

> I began to feel great pressure in my eyes. It felt like the feeling you get when you spin around many times and get that slight headache or when you ride in a moving vehicle. I wasn't too concerned though. The most unusual thing . . . was that with each correct answer, I felt my mind expand. The dream became more lucid and my peripheral vision was greatly enhanced. I also felt my dream body become more solid; I saw my hands and feet with much greater clarity.
>
> What happened next scared me more than anything I ever experienced in my life. I found my consciousness so expanded that for a moment I could not tell if this was just a dream or [another] reality. The feeling was overwhelming. I became very frightened. Everything around me had become too clear to be just a dream, and it felt as if my physical body and mind were converging together with my dream body. It was very frightening. Something in the back of my mind told me that if I didn't stop with the math problems and awaken soon, I would not be able to awaken at all, and I would die. This last word stuck heavy on me. I became very, very nervous and started to panic.
>
> I immediately dropped the paper and pencil and walked away from the desk. But walking this time was different from any I had experi-

enced in a dream. This time I seemed to feel the weight of each foot as it hit the ground. Actual weight. It was like I was there in my physical body. I began to tremble. What was happening was too much for me to comprehend. I just wanted to wake up. When I tried, I found out that I could not. This scared me very badly. . . . Despite my efforts to wake up I found I still could not.

Out of desperation I tried to focus my mind on my physical body. It worked. For an instant I saw my face, in bed, overlap my vision like a double exposure. I then felt my dream body—or more accurately my mind—being sucked up into a vacuum and into a tunnel. The feeling was most unusual; I had never felt it before. This tunnel feeling was the closest thing I could think of to describe the experience. I then felt I was jerked into my physical body. When I awoke, I had that pressure in my eyes still, and it lasted most of the day. During the course of the day . . . I felt a new outlook on my life. I felt better to be alive than I ever had before.

The experience of multiple layers of consciousness and alternate realities is not always frightening. Kelzer speaks of being simultaneously aware of his wife's efforts to make love to him in the early morning while at the same time experiencing a "transformative" lucid dream. "She is extending a sexual invitation to me and I am completely clear that she is touching my physical body and is hoping to arouse me from sleep," he writes. "Still lucid, I gaze with total absorption at the infant Jesus, appreciating so much the beautiful, glowing light that radiates from him continuously. I feel so solidly established in the lucid state and so transfixed by this vision that I know that Charlene's touching my physical body cannot pull me out of lucidity or out of the dream."

It is a fair statement to say that we are on the ground floor in our exploration of consciousness in sleep. Not surprisingly, then, the spiritual or transpersonal questions raised by lucid dreaming are clearly difficult for most people to assess and make some sense of. Even experienced travelers along spiritual paths have expressed caution in using the lucid state. Tibetan Buddhists who produced the first in-depth discussion of lucid dreaming in the "Yoga of the Dream State" viewed lucid dreaming as a potentially dangerous state if pursued outside a serious meditative practice.

In other words, for lucid dreaming to be truly efficacious, it must be placed in perspective.

Doing this is not always easy. The problems encountered may be similar to those some Westerners run into when studying an Eastern religion and/or when meditating. Psychologist Jack Engler, co-author of *Transformations of Consciousness,* believes that many of these difficulties occur when a too heavily burdened "self" attempts to experience transcendence. Before one can realistically hope to move toward transcendence, Engler says, one must clear away the baggage of unresolved psychological issues and integrate the self. The same applies to lucid dreaming: One should first try to deal with ordinary day-to-day problems in lucid dreams before using them as a spiritual vehicle. Further support for this caution comes from a recent study by Mary Darling, a graduate student in psychology at Carleton University. Although other researchers have shown that lucidity can emerge naturally when one increases self-reflectiveness in waking life (through psychotherapy, for example), Darling discovered that when people were *trained* to lucid dream, they scored no higher on scales of self-reflectiveness than did people who were not trained to lucid dream. In other words, forcing lucidity on a system will not necessarily increase one's self-awareness, and as we have been arguing, it may, in fact, interfere with psychological stability.

The problems incurred without this preliminary psychological work can be hard to separate from difficulties often encountered in transpersonal experiences. As transpersonal theorists Ken Wilber and Mark Epstein point out, spiritual pathologies can look psychotic, and the difference can often be found only by looking at the history of the individual involved: The paranoid schizophrenic and the guru may both have visions of a demon or an angel. But the latter will be able to make sense of such a disturbing sight because he or she has been trained to do so.

In lucid dreaming, seeking spiritual insight may present some problems. An example comes from the lucid dreaming history of Scott Sparrow. "I found that at the height of my lucid dreaming, I ran into a brick wall of sorts," he explains. "Lucid dreaming had become evidence of my evolution, a merit badge of sorts. Of course, I thought I was handling it okay; but I had no idea what I was repressing. Who does? Well, all kinds of very angry people began showing up in my dreams and turning rather demonic to boot. A black panther walked in the front door and would not go away no matter how much I told him he was only a dream."

Perhaps, Sparrow suggests, such unpleasant experiences are endemic to any "path." "Maybe we need to fly, then crash, then pick up and pursue the path with more sobriety," he says. We shouldn't think we have failed simply because we have encountered problems. "How I wish," says Sparrow, "there had been someone around me [when I was having trouble] to say, 'This is part of it. Pick yourself up, and you'll make it through okay.' It would have made the path a lot more meaningful, if not easier to tolerate."

Despite the confusion and anxiety that sometimes accompany lucid dreaming, it can be a valuable tool for individuals who are seeking to better understand themselves. The essential question to ask, as psychotherapist Erik Craig has stated, is, " 'How may we best acquire and use the knowledge of this human territory in a way that respects and conserves its essential structure and nature?' . . . There are very, very few opportunities to have life completely thrown at us, to have life explode around us, and for us to be tossed in the middle of it. . . ." Lucid dreaming is such an experience, and if we learn to use it well, we do not yet know how far along the path to self-enlightenment it will carry us.

Chapter 6

The Healer Within

CAN DREAMS KEEP YOU HEALTHY?

Most people wouldn't give it a second thought. The idea of healing themselves in a dream seems as remote as an afternoon jaunt up Mount Everest. But others, like David Pack of Knoxville, Tennessee, think a lot about it. A few years ago during a heated arm-wrestling match, he injured his arm, and despite medical treatment it was still hurting him badly enough six months later that he was unable to continue working in the construction business. As an act of desperation he suggested to himself before falling asleep that his arm be healed. "I recall a man in my dream state twisting and poking around on my elbow and it hurt," Pack explains. "I asked him what he was doing, and he said, 'You have received two healings.' " It was at this point that Pack realized that he was dreaming.

Upon awakening, Pack discovered that his right arm was tingling as though it had gone to sleep. But when the tingling was

100

gone so was the pain. His arm was, as he put it, as "good as new." He was curious, though, about why the voice had proclaimed two healings. He found out the same week when a cyst in his back, which had been bothering him on and off for ten years, finally burst, relieving his chronic pain.

The idea that dreams are somehow involved in our biological well-being is anything but new. Ailing citizens in ancient Greece would sometimes journey for miles for an overnight stay at a temple of healing. There they would go through rituals of purification and lie down on the skins of sacrificial animals, awaiting a dream that would heal, the nocturnal gift of a giving god. The Romans, too, slept in temples for messages of healing from the gods. Their instructions were not always easy to follow: One Roman citizen was instructed to walk barefoot in winter, use emetics, and sacrifice one of his fingers in order to purge his illness. Aristotle, true to form, did not share these beliefs. Seeing no evidence that dreams came from the gods, he reasoned that they sprang from the center of feeling—the heart. That being so, he reflected, it was still possible to diagnose an illness or prescribe a cure from the contents of a dream because dreams mirrored the organic functions of the body.

Today's scientists require more evidence for their convictions than did Aristotle. Indeed, the connection between dreams and bodily functions still lurks in the uncertain terrain of clinical and case studies (never to be discounted in science) and hypothesis. But substantive work is being done, particularly in the area of mental images. And it is here that dream researchers have turned for the first glimpses of how dreams, which are forms of mental images, can reflect or change our physiology.

As far back as the 1930s, researcher Edmund Jacobson found that if you "imagine" or visualize yourself doing a particular action, say lifting an object, the muscles in the arm you were thinking about show increased electrical activity. Subsequent studies substantiated Jacobson's work. Subjects were found to salivate more when asked to produce images of their favorite foods than when they thought of food they dislike. Imagining an object moving across the sky produced more oculomotor (eye) movements than visualizing a stationary object; and generating images of abstract words produced more pupil dilation in subjects than did images of concrete words, which are easier to visualize. In study after study, researchers have found a connection between what people fantasize or imagine and the biological activity involved in actually performing those activities. In one particularly fascinating study, Robert Kuzendorf, a cognitive psychologist at the University of Lowell in Lowell, Massachusetts, attached electrodes to the eyes of twenty subjects, five of whom were capable of producing very vivid mental images. He had each of them look at red and green lights that were flashed in front of their eyes. Kuzendorf found that each color affected the retina differently: Red produced one electrical pattern, green another. He then asked the five subjects who were superb at producing vivid images to imagine the colors one by one. In each case the imagined color produced the same effect on the eye as the actual flashing light. More amazingly, when Kuzendorf flashed a colored light at these subjects and asked them to imagine that it was another color, they regularly reported seeing the other color, and 25 percent of the time their eyes responded as though they were perceiving the imagined, not the actual, flashing color.

Other research has found that the form and function of an image is only partially dependent upon the conscious understanding of the individual. For example, you may have a rough idea of how a ball bounces, but if asked to imagine a ball bouncing, you will be able to do so easily because somewhere along the way you gathered all the information necessary to visualize it bouncing. That information may not be conscious, but it is there and operating in a fashion that may have profound physiological implications.

Just because images produce physiological responses, however, does not mean that the responses are healing ones. The real question is, Do images affect the body's immune system, and if so, in what ways? And that's where psychologist Bruno Klopfer comes in. In 1957 one of Klopfer's patients whom he later referred to only as Mr. Wright was dying of cancer and asked to be given an injection of an experimental drug called Krebiozen. Researchers believed that Krebiozen might prove helpful in the treatment of cancer, and Wright had grabbed onto that medical hunch with all the fervor of a dying man's last hope. Indeed, it was his last chance. He had been turned down for a program testing the drug because he wasn't thought likely to live even three months, too short a period for researchers to evaluate the drug's effects. Believing his client was going to die in a few days, Klopfer gave him an injection of Krebiozen. The results were nothing short of miraculous.

"I had left him febrile, gasping for air, completely bedridden," explained Klopfer. Two days later, however, "the tumor masses had melted like snowballs on a hot stove, and in only these few days, they were half their original size! . . . Within ten days he was able to be discharged from his 'deathbed,' practically all signs of his disease having vanished. . . . Incredible as it sounds, this 'terminal' patient gasping his last breath through an oxygen mask was now not only breathing normally, but also fully active. He took off in his own plane and flew at twelve thousand feet with no discomfort."

Unfortunately for Wright, in a matter of months reports began to appear citing the poor results of Krebiozen on experimental groups. Klopfer noted how disturbed his client was by the news. "After two months of practically perfect health, he relapsed to his original state and became very gloomy and miserable."

Hoping that he could rekindle Mr. Wright's faith in the powers of Krebiozen, Klopfer told him that a greatly improved type of Krebiozen had been developed and that he would receive the improved drug the next day. The news immediately lifted his spirits. "Without much faith and putting on quite an act," Klopfer admits, "I administered the first injection of the doubly potent, fresh preparation—consisting of fresh water and nothing more."

Mr. Wright's recovery was once again startling. His tumors disappeared, his lungs cleared. He rose from his hospital bed "the picture of health," according to an amazed Klopfer. But then the

American Medical Association released its official statement on Krebiozen: "Nationwide tests show Krebiozen to be a worthless drug in the treatment of cancer."

It was a report that killed. Wright returned to the hospital and died in less than two days.

Klopfer is by no means the only doctor to see firsthand the profound effects that a patient's thinking can have on the course of a disease. Since Klopfer first published this story, a new discipline known as psychoneuroimmunology (PNI) has evolved to investigate the role the mind plays in the pattern of disease. PNI researchers have determined that in substantial ways the mind does affect the body's immune system and are working to understand the when, where, and how of such mysterious connections. As physician Leonard Wisneski writes in the *Noetic Sciences Review*, "We now know there is direct communication between our brain and our immune cells." This communication has shown up neurochemically and also anatomically. "There are nerve fibers between the brain and the thymus, the spleen, the bone marrow, lymph nodes . . . ," Wisneski explains, "and there may be some direct communication between the central nervous system and the immune cells by this mechanism."

Finding links between imagery and the immune system is an even more difficult task. Jeanne Achterberg, a psychologist at the University of Texas Health Science Center, points to the central role of emotions as a starting point for an understanding of how imagery may affect immunity. Because both imagery and emotions are located in the same vicinity in the brain, they may share certain biochemical wiring. "Many of the autonomic functions associated with health and disease," says Achterberg, "are emotionally triggered." The same basic communication system that connects our emotional state to our autonomic systems may also exist for imagery. "Verbal messages must undergo translation by the imagery system before they can be understood by the involuntary or autonomic nervous system," Achterberg explains. Although there's no need to examine these messages while we are healthy, if we become ill, gaining access to and controlling our imaginal processes may be more important than we realize. "Consciously accessing and manipulating images," says Achterberg, "may prove to be a way to enter into psychophysiological systems and establish harmony in functions and structures that have gone awry."

One of the first physicians to experiment with imagery as adjunct therapy was O. Carl Simonton, a radiation oncologist in Dallas, Texas. Early in his career, Simonton became intrigued with the personalities of cancer victims. He had seen patients who, though stating that they wanted to recover from their cancer, continued to smoke or drink or persistently skipped treatment sessions. Other patients had talked of how much they had to live for but seemed disinterested in the world and often suffered from depression. The patients who most fascinated Simonton, though, were those who had left the hospital after treatment with little hope for their survival and then kept showing up for treatment years after their initial visit. Curious, Simonton began querying them about their good health and found that their attitudes differed from the other cancer patients in two distinct ways: First, they believed that they had some power to control the course of their disease; and, second, they appeared to have a stronger will to live.

Eventually, he and his wife, Stephanie, a psychotherapist (they are now divorced), decided to see if they could help patients without those positive attitudes learn how to cultivate them. After studying an assortment of psychological approaches—group therapy, meditation, biofeedback, and others—the Simontons derived a method of their own. At the heart of their approach are visual imagery and relaxation. In their book *Getting Well Again*, written with James L. Creighton, they explain the process: "Essentially, the visual imagery process involved a period of relaxation, during which the patient would mentally picture a desired goal or result. With the cancer patient, this would mean his attempting to visualize the cancer, the treatment destroying it, and most importantly, his body's natural defenses helping him recover."

Their success with this imagery therapy was impressive. In case after case, the patient's cancer went into remission after a period of intensive work with imagery. Of course, because cancer is known to go into remission spontaneously, it's impossible to know if the Simontons' treatment was responsible. Indeed, many doctors are hesitant about using this sort of treatment because of the lack of controlled studies. Only a few such studies exist. How-ard Hall in his chapter in *Imagination and Healing*, for instance, discusses several respected studies in which he found that hypno-sis and imagery boosted immunity in some individuals. But phy-sicians also fear that some patients might bypass traditional cancer therapy in favor of behavioral treatment. After all, if you can heal yourself with images, why use chemotherapy? Some doc-tors also worry that behavioral therapy may sometimes cause patients to blame themselves if they don't get well: if, after using the technique, their cancers don't go into remission, patients may think it's their own fault. And imaging therapists are only helpful when used with patients who are good at producing images. Be-cause people do vary in this ability, some will undoubtedly reap the benefits and others will not.

A particularly impressive example of the mind's ability to influ-ence the body has been found within the relatively small percent-age of the population capable of entering a deep hypnotic state. In hypnosis, individuals are carefully guided into a relaxed state and instructed to feel, imagine, and experience ideas or events in a way that alters waking behavior. Warts have receded, smoking stopped, allergies lessened, and blood pressure lowered through hypnotic suggestion. The actual mechanism at work in successful hypnosis is similar to that of other imagery, but it also has another component. "By becoming deeply absorbed in imaging a physio-logical change," explains psychologist Theodore X. Barber, "ex-cellent hypnotic subjects can reinstate the same feelings that are present when the actual physiological change occurs, and the rein-stated feelings can stimulate the cells to produce the physiological change." In other words, deep hypnotic states carry within them the potential to heal.

Both hypnosis and the nonhypnotic therapeutic imagery techniques combine imagery with relaxation. In the early 1970s, Harvard medical school cardiologist Herbert Benson, drawing on the work of TM psychologist Keith Wallace, began studying the ability of TM meditators to lower their blood pressure and pulse. He wanted to see if their ability could be learned by people suffering from hypertension. What he identified was an interesting physiological change brought about through meditation, a "relaxation response" as he called it, in which the mind is cleared of distractions and stress relieved. By repeating a simple sound such as "ohm," the opening syllable of many mantras, over and over again, people could reduce the stress associated with disease. Research has shown that regular meditators tend to appear younger and to be in better health generally than control subjects. Hypertensive patients have been able to decrease their blood pressure and serum cholesterol levels through prolonged meditation. Improvement has also been reported in patients with chronic bronchitis and other respiratory problems. As we explain in chapter 8, regular meditation increases both brain wave coherence and blood flow to the brain. The list goes on.

But unfortunately, not all of us have the discipline to meditate on a regular basis and so can't benefit from the health improvements that frequently accompany deep meditative states. Furthermore, only a small percentage of the population can achieve a deep hypnotic state or daydream vividly and with sufficient clarity to mirror waking reality. But everyone sleeps and everyone experiences the brilliant imagery of dreams whether they want to or not. What if it were possible to harness the independent scenery of the dreamworld to heal?

THE DREAM CONNECTION

Hervey de Saint-Denys, the French scholar who in 1867 published the first book ever written on lucid dreams, was fascinated with how dreams are affected by one's physical condition. A dedicated dream diarist, he found examples of such incorporation in several of his own dreams. In one of those dreams, "I kept trying to light a candle without succeeding," he writes. "Sometimes my matches would not light, at others the candle refused to burn or kept going out. I was so annoyed that I wanted to fling the thing through the window, but I did not even have the strength to raise my arm. Then I woke up and found that I was lying uncomfortably on my left side." Although Saint-Denys was uncertain about the relationship between the candle and the odd position he had taken in his sleep, he was admiring of "the wisdom of nature, which warned me through a dream that I was in an uncomfortable position, so that in trying to chase away a dream which tormented me I also changed my position."

Even before Saint-Denys's book appeared, another early dream researcher, the French scientist Alfred Maury, had himself pinched, tickled, and exposed to light and odors while asleep to see if these sensations would affect his dream. They did—to a limited extent. Contemporary researchers too have begun to document the effect the body has on the content of dreams, finding that in general dreams are most responsive to tactile sensations. Sprinkle water on the face of a sleeping subject, for instance, and you will often find a symbolic expression of wetness in his or her dream. Internal stimuli—a headache, muscle pain, or illness, for example—will also often work their way into dreams, especially in children.

Robert Van de Castle, one of the pioneers of contemporary dream research, has uncovered some fascinating incorporations in the dreams of women. When a woman is ovulating, Van de Castle found, her dreams tend to be friendlier toward men than toward women. But when she begins to menstruate, her dreams will show greater friendliness toward women than toward men. Similarly, the dreams of a pregnant woman may presage her eventual labor. Although some references to the baby will often be found in a woman's second trimester, it is in the third trimester that they abound. Then dreams of labor are common. Researchers at the University of Cincinnati Medical School have found that the woman who has anxiety-ridden and threatening dream images about the baby and her forthcoming labor will usually have an easier and a shorter labor than the woman whose dreams show happier, less fearful, images. It's as if the threatening dreams are acknowledging the painful event that is to come, while the more pleasant dreams deny that reality just as perhaps the woman who is dreaming them is denying the pain that will be sure to accompany birth.

As with waking imagery, "whatever is dreamed is real in terms of physiological responses," writes psychologist Robert E. Haskell in an excellent review of the research on dreaming and illness published in the *Journal of Medical Humanities and Bioethics*. If you dream that you're running, your respiration rate will probably increase. If you dream of something stressful, you'll probably secrete more gastric acid. Almost everyone has awakened from a nightmare breathing rapidly and with his or her heart feverishly pounding away. In fact, REM sleep generally exhibits more fluctuating biological changes than does the waking state. Unfortunately, many dream researchers, though acknowledging the biological variations of REM sleep, believe dreams to be nothing but some excess neuronal baggage, a line of thought that Haskell finds regrettable. "It is this issue of the separation of mind and body that has led to many problems in the health field in general," he writes. "Dreams are often complex constructive cognitive events, not merely neuronal noise."

Despite the discord over this point in the dream community, a number of researchers have documented numerous cases in which severe biological illness has been reflected in dreams. In one study, almost half the dreams of patients about to have surgery were found to reflect imagery of cutting and destruction, being hurt and injured, or of loss of power and mobility. After surgery such imagery appeared in only about ten to fifteen percent of their dreams. Anecdotal evidence of similar incorporations has also been reported. There have been instances in which people have awakened with their legs paralyzed after having dreamed of being paralyzed with fright in a dream. H. A. Savitz, a medical doctor who pays attention to her patients' dreams, tells of one patient who complained of a fluttering feeling in his stomach and reported a dream in which "he fell from a wharf into the water between the wharf piles. A yacht was moored alongside. The yacht squeezed him onto the pier structures." Interpreting this image of being squeezed as a symbol for some sort of internal distress or discomfort, Savitz administered an electroencephalogram (EEG) and found that the man was suffering from a blockage in one of the muscles of his heart.

After studying the dreams of a group of hospital patients, Robert C. Smith, a psychiatrist at Michigan State University, reported a correlation between dreams of death and separation and the health of the dreamer. Patients were asked to relay the content of their dreams, which was evaluated by several different groups of investigators. Patients whose dreams reflected images of death or separation were suffering from significantly worse organic disease than those whose dreams were free of such imagery. And patients who reported no dreams at all had significantly higher death rates than did the other groups, although Smith found this to be true only in the first group he studied.

The temptation may exist to attribute to dreams some quasi-supernatural properties as if they tapped into a secret universe of time and revealed to those with the talent to interpret them important information unknown in waking life. But there is another explanation for the occasional prognostic abilities of dreams. "Psychologically," explains Haskell, "they [prognostic dreams] can be explained in terms of subliminal perception or the dreamer's cognitive processes perceiving cues too subtle to be processed consciously." Mystically prognostic or simply attuned to deeper unconscious information, the sheer number of prognostic dreams merits attention. Consider these two examples:

• A patient who died of liver cancer dreamed six years before his death and five years before the cancer was diagnosed that he was suffering from the disease and that he would live only six to eight years more.

• In New Hampshire, Charlotte Bell noticed a change in the content of her dreams; they seemed to be telling her that she was ill. Even after she consulted several doctors who gave her a clean bill of health, her dreams continued to warn her of disease. She decided to go for one more checkup. This time the physician discovered cancer. Surgeons operated and then told Bell she would need chemotherapy to ensure that the cancer was completely destroyed. But Bell refused. Her dreams, she said, were telling her the cancer was gone. She would be okay without chemotherapy. As it turned out, her dreams seemed to have been right. "Cancer takes from you," she writes. "It certainly took from me. Those last two years I felt old, tired, strung out. I was often cantankerous. Now, I feel good. When people see me now, there has been a uniform reaction. With seeming surprise they all have said, 'You look so good. I'd expected . . . ' and their voice trails off in embarrassment. I giggle and hug them."

Clinical work with healing imagery has found four components to be crucial to the image's effectiveness:

1. The image should be vivid and resonant for the individual.
2. Being involved in the process of imaging is more important than the image itself.
3. The image should be spontaneous and chosen by the individual so that he or she is comfortable with it.
4. The imager/dreamer should feel in control of the process. This is particularly applicable in lucid dreaming.

Although dreams that reveal information about the health of the dreamer are quite common in dream literature, reports of dreams in which the individual has effected a healing are more rare. Here's an example: More than ten years ago Gillian Tinder, who was then twenty-two, began passing out for no apparent reason. An EEG indicated epilepsy. She began medication that immediately stopped her fainting spells. But, she says, the medication "made me feel weird, not in touch." She didn't want to stop the medication and run the risk of more sudden swoons, but she did begin reading extensively about her illness, an endeavor that she believes inspired a dream in which she was hooked to an EEG. In the dream she was instructed to turn lights on and off by

Example of Dream Healing

thinking about them in order to control an aura-laden pressure she felt in her head. She was also told to switch from nightmare-like thoughts to happy ones quickly. "When I woke up," she explains, "I truly believed that the [dream] had happened. It was only when I questioned myself about particulars, such as what was the doctor's name? where was the hospital? and the like, that I realized I had been dreaming." After having this dream fifteen to twenty more times, she felt a need to try the mental exercises while awake. After a week or two of practice, she decided to stop her medication. "For a year or so I was very much aware of the aura," she says, "and it was a conscious effort to turn it off." By using the mental exercises from the dream she was able to fight off the aura. Gradually, she stopped being conscious of doing anything and has not experienced a spell in almost ten years.

Clearly Tinder may have learned some mental techniques for controlling the seizures while reading extensively about epilepsy, but it was the *practice in her dreams* that finally convinced her to try the techniques while awake. The important point here is that she was able to practice in her dreams because after the initial dream, whenever she found herself sitting in the dream chair with electrodes taped to her head, she realized she was dreaming and made a conscious effort to continue with the experiment "as though," she writes, "it were waking reality."

LUCIDITY AND HEALING

Lucidity brings with it various degrees of consciousness within the dream. It is possible then that while lucid, one can consciously *decide* to try to heal a wound, beef up the immune system, or clean out gradually clogging arteries. In 1987, Gackenbach and LaBerge prepared a project for *Omni* magazine in which readers were asked to participate in a two-week experiment in lucid dreaming. Among other things, readers were asked to write a detailed description of any "healing" lucid dream. After analyzing their data, the researchers discovered several cases of apparent dream healing.

In one, Krisanne Gray, a homemaker and mother from Spokane, Washington, related how she has used lucid dreaming to quit smoking, stop biting her nails, lose weight, and rid herself of hives and menstrual cramps. Although she has never seen a doctor for her hives, she is often bothered by them and has controlled them by suggesting to herself as she falls asleep that she needs to calm down. Then when she turns lucid, she creates a cool meadow environment in which she continues to tell herself to be calm. Repeatedly, after this dream experience, her hives will disappear.

Gray handles menstrual cramps in a similar fashion. She reports one particular instance in which on the day she was to play in a tennis tournament her period started and she was plagued with severe cramps. Fearing she would not be able to compete, Gray took a fifteen-minute nap in which she dreamed she was on the bench waiting for the tournament to begin. Cramps were bothering her. At that point she turned lucid and found the locus of pain in her body. She told herself to relax those muscles. When she awoke from her dream, her cramps were gone and she went on to compete in the tournament.

Carl Paoli from Mount Prospect, Illinois, submitted a lucid dream in which he tried to heal himself.

> About a year ago, I sprained my ankle. . . . It was very swollen and it was very difficult to walk. In a dream I remember running for what reason I don't remember, and suddenly I realized I couldn't possibly be running with this ankle so I must be dreaming. At this point I began to come out of my dream, the pain of my ankle started to fade in, but then I reached for my ankle with my dream hands which caused me to tumble in my dream. As I held my ankle I felt a vibration similar to electricity. Amazed, I decided to throw lightning bolts around in my dream. That's all I remember of the dream, but I awoke with next to no pain in my swollen ankle and was able to walk on it with considerable ease."

A young married woman from Texas, who frequently experiences dream lucidity relays a dream that she believes healed a pulled muscle in her chest. She had the dream a week after pulling the muscle, an injury that bothered her almost every time she moved.

> I was reading a book one night before going to sleep about an Indian medicine man who has performed a healing ritual. I turned out the light and began fantasizing about going to Nevada and meeting the medicine man. This moved into a dream where I saw myself walking into a small desert town and down a road to the medicine man's house. I don't remember much else except the medicine man kept repeating over and over, "Believe in me and you will be healed." I remember thinking that I was dreaming and that it was silly to believe that a medicine man could come to me in a dream, but I decided to go with the flow and relaxed as he kept repeating the sentence. I woke about an hour and a half after I had turned the lights out and sat up in bed. I moved my arms and body around. The pain was gone.

Harry Hoots of Waianae, Hawaii, tells of another type of lucid dream healing. In 1977, Hoots was injured during military training near the Arctic Circle. During a survival exercise, he tore ligaments in his right knee, and because of a severe blizzard which had moved in on the group, his buddies could not get him to the hospital for forty-eight hours. The team medic did, however, give Hoots a pain reliever which made him drowsy and he fell asleep.

> During my sleep, my conscious mind became very alert. . . . I observed myself standing in midair, calmly and quietly. All around me was darkness and my body was illuminated. I then began performing what is called a "short set" in yang style t'ai chi ch'uan (a Chinese exercise system I had learned four years previously for health maintenance). I experienced every movement from head to toe, breathing rhythmically with the motions over a period that seemed like hours. I felt during this dream that it was terribly vital that I relax and complete the set in order to regain the full use of my right leg when the injuries healed. This feeling was one more of total confidence than of hope and seemed to be generated from some source other than my normal thoughts and feelings.

After Hoots finished the set of t'ai chi, he drifted from the lucid state and has no recall of further dreaming. By the time he was treated by a doctor, it was too late for corrective surgery (the tissue had been swollen for several days). His leg was put in a cast for six weeks. Then, his doctor said, they would see about corrective surgery. But after the cast was removed, Hoots was haunted by his dream; he felt there was some reason he had dreamed about the exercises. He refused surgery, choosing instead to begin a physical therapy program. "I attained the goals of an eight-week physical therapy program in just four weeks. I was very excited at my progress and . . . while I have no physical proof, I am satisfied that the dream prepared me for proper recovery."

Finally, Patricia (last name withheld), an editor and writer from Rhode Island, explained how her lucid dreams helped her deal with pain caused by intestinal adhesions. For several years, Patricia had undergone numerous surgeries to remove the adhesions. Frequently during this time she experienced lucid dreams in which she felt the severe pain caused by the adhesions and then willed the pain to go away. Although the pain had never been relieved by aspirin or other painkillers, after having one of these dreams, Patricia reports, "I would wake up; the pain was gone."

None of these cases can be called miraculous, but they may demonstrate that during the enhanced state of mental imagery called dreams, one can intuit and perhaps affect the health of the body. At the least certain commonalities can be found among these examples that hint at a pattern of perceived dream healing:

• First, a history of dreaming lucidly accompanies dream control of both lucid and nonlucid dreams.

• Second, there is a definite presleep intent to lessen the physical discomfort.

• Third, action is taken by the dreamer or by a dream character either before or during the lucid state to rid the dream body of the discomfort.

• Fourth, the dreamed actions are, with one exception, quiet, that is, there is an attempt to relax, rather than attack an injured part.

People who feel they have successfully affected their health also often experience the positive results of the dreamed action both in the dream and after they awaken. This is clearly demonstrated by E. W. Kellogg, a frequent lucid dreamer. He writes that in April 1984, while "overenthusiastically" eating Japanese-style shish kebab, he punctured his tonsil with the wooden skewer! Within a few days his tonsil "had grown quite horribly infected and swollen, looking about three times normal size, bright red . . . with yellow lines of pus decorating the exterior." Having sought no medical treatment, he went to bed in this condition with the intention of healing his tonsil. He had a lucid dream in which he used affirmations (positive thoughts) to heal his throat. Kellogg reports that when he awakened from the dream, the "pain had almost entirely disappeared, and the next morning, my right tonsil looked and felt almost normal, only slightly red and swollen. At least 95 percent of the infection had disappeared in less than twelve hours. From the dramatic reduction in pain felt right after the healing experience, I suspect that much of this healing took place during the lucid dream itself. . . . "

The bulk of the scientific work with dream healing has been done with psychotherapeutic and performance applications as described in "Phantoms in the Night," chapter 5 and "Night Coach," chapter 4. Indeed, this mental imagery-based model of dream healing fits well with psychologist Paul Tholey's lucid dream training for athletes in which athletes first image what they want to accomplish, then practice those goals in lucid dreams. Upon awakening they compare their subsequent physical attempts at the goals with their dreamed rehearsals and report improvements. But one pilot study has shed some light on the potential of lucidity to influence immunological processes. Dr. Andrew Brylowski, an intern at the University of Texas Southwestern Medical School, conducted an experiment to see if lucid dreamers could change the level of natural killer (NK) cells in the blood. NK cells are a special type of immune cells that have the ability to recognize invading tumor cells or viruses, seek them out, and destroy them. Levels of NK cells are known to drop during sleep. Brylowski and his colleagues decided to see if a lucid dreamer could *raise* the level of NK cells. Drawing blood from their subject every hour throughout the night, the doctors found that, as expected,

NK activity decreased with the onset of sleep but increased to waking levels following periods of lucidity. Because they found this to happen only one night and because they ran the experiment with only one patient, more research needs to be undertaken to substantiate the findings. Still, this preliminary work is one of the first serious attempts to probe the biological consequences of lucid dreaming.

OF SOUNDER MIND AND BODY

From studying the research, we believe:
- Lucid dreamers are the best candidates for dream healing.
- Lucid dreamers possess personality characteristics that may make them less vulnerable than nonlucid dreamers to stress-related diseases.
- When lucid dreamers do succumb to illness, they are better equipped psychologically to adjust to their maladies.

If imagery has the power to improve our immune systems and if one can learn to influence the vivid images found in dreams to do so, the first steps have been taken toward dream healing. Because lucid dreamers exhibit consciousness in their dreams, they appear to be the best candidates for most effectively being able to do this.

Lucid dreamers also share some personality traits that predispose them to be healthy. For example, they more closely monitor their feelings and thoughts than people who don't lucid dream. In studies looking at the effect of stressful crises (death in the family, loss of job, marital problems) on health, researchers have found that individuals low in self-consciousness will often become ill after experiencing such stress. Similarly, Gackenbach and her students at the University of Northern Iowa conducted a study that suggests that lucid dreamers may process stress through their dreams. In a sixteen-week study, lucid dreamers were shown to experience lucid dreams on nights following stressful days more often than at any other time. These lucid nights in turn were usually followed by days in which the subjects felt less bothered by stress.

Lucid dreamers' capacity for daydreaming and for an active and rich dream life may also protect them from diseases long believed to have a strong psychosomatic component such as duodenal ulcer, rheumatoid arthritis, asthma, and ulcerative colitis. Researchers have found that one of the major psychological trademarks of people who suffer from such diseases is a psychological dynamic known as alexithemia. Alexithemics typically have difficulty expressing their emotions; they are preoccupied with the details of daily life, and have a greatly diminished ability to daydream or to remember their nocturnal dreams. One study, in fact, suggests that alexithemics actually have less active REM cycles than do others. The one sure way they have of expressing conflict and stress is through their bodies, thus the frequent appearance of disease. Conversely, the lucid dreamer's enhanced expression of the imaginal while awake and asleep may be intrinsic to good health. Indeed, dreams in general may play a role in health simply by helping us express our emotions. Rosalind Cartwright, one of the leading dream researchers in the world today, has conceptualized the dream as an emotional, problem-solving process. In other words, dreams enable us to work out problems of an emotional nature. In her work she has uncovered many differences between the dreams of people who successfully adapt to the changes in their lives and those who do not.

THE PATH TO OPTIMUM HEALTH

As we mentioned earlier in this chapter, there are many health benefits associated with the practice of meditation. The goal of meditation is to transcend waking, sleeping, and dreaming consciousness. The evolved state of consciousness that follows such transcendence is markedly different from the others and observes, or witnesses, them. An individual who has reached this level of consciousness can observe his or her dreams. Furthermore, consciousness during sleep has not only been identified during REM sleep, but also during stage two, or non-REM, sleep, where dreams are much less likely to occur. It may follow then that if one is regularly lucid during sleep or a witness to it, the health benefits of regular meditation will also occur. As of this writing only a few tantalizing bits of research support this hypothesis. For example, Gackenbach has found that women lucid dreamers tend to be healthier in general than the norm. (This was not true of male lucid dreamers, however.) But both sexes who report having spontaneous lucid dreams were found to have healthier vestibular systems, the balance apparatus in the inner ear, than did those who have never had a lucid dream.

Only careful scientific investigation will be able to substantiate the role lucidity plays in health and whether, as we are suggesting, the greatest health benefits, those similar to what have been found in meditators, also exist in the small portion of the population who experience lucid dreams spontaneously.

PART TWO

BIOLOGY
AND
CONSCIOUSNESS

Chapter 7

Dreaming Buddhas

UFOs, BUTTERFLIES, AND THE CASE FOR MEDITATION

Occasionally, a story moves from the obscurity of an ancient text and into popular consciousness. Something in it captures the imagination, and suddenly, considering the number of years it has remained unnoticed, it's everywhere. So it goes with the story of Chuang Tzu and the butterfly. Once only readers of Asian philosophy knew this Taoist tale, but as interest in the East—and dreams—has surged so too have translations of Chuang Tzu's story. It even managed to make its way onto national television in the 1970s in an episode of "Kung Fu." Here is one version:

Once I, Chuang Tzu, dreamt I was a butterfly, a butterfly flying about, feeling that it was enjoying itself. It did not know that it was Chuang. Suddenly, I awoke and was myself again, the veritable Chuang. But I cannot know if as Chuang I had dreamt myself to be a butterfly, or if now as a butterfly I am dreaming myself to be Chuang. But between Chuang and a butterfly there must be a difference.

There must be a difference, but what is it? As the Taoist philosopher so poetically points out, dreams call into question our definitions of reality. We are aware while awake of another realm in which our experiences, desires, and fears come to life in unexpected ways. But while dreaming, we are lost in amnesia, forgetting our waking lives and accepting whatever comes along as real; unless, of course, we turn lucid and become aware of both our lives, the one we are dreaming and the one we know while awake. In Western culture, the first mention of lucid dreaming came from Plato, but there is no reason to suppose that the Egyptians or Babylonians or indeed even our Cro-Magnon ancestors did not also occasionally awaken within their dreams. One can only imagine what ancient shamans made of such strange and alluring experiences. It was commonly believed in antiquity that the soul left the body during dreams and journeyed into the land of spirits. To turn lucid then could have fed that belief; to witness a dream with the conscious mind could have served as proof of the "reality" of the dreamworld.

Such experiences also lead to other conclusions. The earliest record of any sophisticated use of lucid dreaming was the "Doctrine of the Dream State," a Tibetan Buddhist guide to becoming conscious in the dream. Tibetan yogis believed that by recognizing the illusory nature of dreams, one could more clearly understand the illusory nature of reality as a whole. If one gains mastery over dreams, according to this Yoga (or teaching), "whether in the sleeping-state or in the waking-state one realizeth both states to be illusory." In order to help students obtain this insight, the doctrine presented several meditations to induce lucidity and directions for what to do once conscious awareness had been achieved. "If," the doctrine instructed, "the dream be about fire, think, 'What fear can there be of fire which occurreth in a dream!' Holding to this thought, trample upon the fire. In like manner, tread under foot whatever be dreamt."

This conscious action within the dream, according to many Buddhist and Hindu teachings, is a necessary step on the path to enlightenment. Enlightenment is generally viewed as either a release from the suffering that forms the core of human existence, or the recognition that life is bliss. The Buddhist idea of *duka*, or suffering, also includes what Harvard professor Jack Engler calls "existential malaise" and what Freud referred to as "ordinary human unhappiness"—the feeling that something is slightly askew at the core of our lives. The Buddha himself declared that the only thing he taught was suffering and the way out of suffering. The way out, the Buddha said, included the practice of meditation, the retraining of the mind to see through itself. Meditation would teach you to be in and of each moment. Although the word *detached* is often used to describe the gradual awakening of the mind that accompanies meditation, it is misleading. "If you put your self totally into each moment with nothing left over," Engler explains, "that is what is meant by detachment."

Meditation enables one to see that all perception is a construction of "reality." Even the distinctions we make between the world we see when awake versus the one we live in in our dreams are illusions. That is why the Tibetans were so interested in becoming conscious in their dreams. It was a step toward the experience of one mind. To be enlightened means to be conscious of the illusion always . . . while awake or dreaming, and even in dreamless sleep. Although many different types of meditation exist, all seek to refocus attention in a way that enables the individual to transcend the limitations of ordinary perception. Daniel Goleman writes in his book *The Meditative Mind*, the "key attributes of this state are always the same: loss of sense awareness, one-pointed attention to one object to the exclusion of all other thoughts, and sublimely rapturous feelings."

In some meditation schools attention is refocused through concentration on a mantra, koan, or object. Other schools take a different approach, instructing students to observe their thoughts and images, to become aware of each passing moment and thereby become detached from the events. One's focus is then centered on the present moment; the mind observes itself observing life as it unfolds. It is a state strikingly similar to that found in lucid dreaming, and as Harry Hunt, a psychologist at Brock University in Canada, has speculated, such "systematic meditation might have been 'invented' as an attempt to attain within wakefulness the sort of mental clarity, exhilaration, and simultaneously detached openness that emerges as lucid dreaming."

FRAMES OF MIND

In order to gain some theoretical understanding of lucidity, it is necessary, as William James, author of the 1902 classic book *The Varieties of Religious Experience*, wrote, to place things in their "series," to identify the similarities and differences between lucid dreaming and other mental states that are similar to it. Of those states, meditation is the one most closely related to lucid dreaming, but before we continue our discussion of it, we need to examine three other related states—out-of-body experiences (OBEs), near-death experiences (NDEs), unidentified-flying-object (UFO) experiences. Another relative of the lucid dream—the ordinary dream—was discussed in "Looking Inside the Dream," chapter 3. By examining these related states of consciousness, we can come to a better understanding of the mental mechanisms responsible for each one. Each state, including lucid dreaming, is a transitional state that may carry one closer to the experience of a higher state of consciousness known as "pure consciousness." This ultimate state of consciousness will be discussed briefly at the end of this chapter and in depth in "The Evolving Soul," chapter 10.

Much of the early lucid dream research was carried out by parapsychologists who saw many similarities between lucid dreaming and out-of-body experiences. Although their research has often been dismissed by other scientists, many of the areas pioneered by parapsychologists are now being taken seriously, though consciousness in all its multifariousness is certainly a trickier subject for scientific research than, say, electrical engineering or plate tectonics. The study of consciousness is coming into its own through the diligent work of determined scientists who reject the fuzzy thinking that has so often characterized investigations of the mind. When, for instance, parapsychologist Susan Black-more was attending a scientific conference on vision, she found herself sharing a few pints of Bulgarian beer with a group of visual scientists. They were curious about her interest in lucid dreams and out-of-body experiences. "Why are they interesting?" one of them asked. Blackmore, who is with the Department of Psychology at the University of Bristol, began, in her words, "muttering about how nice they are, how difficult to induce, how exhilarating if you succeed, about the clarity of consciousness . . ."

Her inability to articulate just why it was she found the focus of her studies interesting made her realize that it was a question that needed to be answered if OBEs and lucid dreams were to be of interest to other scientists. In a paper published in *Lucidity Letter*, a journal devoted to the scientific study of lucid dreaming, she tried to explain in more detail than she was able to over a few beers what it is that makes both phenomena grist for the scientific mill. "Lucid dreams and OBEs are so interesting . . . because they tell us so much about ourselves," she writes, "about consciousness and about the illusions with which we live most of our lives."

Blackmore suspects that OBEs and lucid dreams are different expressions of the same underlying state in which, for whatever reasons, one's consciousness is expanded. If you were to experience an OBE now, you would suddenly find yourself looking down upon your body, perhaps flying around the room or out the window. In a lucid dream, you might also fly, but there will likely be unexpected dream elements—a three-eyed monster, for example,—popping into the scene unexpectedly. In both states, though, you will most probably feel "more" conscious and closer to the center of yourself. A lucid dream, Blackmore explains, "is a rare chance to feel perfectly conscious while experiencing the contents of your imagination. If you only have the skills to do so, you can experience anything you can imagine as real."

Many people who have an OBE may have two conscious selves, one that remains in the body and participates in whatever activity is going on and one that floats above the body, a silent observer.

When this sense of two selves occurs during sleep, some people may not realize they are sleeping, believing instead that they are awake, which of course they are—awake within a dream. Dreamers may interpret this experience as a lucid dream in which they travel through an unfamiliar dreamscape or as a mystical experience, a journey through a spiritual realm that exists outside normal waking or dreaming consciousness. Blackmore explains that these same two interpretations have been dominant among researchers. One group hypothesizes that the "soul, astral body, spirit, or whatever," says Blackmore, "leaves the body temporarily in an OBE and permanently at death." Psychological theories, on the other hand, she says, "deny that anything leaves the body and posit that the experience is one of the imagination." Most current theorists favor the latter view, but to say OBEs fall within the realm of imagination is in no way to reduce their meaning to or impact on those who experience them.

OBEs have been known to occur in other states of consciousness, arising during meditation, while under the influence of psychedelics, and during times of extreme stress. But they most frequently occur as one is lying prone and likely to be falling asleep or dreaming. "It is," Harry Hunt explains, "as if a dreaming sequence starts but, atypically, awareness of one's actual setting in time and space is not dislodged as in most dreams." Rather, the dreamer integrates "the imaginal participations of the dream with a detached self-awareness that knows one's actual context for what it is." To put it another way, if Chuang Tzu had been lucid when he dreamed of being a butterfly, he would have known that he was Chuang Tzu, and if he had experienced an OBE dream that he thought was real, he would have realized that his physical body was in bed but he would have thought he was awake. Another possibility would be if he had had an OBE-lucid dream. Then he would have seen his physical body in bed, but he would have recognized that he was dreaming. This last variation is probably the most accurate. WRONG

Because of the phenomenological similarities between lucid dreams and OBEs and the fact that they both reliably occur in the same people, Blackmore argues that they are caused by the same sort of thought constructions. In each experience the brain remodels or restructures perceptions differently than it does in ordinary waking consciousness. This reconstruction is often the result of severe stress. Gackenbach, for instance, experienced her one and only nondreaming OBE while giving birth. "After thirty-two hours of labor with my first child," she explains, "I was extremely fatigued and in enormous pain. The fantasy kept running through my mind in between screams of pain that I wanted to jump off the birthing table and run away. Quite suddenly I found my 'self' viewing me from above and behind my body. I remember thinking to myself, 'This is more like it,' and feeling a great sense of relief, but alas I quickly found myself back in my body with my daughter eager to exit."

Hunt's description of lucidity and OBEs as experiences of "intensified self-reference" (a part of the mind is detached and observing while at the same time one continues to participate in the dream or the life event) also applies to several other states. Near-death experiences in which an individual comes close to dying is one. Two studies have found that people who have NDEs are more likely to experience dream lucidity. Descriptions of NDEs share much of the same imagery as some lucid dreams, OBEs, and deep meditation: There are the mandalalike patterns of light, the bright white light of the void, and the tunnel through which one journeys. Following an NDE, people commonly feel as though they were in an altered state of consciousness. Having seen the "other side," they often come away with extremely positive feelings about their lives. It is a feeling they don't want to lose. In a recent article, psychologist Kenneth Ring relates the NDE of "Jayne Smith." During the birth of her second child, Smith experienced "ecstatic gratitude and cosmic knowledge during which she almost immediately lost all body awareness and says she existed, while cradled in the light, as pure consciousness."

Not only do NDEs often include an out-of-body experience, they also sometimes fold back on the lucid dream, as in the case of retired physicist John Wren-Lewis. He became concerned one night that the wine he had imbibed might disrupt the mystical consciousness that had resulted from his near-death experience. In a dream that night, he turned lucid: "I knew this as a dream in which my ghostly invisibility symbolized my post-NDE state, and the dream characters who could see me were the people who in waking life recognized that I was living in heaven here on earth, dead to 'this world.' " Wren-Lewis realized that he was having this dream in order to explore his concern about the effects of the wine on his newfound consciousness. As he became aware of lying in his bed in his apartment in Australia, he saw

> that the real threat to my mystical consciousness lay not in drink itself but in getting caught up in an internal dialogue about drink. To celebrate this breakthrough in dream terms I walked straight through the wall of the dream room. As I emerged into the street by Sydney harbor my dream was flooded with mystical consciousness, not as something new, but as a simple recognition of what had actually been there all along, the exact same sense I have when I click back to the mystical consciousness in waking life. I flew over the water, borne by a wind I knew to be the breath of God on creation's first morning, and fainted at the beauty of it all—to wake in bed, my eyes brimming with tears of gratitude.

In this instance Wren-Lewis used a lucid dream to reaffirm the mystical (perhaps "pure") consciousness that came from a near-death experience.

UFO "experiences" may also share some characteristics of lucid dreaming, OBEs, and NDEs. In fact, it may be that a fair number of such experiences are actually misinterpreted dreams. In such an experience, the individual believes he or she has been abducted, studied, and even experimented upon by aliens. Often the abductee blocks the memory of what is generally a painful and terrifying event and only under hypnosis do the details surface. In some cases, however, those blocked memories may be forgotten dreams, or, as Ring puts it, "At the phenomenological level, NDEs and UFO [experiences] are of course quite dissimilar, but it is in their 'deep structure,' as it were, rather than in their surface contextual manifestations that important commonalities can be discerned."

Veteran lucid dreamer Alan Worsley, for example, explains that occasionally when he induces lucid dreaming by lying still for up to two hours or more on his back, he too has found himself at the mercy of aliens. "I am not given to superstition or believing in 'unnecessary entities' but perhaps the term 'dream' is a little too bland to do justice to the ultra-realism of these experiences," he explains.

> For instance, if one "dreams" as I have, in rich tactile and auditory imagery, of being examined in the dark by robots or operated upon by small beings whose goodwill and competence may be in doubt, or abused in various ways by life-forms not known to terrestrial biology, it can be very difficult to keep still. I have found that if I do not keep still this peculiar state of consciousness usually evaporates in a moment. That can be very useful as an escape route but it can be annoying to lose it when the success rate is not high and each attempt takes two hours or more. I like to regard myself as at least a moderately intrepid investigator, but I have to admit that in spite of being intellectually of the opinion that what was happening was only internally generated imagery, I have flinched during these episodes on more than one occasion. . . . I suspect that many 'UFO abduction' experiences, as well as out-of-body experiences are examples of the same kind of thing.

An extraordinary example of how OBEs, NDEs, UFO experiences, and lucid dreams are interconnected comes from Mark, a successful businessman in North Carolina. Since early childhood, Mark has been able to have OBEs at will. He explains that they are tranquil and nonthreatening. Also it is common for him after about one and a half hours of sleep to turn lucid and maintain that consciousness the remainder of the night. He reports that at all times he is in total control of the process, and reports a feeling of complete but relaxed consciousness. As a teenager he and his mother had their first UFO abduction experience (at the same time) in which they were taken by aliens to a spaceship to be examined. Throughout that experience Mark continually assured himself that he was dreaming. Although he awoke with mud on his feet—the aliens had led them through a muddy area—it should be noted that he also is a frequent sleepwalker. Clearly Mark has had a lifetime of extraordinary experiences with consciousness that allow him to move fluidly from one imaginal state to another.

It is important to point out that the felt reality of all these experiences—OBE, NDE, lucid dream, and UFO abduction—is profound. And it is perhaps because of that intensity of feeling that the unsophisticated observer often concludes that the experience is "real" in the way that driving to work is "real" or putting the kids to bed is "real." Although we are arguing that these experiences do not represent "objective" reality, we do agree that there may be other explanations. Such experiences challenge our concepts of what "real" is. It would be a mistake to dismiss these experiences as being "outside" of accepted reality. As we illustrate in other portions of this book, such experiences, especially lucid dreaming, challenge our notions of what it means to be "awake" and also what we mean by reality.

THE MEDITATIVE EDGE

Despite the parallels to lucid dreaming, none of the states of consciousness we have discussed so far can be seen as causing or accounting for the lucid dream. A stronger and more direct parallel can be found between lucid dreaming and meditation. It is the one technology that can lead not only to lucid dreaming, but also beyond it to higher states of consciousness. The lucid dreamer's facility for self-reflectiveness, of recognizing the self in the midst of a dream, is strikingly similar to self-reflective consciousness in "mindfulness" or "insight" meditation, says Harry Hunt. This is the meditation practiced in Zen, Theravada, and Tibetan Buddhism. And TM psychologist Charles Alexander believes the same is true of the yogic tradition. In both meditation and lucid dreaming, once a detached but receptive attitude has been integrated into the waking or dreaming consciousness, strong feelings of exhilaration, freedom, and release occur. There is, Hunt explains, "an unusually broad sense of context and perspective, a 'balance' of normally contradictory attitudes, and the felt sense of one's own existence (that special 'I am' or 'being' experience). . . ."

Without this heightened sense most of us become consumed by everyday living, untouched by the "awe" of life and the stark inevitability of death. This, explains Hunt, is "the full human context to which on rare occasions we spontaneously 'wake up.'" In the same way, we remain unaware that we are dreaming, until the moment we turn lucid. Both types of sudden awakenings "can have quite an impact," admits Hunt. But both are frequently short-lived.

At virtually every level of analysis there are strong parallels between lucid dreaming and meditation. The content of both experiences, for instance, is similar, as are the personalities of meditators and lucid dreamers. The physiological changes that occur in both meditative states and lucid dreaming also resemble one another. And, perhaps most important, the practice of meditation has been associated with the frequency of lucid dreaming.

But if lucid dreaming is a form of meditation or at least directly related to it, then in order to understand it, we must also understand meditation.

Although many Westerners associate meditation with the Eastern religions, it has been practiced in one form or another in all religions and in most societies. "American Indians practice a form of meditation remarkably similar to zazen [Zen meditation]," explains meditation researcher Michael A. West.

> In Africa, in the Kalahari desert, the people of the !Kung Zhu/twasi practice a form of ritual dancing (like Islamic Sufi dancing) that activates a postulated energy source and produces an "ecstasy" experience. Many tribal groups practice such ritual dancing coupled with chanting to produce altered states of consciousness. . . . The Eskimo would sit facing a large soft stone and using a small, hard handstone would carve a circle in the large stone continuously to produce trance. . . . Meditation has long been used within the Christian religion and

many of the Christian techniques are identical to those used in other religions, cultures, and times.

What is clear in all these practices is that meditation requires no complicated preparations to induce a change in consciousness. One need only sit quietly and enter deeply into one-mindedness. This can take place by concentrating on one's breathing, a koan (in Zen), or, more common in Western religions, a prayer. While in this state of concentrated mindfulness, thoughts slow, the cognitive system becomes less noisy, and one may experience oneself alone. "I am now a being unto myself," as one meditator put it. "I am separate from lover, friend, mother, father, therapist, whomever . . . but in my meditation I do not sense this separateness as loneliness, I know it as closeness to myself and to life."

For the past two decades Western scientists have been addressing the question of meditation: what it is, how it changes an individual's perceptions, why people are drawn to it. Several models have emerged to explain these questions. One model views meditation as a mechanism that serves to reduce stress and anxiety. Meditation has been used successfully in psychotherapy and on an individual basis to reclaim equanimity. Another model views meditation as nothing more than light sleep, a controlled version of the feelings and imagery that most people experience as they fall asleep. Other researchers have suggested that meditation is a form of self-hypnosis because, like hypnosis, it enhances internal attention. As Deane H. Shapiro, Jr., of the University of California, Irvine, explains, meditation is "a family of techniques which have in common a conscious attempt to focus attention in a nonanalytical way and an attempt not to dwell on discursive, ruminating thought."

Each of the current meditation models sheds some light on the nature of meditation, but each is incomplete. Meditation is a procedure, a technology, and as such it facilitates outcomes, such as stress reduction and consciousness during sleep. These outcomes are a natural part of the biology of the human system and can surface spontaneously without meditation. But meditation clearly increases the likelihood of attaining these outcomes.

If meditation is more than the sum of its parts, what is it? Virtually all meditation schools contextualize the practice as a spiritual path that leads to union with the higher self, nature, God, or "pure" consciousness. We will focus on one of the schools—transcendental meditation—because it has been extensively studied scientifically and because it has been the most influential meditation group in the West. Indeed, in the thirty years since its founder, Maharishi Mahesh Yogi, "rediscovered" a simple, enjoyable meditation technique, the movement has trained about three million people.

Of course the kinds of "success" enjoyed by the TM movement do not mean that it represents the "right" path for the spiritual seeker, or that it is above criticism. In *Spiritual Choices*, a book by some of the most influential leaders in contemporary transpersonal psychology, TM was strongly criticized. Although such criticism is by no means uncommon, it has been more often leveled at the movement than at the meditation technique. Rather than align themselves with other "New Age" groups, the TMers have chosen to go it alone. Their isolationism, which has been perceived as arrogance, or excessive dependence on one teacher, by other New Age groups, is actually part of what they see as their role as disciples: They are attempting to honor the Maharishi's insistence that the teachings be kept pure. Perhaps the Maharishi's fear is that TM will be watered down by the teachings of other groups. It is a lesson well learned from Christianity. According to some historians, only one hundred years after Christ's death his teachings had been radically changed.

But the Maharishi is also committed to the scientific study of his teachings. Rather than convert people exclusively through proselytizing, the TM movement has opted to prove its teachings through the diligent and often unrewarding path of science. In the past twenty years, TM scientists have amassed more than 300 research studies from more than 160 independent institutions in 27 countries and from disciplines as diverse as physics, literature, psychology, and biochemistry. Initially their scientific studies lacked adequate controls, but today TM scientists are, by and large, putting out work that is methodologically sophisticated and reputable. In one of their recent studies, for instance, TM scientists paid $7,000 (out of their own pockets) to have data scored and analyzed by independent scientists in order to verify their objectivity. In part, the value of their research lies in their ability to carry out in-depth studies on meditators. Serious meditators in other traditions are typically resistant to taking part in scientific research, a fact that led Harry Hunt to say that as far as a body of research on meditation is concerned, the TM work is "virtually the only game in town."

TM, or Vedic, science expands upon modern science in what it is seeking to understand. "Through its objective approach," explains the Maharishi, "modern science reveals that which is perceived, the object. The subject, the perceiver, remains separate from it. . . . Vedic science . . . extends and fulfills the objective approach of modern science by incorporating the knower and the process of knowing into the field of investigation."

The Maharishi conceptualizes meditation as a tool for the development of consciousness. Unlike contemporary physiology, Vedic science does *not* view consciousness as a *by-product* of a complex nervous system. Rather, it contends that consciousness is the primary reality from which matter and life arose. By meditating, an individual can more fully experience this primal experience of consciousness, which in TM is called "pure" consciousness. According to Vedic belief, there is no mental content, no thoughts, feelings, or perceptions in pure consciousness. Rather it is an experience of "self" or "amness." It is the center of one's being, "a state of knowing-ness, rather than knowing particulars," in the words of TM psychologist Charles Alexander. Meditation enables the individual to tap into this state and over time helps to establish and maintain it.

Through TM meditation, one begins to access pure consciousness by developing a "witness," a silently observing part of the self that witnesses all other states of consciousness (waking, sleeping, and dreaming) without trying to change them. This is a difficult concept to comprehend because for most of us it is something we have never experienced. But imagine it this way: You are sitting beneath a tree reading a book. You may find your mind wandering a little as you read, suddenly remembering perhaps that you need to buy milk or call your mother. Your conscious mind may vacillate between intense concentration on what you are reading and a pleasant daydream. But if you have developed the "witness," no matter what you are thinking at any given moment, there will be a part of your mind that watches what you do and listens to what you say to yourself. The witness stands apart from all other states of consciousness, calm and relaxed, a comforting backdrop to the wild emotional and intellectual gymnastics of waking consciousness. This part of yourself, however, should not be confused with the part that monitors and comments on your mental activities. The silent witness makes no value judgments, it just is, being, or the Self.

Now imagine that you are dreaming: No matter what you are doing in a dream, the witness is there observing, not trying to change or control what happens, as the awakened consciousness in a lucid dream might, but just watching. Here is an example of the witness in a dream from a long-term TM meditator: "Sometimes whatever the content of the dream, I feel an inner tranquility of awareness that is removed from the dream. Sometimes, I may even be caught up in the dream but the inner awareness of peace remains."

The witness will also be there when you are not dreaming, when you are in the deeper stages of sleep. In its purest form, witnessing produces a consciousness devoid of content, thought, or sensations. "It is a feeling of infinite expansion and bliss and nothing else," explains one TM meditator. "Then I become aware that I exist but there is no individual personality, and then I become aware that I am an individual but no details of who, where, what, or when. Eventually these details fill themselves in and I come awake."

Another meditator says that the experience "is like an amplifier turned on, but with no sound. The experience fades as boundaries of dreams or the waking state gather, gain definition, and overshadow."

The development of this state of mind lies at the heart of many meditation traditions. Not surprisingly, some traditions view lucid dreaming as a form of sleeping meditation, a necessary precursor to the emergence of the witness. Hunt, for instance, points out that in Tibetan Buddhism once a disciple has "attained a relatively stable dream lucidity, he [or she] may practice confronting fearsome deities or use the opportunity to deepen his [or her] meditative absorption in preparation for 'lucidity' during Bardo." (In Tibetan Buddhism the Bardo is the realm through which the soul travels after leaving one body in death and before being reborn into another.)

Alexander and his colleagues at the Maharishi International University in Fairfield, Iowa, believe witnessing to be a more advanced stage of consciousness than lucid dreaming. During lucidity, one part of the mind is active and involved in the dream while another is observing it, aware of the true nature of the state while still involved in it. The reverse seems to be true of witnessing. The awareness of the observer is more dominant than the actively engaged participant, yet it is also quiet and removed. The separation of the two roles is clearer, and thus witnessing in a dream emerges as quieter.

At what point, though, does one stop being in a lucid dream and begin witnessing? Although it can be described as a continuum and is sometimes experienced as such, witnessing typically emerges spontaneously. Suddenly, one has the sense of just "being" there.

The goal of meditative practice is, in essence, to bring what the attentive and receptive mind achieves in meditation to other settings—to sleep, to dreams, to everyday life. Lucid dreaming is an early form of witnessing consciousness that may arise naturally in some people and may be induced by the practice of meditation in others. Viewed in this context, the study of lucid dreaming may tell us as much about the development of higher states of consciousness as it does about dreaming.

Chapter 8

The Paradoxical Dream
DECODING THE DREAMING BRAIN

It was one of the most satisfying night's sleeps Alan Worsley would ever have. Lying in a sleep lab at Hull University in England with electrodes taped to his head, Worsley couldn't have been particularly comfortable, but he drifted off to sleep the night of April 12, 1975, knowing that if he and fellow graduate student Keith Hearne were successful, they would have the first scientific evidence that lucid dreaming is indeed a phenomenon of sleep. In some respects their experiment was simple: If Worsley, who has been a prolific lucid dreamer since the age of five, experienced a lucid dream, he would try to move his eyes in a prearranged manner, signaling to Hearne that he was lucid. Electrodes placed near Worsley's eyes would provide a polygraph record or electro-oculogram (EOG) of those eye movements as well as the ones associated with rapid-eye-movement (REM) sleep. In addition, an EEG (electroencephalogram) would record Worsley's brain wave activity, and another device would record muscle tone. Taken together, the charts of these instruments would show what stage of sleep Worsley was in when he signaled.

"Having already acquired the capacity to exert voluntary control of dreams while knowing I was dreaming," explains Worsley, "I was confident before we began the experiment that I could move my eyes from left to right a certain number of times."

His confidence was not misplaced. "With my first laboratory lucid dream," Worsley writes, "we succeeded with this simple technique for marking the onset of awareness of dreaming. This single instance in itself demonstrated that lucid dreams could occur in REM sleep; that the dreamer was able to remember a task and carry it out; that he was able to signal that he was doing so; and that he could count the eye movements and make them at the agreed rate."

Across the ocean and two years later, completely unaware of Worsley and Hearne's work, Stephen LaBerge and his colleagues at Stanford University conducted the same experiment—this time with LaBerge as the dreamer. After turning lucid, LaBerge recounts, "I decided to do the eye movements that we had agreed upon as a signal." He moved his dream finger vertically, following it with his eyes. After he awakened, he and his associate Lynn Nagel observed "two large eye movements" on the polygraph sheet that coincided with LaBerge's memory of what he had done in the dream. Independently, researchers at several other universities also began testing lucid dreamers' abilities to signal from the dream state and found that no matter what the prearranged pattern of movements, the dreamers were able to routinely signal correctly while asleep and dreaming.

Although Hearne claims priority in capturing the first "signal-verified" lucid dream, Stephen LaBerge and his colleagues at Stanford have done the bulk of the work on the physiology of dream lucidity. Perhaps more than any other researchers, they have proven that lucid dreaming does indeed take place during sleep. Before their studies, most dream researchers doubted that lucid dreams occurred during sleep. Instead they believed that the dreamers who said they were conscious in their dreams had simply awakened and were experiencing vivid sleep imagery, which they mistakenly interpreted as dreams. Indeed, rapid-eye-movement sleep is sometimes interrupted by momentary periods of wakefulness. Perhaps lucid dreamers were mistaking these microawakenings for consciousness in dreams. To many sleep and dream researchers, lucid dreams were simply a philosophical impossibility. By definition, dreaming was a state in which one was not aware that one was asleep. Therefore, no matter what the dreamer might believe, lucid dreams were not dreams.

With the weight of scientific opinion against them, lucid dream researchers gradually accumulated the evidence required to prove that lucidity did occur during sleep. Anecdotally, the case was strong. Lucid dreamers reported that they experienced no sensory input from the outside world while dreaming. When they attempted to notice external noises, say the ticking of a clock near their bed, or feel their pillows or sheets, they could not. Though awake within their dreams, they were quite profoundly shut off from waking reality. To support this empirical evidence, various physiological studies were designed to map the onset, duration, and content of lucid dreams. The first thing the researchers wanted to find out was what stage of sleep people were in when they experienced lucid dreams. Did they occur while one was drifting off to sleep, during REM sleep, or in another stage of sleep? The answer came quickly: Lucid dreams occurred most frequently during rapid-eye-movement sleep. In one study conducted at Stanford, LaBerge, Lynn Nagel, and veteran dream researcher William Dement found that a whopping 92 percent of signal-verified lucid dreams took place during rapid-eye-movement sleep. Subsequent sudies at other universities also recorded REM-sleep lucid dreams.

The evidence that lucid dreams are a by-product of REM sleep goes beyond the ability of dreamers to signal. A complicated array of physiological factors lends support. REM sleep is composed of two related but distinct phases. One phase is characterized by fluctuating physiological activities: muscles twitch, heart rate increases, and of course, the eyes move erratically. The other phase is calmer: the movements subside, creating a period of quiet REM. Lucid dreams seem to occur most regularly during the height of the energetic phase and are characterized by both dense eye movements and increased heart and respiration rates that exceed those found in nonlucid periods of the same REM episode. This increased activity, LaBerge suggests, may be a necessary background for lucid dreaming.

LaBerge discovered that REM-state lucid dreams are initiated in two ways. The first type are "wake initiated," that is, they begin during brief periods of arousal and then continue on as the subject returns to sleeping REM. Usually, the dreamer experiencing this type of lucidity will be aware both of having been momentarily awake and of having gone back to sleep. The majority of lucid dreams, however, begin with an ordinary dream. Known as "dream-initiated" lucid dreams, they usually occur after "something" causes the dreamer to suddenly become aware that he or she is dreaming. It's the "oh, this is a dream" sense, attested to by almost all lucid dreamers.

Although lucidity appears to be primarily a product of rapid-eye-movement sleep, it is not exclusively one. Lucid dreams have sometimes been found to arise during other stages of sleep. Most lay people consider the wonderfully dramatic scenarios we call dreams to be the primary work of the sleeping brain, but in fact many dreams are thoughtlike and less dramatic than REM dreams. These "quasi-dream experiences," as dream researcher David Foulkes calls them, take place during periods of sleep other than REM and are more likely to rehash daily events than do REM dreams. Foulkes explains that these dreams tend to be less distorted than REM dreams and more likely to make sense to the dreamer. Often they will continue a theme begun in a REM dream but in doing so will tend to resemble waking thinking patterns rather than the more bizarre patterns typical of REM dreams.

One of the most interesting examples of lucid dreams that take place outside of rapid-eye-movement sleep comes from a study by Joseph Dane, a clinical psychologist at the University of Virginia.

He guided a group of women who reported no previous experience with lucid dreaming through a series of techniques designed to induce lucidity. This included suggesting to them while hypnotized that they would have a lucid dream. During one night of monitored sleep-lab stays, all but one of the women were able to signal that they had turned lucid, and almost all of them did so from a stage of sleep other than REM.

WHEN DREAMS APPEAR

The sleeping brain, like its nocturnal companion the moon, goes through a series of periodic phases. When you first drift off to sleep, or even when you close your eyes and relax, the brain begins to produce alpha rhythms, the hallmarks of a relaxed brain. As you slip deeper into sleep, you probably begin to experience vivid and dreamy visions and forms. Your brain waves slow to four to six cycles per second, and the amplitude of the waves decreases. You are now in stage 1 sleep. Soon after reaching this stage, short bursts of wave activity occur. The images you see now will probably seem more realistic than what you experienced in stage 1. Gradually, your brain waves slow even more, turning into delta waves, which indicate that your brain is at the ebb of its electrical activity, and you descend to stages 3 and 4, the deepest sleep. Although these stages might seem like the best environment for dreams, they are not. If you were awakened now, you would report few images; your mentation would more closely resemble that of waking thought than of dreams. In fact, dreams, as we commonly think of them, do not occur until you have reached stage 4 sleep and then ascended back up through stages 3 and 2 to what is called "emergent" stage 1. At this time, your body's muscles are virtually paralzyed, and REM sleep begins. This unexpected paralysis as you move toward lighter stages of sleep is another reason REM sleep is considered paradoxical. It's as if you are at a tennis match. Before the action begins, you are free to move about, buy a soft drink, talk to a friend. But when the umpire asks you to be seated, movement ceases; you become wrapped up in the game. As in REM sleep, your eyes do most of the moving. But at the end of the set, you stand up again. The dream is over.

Lucid dream researchers have studied these fluctuations in the brain waves of lucid dreamers, looking for how they might vary from the norm. Canadian psychologists Harry Hunt, Robert Ogilvie, and Paul Tyson have been particularly interested in variations in alpha waves, the waves that are produced when you are in a state of relaxation. If Hunt's model is correct and lucidity is related to the meditative state, higher levels of alpha should occur during lucidity. When you meditate your brain becomes more relaxed and you begin to produce alpha waves. If lucid dreaming is similar to meditation, one might expect to find an increase in alpha waves there, too. Indeed, Hunt and his colleagues found that alpha waves increase early on in lucidity and during prelucid dream experiences, such as false awakening (you wake up to find you are still dreaming).

A recent study by Dutch psychologist Jan Meirsman sheds additional light on the association of alpha waves to lucid dreaming. He studied the REM sleep of six TM-Sidhi (advanced) meditators who claimed to witness much of each night. He found that alpha waves increased to a level in these subjects that was much higher than in nonmeditating control subjects. Again we see that a change that first occurs in lucid dreaming may become even more pronounced as one moves into higher states of consciousness.

DREAMED REALITY

If you are having a lucid dream and decide to move your eyes to the left and then to the right, your eyes will physically move in those directions. That's why people can signal from the dream state that they have turned lucid. But the control a lucid dreamer has over his or her biological states extends beyond the eyes. The Stanford group has demonstrated that lucid dreamers can voluntarily control their respiration and that they are capable of abbreviated versions of small movements. LaBerge, for instance, has signaled from a REM-state lucid dream by slightly clenching his fist. Of course, his ability to do this led some researchers to conclude that he was not asleep, or at least not in REM sleep.

Even when the muscles used by a lucid dreamer do not move, researchers have found increased electrical activity in that muscle group. In experiments by Morton Schatzman, Peter Fenwick, and Alan Worsley, the latter carried out a variety of muscular movements while lucid. Here's his dream in which he tries to work the muscles in his feet:

> I gave the eye-movement lucidity signal. I got up with all my wires attached. Being careful not to dislodge the electrodes, I placed the toes of my right foot against the base of a bench and my right heel on the floor. Standing with most of my weight on my left leg and holding the top edge of the bench with my hands; several times I pushed my right foot down against the base of the bench and against the floor. Each time I pushed down with my foot, I pulled upward on the bench with my hands. . . . I did a series of about seven quick downward thrusts with my foot at a rate of nearly two a second.

For these movements and the others that Worsley dreamed of, the researchers found increased electrical activity in some of the muscle groups that were being tested. In other words, despite the paralysis of REM sleep, the dreamer's conscious effort to move a muscle stimulated some electrical activity in that muscle.

Another example of this mind-body parallel during lucidity can be found in LaBerge's work on dreamed sexual activity. Starting largely with Patricia Garfield's popular 1974 book *Creative Dreaming*, stories about the joys of lucid dream orgasms began circulating in the dream community. The orgasms experienced in lucid dreams, some contended, were more intense than waking ones. Curious about the physical reality of such reports, LaBerge enlisted three subjects, one female and two male, for an experiment. While in a sleep lab, they were to signal to him three times: first, at the onset of lucidity, second, when they first began sexual activity; and third, when they experienced orgasm. In addition to wearing sensors on their heads to test brain waves, the woman was asked to wear a vaginal probe and the men a penile strain gauge to measure their sexual response. The woman's lucid dream began with a long sequence of flying. At one point, she flew through an archway and spotted a group of people. She descended upon the group and tapped the first man she saw on the shoulder. "He came toward her," LaBerge recounts, "as if knowing exactly what he was expected to do. At this time, she signaled again, marking the beginning of sexual activity. She says that she must have already been excited from the flying, because after only fifteen seconds she felt as if she were about to climax. She signaled a third time, marking her experience of orgasm."

After examining the physiological data obtained while the woman was dreaming, LaBerge found marked increases in both respiration and vaginal blood flow that corresponded to the activity in her dream. Further, those physical responses were comparable to ones found in waking orgasms. She had indeed experienced an orgasm. LaBerge recorded similar responses in the men, but unlike the woman, who showed vaginal muscle contractions (or physical orgasm), the men did not ejaculate. LaBerge hypothesizes that the brain impulses that arose from their lucid dreams were not strong enough to trigger ejaculation. Sexual lucid dreams for men are apparently quite different from wet dreams, which LaBerge suggests occur primarily in adolescents and men who have no regular sexual outlets.

In the same way that lucid dream orgasms are "felt" by the dreamer to be intensely real, other images and events in lucid dreams are often perceived as "superreal" or "more real" than waking reality. It's enormously difficult to scientifically document subjective interpretations of a dreamed experience, but lucid dream researchers are investigating certain physical aspects of lucidity that may shed light on the way we construct waking and dreaming reality.

In one study, for instance, LaBerge instructed two subjects to track their fingers in the following ways: (1) while they were awake with their eyes open, (2) while they were awake with their eyes closed and imaging their finger, (3) while they were in a lucid dream with their dream eyes open, and (4) while they were in a lucid dream with their dream eyes closed, again imaging their finger. LaBerge found that the subjects showed the same sorts of eye movements when they were lucid and tracking their finger with eyes open as when they were awake and tracking their finger with eyes open. These eye movements differed from those measured when the subjects had their eyes closed. Similarly, the eyes when closed moved the same whether the subject was awake or lucid dreaming.

In a related study carried out at Saint Thomas's Hospital in London, psychologists Morton Schatzman and Peter Fenwick found that Worsley was able to stare at a fixed object in his dream while, at the same time, he slowly moved his dream head from side to side. The eye movement patterns produced resembled those that would have been produced if he were awake. Given that head and neck movements (and all others) are suppressed during rapid-eye-movement sleep, how could this be? "Some part of his brain . . . must have 'assumed' that his head was going to move and then was moving and, accordingly, that his physical eyes would have to move relative to it, in order to maintain the fixation," the researchers explain.

The bottom line here is that as far as the brain was concerned his "neck" had moved, thus the response of his eyes. Worsley's dreamed event, like those of LaBerge's subjects, was a lived reality in the brain. The brain constructed the dream reality *and* responded to its own construction *as though it were real.* This finding supports the view of University of Northern Iowa psychologist Jack Yates, who showed in the prestigious journal *Psychological Review* that our brains create a mental model of the world and that it is within this mental model that we live.

The implications of this view are far-reaching. The power of waking mental images to influence health, sports performance, smoking habits, and self-esteem has been well documented. If, as is suggested by lucid dreaming studies, imagery produced within a lucid dream is more like reality than images produced while awake, then the lucid dream may in fact be a more powerful state in which to use mental imagery to enhance psychological and biological change. However, as we have discussed before, dreaming or simply recalling what you dream does not in and of itself restore the body and the mind to the degree found when you practice meditation *and* pay attention to your dreams. Nor is dream recall on its own as beneficial as working with dreams on your own or in psychotherapy. If, as we are maintaining, lucidity in dreams is related to waking meditation, then dream lucidity offers us a unique experiential touch point for the psychotherapeutic and meditative traditions. In fact, lucid dreaming is enhanced in both quantity and quality by the practice of either or both traditions.

DEEPER DREAMING

Let's focus on the meditation link. Lucid dream researchers continue to probe other physiological measures in their effort to understand fully what lucid dreaming is. One of the more curious aspects of the phenomenon is its paradoxical nature. Although there appears to be more brain and other nervous system activity during lucid dreaming, some research has also indicated that the body's muscles are actually "more asleep" than they are during nonlucid REM dreaming. For example, Andrew Brylowski, an intern at the University of Texas, measured a spinal reflex, which is stimulated at the knee, known as the Hoffman or H-reflex in a subject while in REM sleep and again after the subject had turned lucid. The H-reflex, which indicates the degree to which the body is "awake" or paralyzed, is measured in waking subjects by electrodes, which chart the electrical activity in the knee. When awake, a person's H-reflex is pronounced, but during sleep, especially rapid-eye-movement sleep, it is markedly suppressed. Brylowski found that this reflex is even more suppressed during lucid REM sleep than during ordinary REM sleep, indicating that the lucid dreamer's body is significantly more paralyzed than it normally is during REM. In other words, when you are experiencing rapid-eye-movement sleep, you are essentially paralyzed from the neck down, but when you are lucid in REM sleep you are even more profoundly paralyzed. It is similar to when your arm falls asleep. At its worst, its deepest paralysis, you cannnot move it at all—that's what your body's like during lucid dreaming. As you begin to have some sensations in it, but still cannot move it— that's what your body is like while you're in REM sleep, but are not lucid.

The dampening of this physical reaction during lucidity may have implications for Hunt's theory of lucidity as a state closely related to meditation. Researchers at the Maharishi International University (MIU) report that advanced meditators who have just ended their meditation recover the full functioning of the H-reflex more quickly than do others. It's the two sides of the coin phenomenon: Lucid dreamers suppress their nervous system more than usual because it may be beneficial to their experience; meditators, once they come out of their meditation and back into the "real" world, can activate their reflexes quickly. Both abilities suggest that the bodies of lucid dreamers and those of meditators are highly adapted to whatever state they are in. At this point, of course, such a statement is speculative at best, and much more research must be carried out to substantiate this theory.

Although LaBerge's work suggests that during lucidity one is moving toward waking (the nervous system is more active during lucidity than during ordinary dreaming), Brylowski's study suggests the opposite—one is really moving toward "deeper dreaming" (more paralysis) when lucid. Rapid-eye-movement sleep has always been considered paradoxical because the increase in bodily arousal is accompanied by the body's inability to move. You know what we mean if you have ever awakened breathing rapidly —that's the high arousal typical of REM sleep. You might also have found it difficult to move immediately or easily, still feeling as though your body was somewhat asleep. Because the body is even more aroused and more paralyzed during lucid dreaming, it may be viewed as paradoxical dreaming.

Some studies that have compared various measures of bodily arousal during meditation with those during sleep have found that the rate at which the body consumes oxygen along with the rate at which the heart is beating is about the same in both states, despite the fact that in meditation one is awake. Furthermore, some studies suggest that waking meditation actually provides a deeper rest than sleep. One might then ask, how can lucidity be a form of meditation, if the body is also aroused? We are suggesting that lucidity acts as a transitory state between sleep and the classic state of "restful alertness" sought in waking meditation.

Charles Alexander, a developmental psychologist at MIU, makes a distinction between dream lucidity and dream witnessing (see chapter 10 for a more detailed discussion of these issues). "Typical dream lucidity," he says, "represents a step beyond ordinary dreaming, and witnessing represents a step beyond ordinary dream lucidity. If you took dream lucidity to its ultimate state, then it would be synonymous with the experiences of transcending consciousness." In other words, lucidity may act as a developmental bridge from ordinary dream consciousness to transcending (also called witnessing or pure) consciousness. And the differences found between meditation and lucid dreaming sleep may disappear once the dreamer has reached the stage of witnessing, that is, once he or she has become an inactive participant in the dream and is, at the same time, observing it, but without any emotional involvement in, or attachment to, the dream. Witnessing has been conceptualized as the fourth major state of consciousness, existing alongside waking, dreaming, and sleeping. Once one has reached this level, he or she may often or continually be an observer of him- or herself in the other states (waking, dreaming, or sleeping).

Gackenbach, along with Alexander and William Moorecroft of Luther College in Decorah, Iowa (and technical advice from LaBerge), devised an experiment to see if there were any distinct physiological differences between the lucid dreams of LaBerge's subjects and a subject who was believed to be witnessing his dreams. They contacted an advanced TM practitioner who agreed to participate. The man, who was twenty-eight years old and had been meditating for almost six years, claimed that he witnessed at all times, including during sleep. He had taken a series of psychological tests, which indicated, among other things, that he was not pathological and did not have a tendency to endorse misleading or grandiose-sounding statements. But what made his reports especially reliable was that he also scored exceptionally high on two physiological measures associated with experiences of pure consciousness.

As expected, the man was capable of signaling that he was dreaming, and as with other lucid dreamers, his heart and respiration rates increased *with the eye movement signals*. But unlike other lucid dreamers, these signs of physical arousal dropped off dramatically once the eye signal had been made. It appeared as if the man's response was the dreaming equivalent to deep meditation. This lucid dream study suggests, as the researchers reported, "that the restfully alert state of Transcendental Consciousness was only momentarily disrupted during the signaling task and then quickly returned to the low arousal, silent, wakeful condition." Again, this was a study that evaluated only one subject and should be replicated with other advanced meditators before any conclusions can be drawn.

Finally, a recent study by Meirsman suggests that meditation serves to stabilize the experience of consciousness in sleep. In lucid dreamers the physiological changes that accompany lucidity vary from one person to another. Meirsman found that with meditators who were experiencing witnessing dreaming there was virtually no variation in those same physical measures. This is among the first studies to support the view that meditation does contribute to the continuity of consciousness in sleep and helps to stabilize it.

THE HOLISTIC BRAIN

Myths arise from science as well as from literature. One of the most pervasive modern myths concerns the functioning of the left and right hemispheres of the brain. Although the myth is based on Roger Sperry's work with split-brain patients in which he demonstrated that each hemisphere carries out specific and quite different functions, the idea has been vastly distorted. The left brain, as Sperry found, does specialize in language; the right, in spatial abilities, which are represented by such things as a good sense of direction. But the idea that the right brain is the seat of creativity and the left of logic, that artists and writers are right-brained and accountants and other "noncreative" types, left-brained, is overstated. Jerre Levy, a biopsychologist at the University of Chicago, points out that "the two-brain myth was founded on an erroneous premise: that because each hemisphere was specialized each must function as an independent brain. In fact, just the opposite is true." She points out that though each hemisphere may have special functions, all activities require input from both hemispheres. For example, reading a story may be primarily a function carried out by the left hemisphere, where language facility is based in most people. But, as Levy explains, "the right hemisphere may play a special role in decoding visual information, maintaining an integrated story structure, appreciating humor and emotional content, deriving meaning from past associations and understanding metaphor." Similarly, Levy explains, "there is no evidence that either creativity or intuition is an exclusive property of the right hemisphere."

This more holistic view of the brain can be measured in part by examining (through EEG measures) how the left and right hemispheres are working together. One measure of how well they are working together is called EEG coherence. Deepak Chopra, a physician and the author of *Return of the Rishi*, explains coherence in this way: "It is really a measure of the integration of the neurons everywhere in the central nervous system. A good analogy would be when you go to hear the Boston Symphony, and you arrive before the performance while players are still practicing on their own as they tune up. Each performer is playing his instrument on the right notes, the right frequency, but the overall result is chaotic. There is no constancy in the relationship between the performers, and therefore what you get is noise. Once the performance starts, they are still playing the same notes on the same instruments, but there is a constancy of relationship—there is music. This constancy of relationship is coherence."

Coherence has been related to cognitive functioning. A Russian scientist, for example, found that during coma there was a marked decrease in coherence as measured by an EEG, that there was less communication between the left and right hemispheres. As coma patients recovered consciousness and speech, the level of coherence rose.

Coherence has also been found to be lower in the mentally ill than in people without severe mental illness. But coherence in most of us varies depending on what we are thinking and doing. As psychologist Rosanne Armitage says, "a central nervous system which has access to the specialization of both sides of the brain at the same time would be expected to excel at a variety of tasks."

Research has also shown that individuals who meditate exhibit greater coherence than controls. A group of Chinese scientists found increased coherence levels in individuals practicing the meditative breathing exercise "qigong." TM researchers report that those who experience the feeling of transcendence (pure consciousness) during meditation exhibit surges in coherence that are higher than those generally found during meditation. Evidence also shows that coherence levels rise during rapid-eye-movement sleep in the same manner as it does during transcendence. Because lucid dreams occur more frequently during REM, Gackenbach argues in a chapter in *The Mind in Sleep,* vol. 2, that coherence should also surge during lucidity and especially during witnessing.

Coherence may also be related to our ability to recall dreams. Individuals who recall more than the average number of dreams (most people remember between two and three a week) have been found to exhibit levels of coherence upon awakening that were nearly as high as their individual levels during REM sleep. In people who recalled fewer dreams, coherence levels dropped upon awakening. Carrying over the higher rapid-eye-movement levels of coherence into waking, therefore, serves to help us remember our dreams.

But more importantly, increasing coherence in sleep or while awake is a way to help our brains perform at their best. And if, as Globus suggests in the first chapter of this book, dreams are the brain's harmonious solutions to our life events as they are played out during sleep, then increasing the level of communication within the brain—turning the noise in our brains into music (coherence)—may enhance the harmonious solutions at our disposal. Most of us will need to use a technology such as meditation to push our brains into high gear, but once having done so, the possibilities, as we will see in chapter 10, abound.

Chapter 9

The Right Stuff

WHAT IT TAKES TO BE A LUCID DREAMER

Maltese falcons . . . pots of gold . . . Pulitzer Prizes . . . tall, dark strangers. . . . We know what dreams are made of, but what about dreamers? As we have alluded to in other chapters, people who have lucid dreams share certain physiological and psychological traits. In this chapter we'll take a closer look at those characteristics, but first we thought you'd like to see how you fit the profile of the lucid dreamer. The following questions are examples of the ones dream researchers ask. They should help you understand some rather complex psychological processes and give you a clearer idea of your lucid dreaming potential. Remember, this is not a test or a complete profile, just a cursory assessment. We suggest you answer the questions first, jotting down your answers; then go on to the rest of the chapter.

PART I

1. How many dreams do you recall on the average per week?
   ___ none ___ four ___ eight ___ twelve ___ sixteen
   ___ one ___ five ___ nine ___ thirteen ___ seventeen
   ___ two ___ six ___ ten ___ fourteen ___ eighteen
   ___ three ___ seven ___ eleven ___ fifteen ___ nineteen
   ___ twenty +

2. Check one of the following regarding your experience with and interest in meditation:
   ___ a. no experience, no interest
   ___ b. no experience, moderate interest
   ___ c. no experience, very interested
   ___ d. some experience, but not currently regular, no interest
   ___ e. some experience, but not currently regular, moderate interest
   ___ f. some experience, but not currently regular, very interested
   ___ g. currently regularly meditating. If you checked "g," please give the following details:
      (1) number of months you have been meditating _____
      (2) average length of time per day that you meditate _____

3. Your sex: ___ male ___ female

4. This is a test of your ability to find a simple form when it is hidden within a complex line drawing.
   a. Find this simple form: ●

b. Find this simple form: ■

5. Please indicate the degree to which the following conditions apply to you:

severe   moderate   none at all
 5   4   3   2   1

a. a history of ear problems _____
b. a major physical handicap that impairs movement _____
c. a vision problem not correctable by glasses _____
d. a history of motion sickness _____

6. Indicate the ease with which you could perform in each of the following activities:

very easy   moderately easy   not at all easy
 5   4   3   2   1

a. standing on one foot _____
b. standing on a board that is balanced on a ball _____
c. standing toe to toe on a wire hung one foot off the ground _____

7. Indicate the frequency with which you have had out-of-body experiences. These are experiences in which you felt that "you" were located "outside" or "away from" your physical body, that is, the feeling that your consciousness, mind, or center of awareness was at a different place than your physical body.

1: never   3: 3 or 4 times   5: 7 or 8 times
2: 1 or 2 times   4: 5 or 6 times   6: more than 9 times

8. The items of this test will bring images to your mind. Rate each image by reference to this scale:

clear and vivid as the actual	moderately clear and vivid	no image only know I am thinking
5	3	1

Imagine each of the following sounds in your mind's ear and classify by the degree of clearness and vividness specified above:

a. the crackle of a forest creek ___
b. the barking of a dog ___
c. the cry of a baby ___
d. the breaking of glass ___

Imagine each of the following acts in your mind and classify by the degree of clearness and vividness specified above:

a. touching your shoulder ___ b. skipping on a sidewalk ___
c. writing with a pen _____ d. rolling over in bed _____

9. Answer each of the following as true or false of you.
a. I can be greatly moved by eloquent or poetic language. _____
b. Sometimes I experience things as if they were doubly real. _____
c. When I listen to music, I can get so caught up in it that I don't notice anything else. _____
d. While acting in a play, I think I could really feel the emotions of the character and "become" her or him for the time being, forgetting both myself and the audience. _____
e. I often have "physical memories"; for example, after I've been swimming I may still feel as if I'm in the water. _____

10. Two-dimensional rotation task: At the left of the sample below there is a triangle with a circle in one corner and one side darkened. Now look at the triangles A, B, C, and D and notice that each has a circle in one corner and a darkened line for one side. Find the one triangle out of the four that is just like the sample.

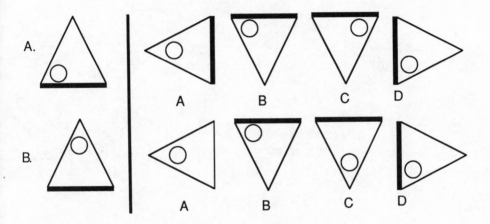

11. Three-dimensional rotation task: In somewhat the same manner as the last task, look at the object to the left below. One of the four drawings to the right shows the same object. Can you find it?

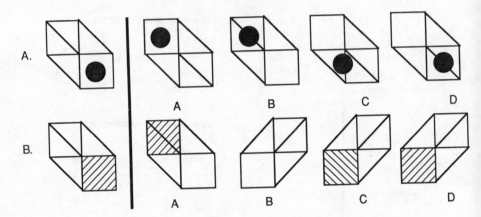

12. What grades did you earn on the average in either high school or college in the following subjects?

_____ English

_____ Mathematics

13. Below are two shapes. Think of a way that you can make a picture from these shapes. Be sure that you include both shapes in your picture. When your picture is complete give it a title that fully characterizes it.

 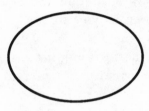

Your Title: _____

14. Assuming you had the available time and money, how interested would you be in trying each of the following activities? Using the rating scale below, indicate the degree of interest these activities hold for you.

Not at all   Extremely
interesting   interesting
  1   2   3   4   5

    a. A famous Eastern teacher has established a retreat near you. He will be offering individualized training in meditation, and you have been invited to work with him. _____

    b. A parapsychologist at a leading university has devised a new technique for developing telepathic powers. He is offering you an opportunity to enter his training program. _____

    c. A master hypnotist has offered you a personalized program in hypnosis designed to explore your unconscious and to help you resolve hidden inner conflicts. _____

15. Rate the extent to which each of the following items is characteristic of you along this scale:

Extremely   Extremely
uncharacteristic   characteristic
  1   2   3   4   5

    a. I'm always trying to figure myself out. _____

    b. I reflect about myself a lot. _____

    c. I'm generally attentive to my inner feelings. _____

    d. I sometimes have the feeling that I'm off somewhere watching myself. _____

    e. I'm aware of the way my mind works when I work through a problem. _____

16. Check all of the adjectives that describe how you *generally* feel.

___ calm	___ worried
___ tense	___ relaxed
___ rested	___ stressed
___ anxious	___ peaceful

QUIZ KEY

For the most part these are not the actual items used in testing. Rather, they have been designed to give you an understanding of each concept. The ability to lucid-dream is associated with:

1. high dream recall
2. the regular practice of meditation
3. being female
4. the ability to find hidden forms
5. a lack of balance-related problems
6. the ability to balance
7. having out-of-body experiences
8. having high vividness of auditory (first set of items) and kinesthetic (second set of items) images
9. ability to become absorbed in activities (highest score: all true)
10. an ability to rotate objects in mental space:
    two-dimensional items:
    (a) the answer is B
    (b) the answer is C
11. and three-dimensional items:
    (a) the answer is A
    (b) the answer is D
12. intelligence (high grades in English and mathematics)
13. creativity as indicated by a detailed and unusual figure drawn
14. extremely interested in these risky ventures for the inner self
15. aware of their private inner lives (high scores on all items)
16. not anxious

PART II: THE LUCID PROFILE

"I did not try to have lucid dreams," explains Baptist minister George Gillespie. "They just started. *They* came to *me*." But once begun, they continued to come, five hundred of them in ten years, and he is not alone. Like any skill, lucid dreaming has its Olympians; like any endeavor, some people excel and some get left on the sidelines. Current estimates suggest that 58 percent of the population have experienced a lucid dream at least once, but only 21 percent are likely to have a lucid dream once a month or more often. What is it that enables one person and not another to be conscious during a dream and fly, face a forbidding stranger, or solve some daytime dilemma? Intrigued by this question, Gackenbach began looking for common characteristics among lucid dreamers. After testing thousands of individuals, both those who had experienced lucid dreaming and those who had not, she began to draw a profile of the typical lucid dreamer. Her profile is based almost entirely upon nonmeditating individuals who do not pay attention to their dreams and thus can be said to characterize the spontaneous emergence of lucidity in sleep. The first two items of our quiz concern the two major predictors of lucid dreaming— the number of dreams one remembers and whether or not one meditates.

Dream Recall (Question One)

The average person recalls only two to three dreams per week. If you remember more than that, your chances of having a lucid dream increase. There are several reasons why one person remembers eight or ten dreams a week and another none. People who pay attention to their inner lives will often recall more than the average number of dreams. Sometimes certain stressful situations also produce particularly vivid dreams that are more likely to be remembered. And even the manner in which you wake up can influence how many dreams you remember: People who awaken abruptly tend to recall fewer dreams than those who wake up slowly.

Meditation (Question Two)

As we detailed in chapter 2, simply practicing meditation increases the likelihood that you will dream lucidly. This is probably true for the two major styles of meditation (concentrative and mindfulness) as well as for methods that combine these basic forms, such as TM. In part, this is probably true because the practice of meditation increases brain coherence and thus consciousness in sleep as well as more archetypal dream content, and results in higher dream recall. Meditation can be defined more broadly here. For example, spending part of each day in deep prayer may also increase your chances of dreaming lucidly. Gackenbach and her colleagues have found that nonmeditators who merely express *interest* in meditation are more likely to have lucid dreams than people who show no interest in meditation at all. To be fair, they will probably not have as many lucid dreams as serious meditators, but their interest indicates a desire to experience internal states of mind, which may be essential for the development of lucid dreaming.

Sex, however, also plays an important role in the profile of the lucid dreamer.

Neuronal Androgyny (Question Three)

Under certain circumstances females experience more lucid dreams than do males. In a study of 106 nonmeditators and 45 meditators, Gackenbach found that women who meditated reported significantly more lucid dreams than men who meditated. This sex difference also occasionally showed up among nonmeditators who expressed an interest in meditating. Again brain coherence comes into play in explaining this female edge in lucid dreaming. Rosanne Armitage and other researchers at Carleton University in Canada found that women, to a greater degree than men, tended to exhibit the high coherence found in rapid-eye-movement sleep and lucid dreaming after they awakened. This high coherence in turn enabled them to recall more dreams. In addition, French-Canadian psychiatrist Pierre Flor-Henry discovered that women generally have higher levels of coherence than men. Perhaps it is this increased communication among the parts of the brain that makes it easier for women to remember their dreams, to dream lucidly, and also to experience transcendence (pure consciousness) during meditation. Although no studies have looked at sex differences in meditation experiences, there is some anecdotal evidence that suggests women have more intense experiences, including those in which they "transcend." As one long-time meditator said, "The ladies do seem to report more spectacular experiences in meditation."

Interestingly, the advantage that increased levels of coherence may give women in sleep and meditation does not always serve them well in waking life. In many endeavors, the more segmented, or specialized, your brain is, the more successful you will be. Researchers have found that most men's brains are more clearly specialized or lateralized for certain functions (say, following road maps or finding their way out of a forest) than women's. To some extent, both sexes are limited by the natural organization of their brains. But, as Gackenbach and her husband-colleague Thomas Snyder, a neuropsychologist at the University of Alberta, discovered, these limitations may not be etched in stone. Their studies and those of meditation researchers indicate that females who meditate and/or lucid dream retain the normal levels of coherence for females but they also exhibit greater brain lateralization than do women who do not lucid dream or meditate. Similarly, men who meditate and/or lucid dream may also maintain the advantages inherent in the male brain while increasing their coherence. It appears that meditation and lucidity move us toward the neuronal equivalent of androgyny by allowing our brains to function more holistically in all aspects of our lives.

That meditators and lucid dreamers of both sexes show greater lateralization and higher coherence levels may also hold the key to understanding how the brain processes information and perhaps shed some light on the nature of higher states of consciousness. According to David Orme-Johnson and his colleagues at MIU, each individual's brain can engage in both specialized and general functions: It is capable of concentrating on a mathematical formula or taking in the general ambience of a new restaurant. The brain can line up an arrow with a bull's-eye or it can process the sight, smells, sounds, and texture of a sunny beach. When the mind is focusing on a particular task, it will probably be using one section of the brain more than the other, and the portion that is most involved in the performance of the task at hand will be low in coherence. This is because in order to perform a specific task well, the portion of the brain best suited for carrying it out must be called into play. To deal a deck of cards, for instance, special physical responses need to take charge. This doesn't mean the rest of the brain is inactive; rather, it increases in coherence, serving to integrate the function being performed (dealing the cards) with other aspects of the environment. The dealing of the cards occurs in a "field" of the card table, friends, and a can of beer. The portions of the brain not engaged in the task at hand serve to integrate and more fully engage the brain in the activity. So if, to use another example, you are reading a story, the left hemisphere, which is doing the bulk of the surface processing, will be low in coherence, while the right hemisphere, which will be giving emotional context to the words, will be high in coherence.[1]

The point is that not only does meditation—and we hypothesize lucid dreaming—make the brain more integrated (coherent), but it also appears to do so even while one is *not* meditating or dreaming, and consequently it helps the individual to engage more efficiently in specific tasks.

Second Sight (Question Four)

You are in a darkened room, looking at a luminous frame on the wall. A rod, also luminous, is in the center of the frame but is not attached to it, appearing instead to be floating there. Your task is to instruct the experimenter to move the rod so that it will be parallel to the wall. You can't touch the rod or the wall; you must stand at a distance in the dark and give your instructions. Could you do it?

---

[1] The MIU researchers suggest that the site of the witness, during both waking and sleeping, is that part of the brain that is high in coherence.

Researchers have known for years that some individuals are capable of making accurate perceptual judgments about where they are or where an object is in space no matter how many distorting cues exist to confuse them. They're the people who can find their way out of a forest after being turned around. They can make accurate judgments even in the dark. Apparently, they employ some internal barometer that tells them where things should be. Other people do not have this ability; a confusing cue will throw off their judgment. Those who are good at orienting themselves in space are said to be field-independent—they do not need correct sensory information to make accurate judgments about where something is in space. A variation of finding your way out of a forest is being able to find a simple figure embedded in a complex one. If you correctly identified the embedded figures in question four, you may be fairly field-independent. Lucid dreamers and meditators, as well as those who remember more than the average number of dreams, are more field-independent than others. Their ability to easily orient themselves in space, be it in the real or dream world, may be another key to understanding the relationship between lucid dreaming and meditation. Not surprisingly, these sorts of spatial-orientation skills feed back to coherence and its association to meditation and lucid dreaming: Individuals who are field-independent also exhibit higher levels of coherence than those who are not.

The Power of Balance (Questions Five and Six)

If you answered that you frequently have ear problems or experience motion sickness (question five), or that you suffer from a physical or visual handicap, you would probably be rejected for Gackenbach and Snyder's studies for ethical reasons. That's because one of the physiological tests they administer is something called caloric stimulation. After having you lie down and hooking sensors to your eyes, they slowly pour either warm or cool water in each ear, a process that creates tremorlike oscillations of the eyes. In individuals whose vestibular systems (the elaborate inner canals and other parts of the ear) are fully functional, these oscillations are regular and pulsing. The lines on the polygraph chart will zigzag in sharp mountainous peaks and valleys. But in people who have some disturbance with the system that controls balance, the lines on the polygraph will either flatten out or become very irregular. Pouring water into the ears of these individuals can be tantamount to throwing them on a speeding merry-go-round. Their systems may be so disrupted that they vomit or fall off the bed. Even without water in their ears, such people will probably experience motion sickness and possibly earaches, which is why researchers won't choose them for this type of study.

Interestingly, these people might also have a difficult time learning to lucid dream. This is because there appears to be a connection between healthy vestibular systems and lucidity. In Gackenbach and Snyder's studies, those who reported having at least one lucid dream a month also had good vestibular physiology. Those who had never had a lucid dream, on the other hand, were found to have some problem with their ears, even though they hadn't reported being bothered by motion sickness or earaches. The reason for this finding probably has to do with the vestibular system's role in controlling balance and thus helping to orient an individual in space. It enables us to know where we are when awake in the physical world *and* where we are when we awaken within the mental constructions of our sleep. For instance, a common activity in lucid dreams is flying, but learning how to soar, float, climb above trees, take off, and land requires a sense of balance and thus an ability to locate oneself in internal space. There may be a biological explanation for why the vestibular system is important in lucid dreaming. The vestibular nerves are located in the brain stem, the point at which the brain and spinal cord connect. Research indicates that these nerves contribute to the production of REM, the characteristic eye movements that accompany dreaming. In fact, these nerves are particularly active in the phase of REM that is associated with lucid dreaming.

In addition to this obvious use of balance while dreaming, both emotional and cognitive balance come into play in lucidity. Usually inexperienced lucid dreamers get so excited by the realization that they're dreaming that they wake up. With experience, they learn to restrain their emotional outbursts while maintaining conscious awareness and continuing to dream. Furthermore, early in the process of lucid dreaming, one must balance the verbal thought "This is a dream" with the other verbal chatter in the dream. Although this sort of emotional and cognitive balancing act might seem unconnected to physical balance, we suggest that it is not. If, as some psychologists argue, the root of thinking is not verbal but rather a combination of sensory systems working together (which in turn creates a spatial quality to preverbal experience), then it becomes clearer that the role balance plays in spatial orientation may influence our capacity to gain and maintain consciousness in dreams.

One further note about balance. We often think that our body balance functions in response to gravity, but recent research indicates that our body balance is not determined by gravity but rather operates in reference to the surroundings, or medium. Mediums can be physical, such as the earth or the ceiling of a room, or they can be mental, such as a dreamed treetop. Furthermore, according to Jack Yates, a cognitive psychologist at the University of Northern Iowa, all mediums are mental, that is, everything we sense and perceive is reconstructed in the brain as a mental model. Balance then helps to orient us in mental space, which is the only space we experience.

The importance of good vestibular physiology for lucid dreaming was further substantiated in an experiment testing body balance. If you are good at standing on one foot and suspect that you would be proficient at balancing in other balancing tasks (question six), you might do well on the stabilometer—a skateboard-size device that rests on a fulcrum, like a teeter-totter. Your job is to balance yourself on the board; each time you err past a certain degree, you hear a click as the machine registers the movement. Snyder and Gackenbach used the stabilometer to see if lucid dreamers were better at this task than others. They found that they were. From this experiment and others they were able to conclude that lucid REM sleep can be characterized as a state of enhanced inward attention—more so than nonlucid dream sleep —similar to that found in waking meditation.

Imagination (Questions Seven, Eight, Nine, Ten, and Eleven)

Given the enhanced inward attention that characterizes lucid dreaming, it is not surprising that lucid dreamers experience more vivid imagery (question eight) and become absorbed in activities (question nine) more completely than do people who have never had a lucid dream. Lucid dreamers also regularly experience more types of spontaneous waking imagery, such as daydreams, hallucinations, out-of-body experiences (question seven), and hypnogogic imagery (the images you see as you drift off to sleep). Lucid dreamers can easily imagine running upstairs, springing across a gutter, or drawing a circle on a piece of paper. Compared to others, their imagining will be extremely vivid. Similarly, their ability to imagine sounds—the honk of an automobile horn or the clapping of hands—is greater than that of people who don't dream lucidly.

The curious aspect of lucid dreamers' propensity for imagining is that it is not the visual components of the imagined event that are perceived as more real, but rather the sounds and the sensation of touch. The lucid dreamer excels in hearing sounds, feeling surfaces, and consequently moving about in space. These imaginal abilities of the lucid dreamer (especially the one who meditates) are due to his or her ability to become absorbed in an activity (question nine). Again, this ability to focus attention is highly reminiscent of the perceptual style sought by meditators.

Related to this is the lucid dreamer's ability to imagine and then manipulate three-dimensional objects in space (question eleven). Although lucid dreamers don't exhibit any greater ability than others for rotating two-dimensional images (question ten), we have included an example as a warm-up for the three-dimensional tasks. Apparently, one's ability to engage in difficult spatial tasks, such as the rotation of three-dimensional drawings, is linked to the ability to lucid-dream. Once again this illustrates lucid dreamers' ease at maneuvering in mental space. Interestingly, and somewhat surprisingly, given the often cited male superiority at such tasks, this ability is especially common among female lucid dreamers.

Intellectual and Creative Abilities (Questions Twelve and Thirteen)

Gackenbach has found that selected female lucid dreamers score higher on scales of verbal and numerical intelligence (question twelve) than do their nonlucid-dreaming counterparts. This is not true of male lucid dreamers, who perform less well on this sort of test than do males who do not lucid-dream. This unexpected finding about males who lucid-dream, Gackenbach hypothesizes, may be evidence of the neuronal androgyny that we spoke of earlier. It may be that the brains of lucid males are less "masculinized" and therefore less specialized for the sorts of tasks in which males traditionally excel.

The same seems to be true of creativity (question thirteen). Female lucid dreamers are superior to women who don't lucid dream in nonverbal creativity. Male lucid dreamers score pretty much the same as nonlucid males. Both male and female meditators, even those who don't lucid dream, have been found to score high on both measures of creativity and intelligence.

For the Thrill of It (Question Fourteen)

If your score for question fourteen was high, you may be someone who enjoys taking risks, not physical ones like skiing down the advanced course when you've been on skis for only a day, but internal risks, like taking a course on developing your psychic abilities, or learning to lucid dream. The idea that lucid dreaming may be related to risk taking was first examined by Joseph Dane, a clinical psychologist at the University of Virginia. He developed a questionnaire to assess the degree to which an individual likes potentially risky situations. Gackenbach and her students at the University of Northern Iowa pursued Dane's original idea and discovered a strong link between that willingness and lucid dreaming. Frequent lucid dreamers, they found, were significantly more likely to take on new internal experiences than were control subjects. No wonder, then, that their dreams turn lucid, freeing them to explore the vast, unknown terrain of the imagination.

Inner Lives (Questions Fifteen and Sixteen)

As mentioned earlier, lucid dreamers tend to be somewhat more androgynous than other people. They exhibit holistic personalities, blending anima and animus (female and male characteristics) more completely than others. They are often strong in aspects of their lives in which others of their sex are weak. Male lucid dreamers, for instance, tend to pay more attention to their inner lives (question fifteen) and to be more open about their feelings than nonlucid males. Female lucid dreamers are more field-independent and tend to take more risks than do women who don't lucid dream. Within this androgyny, though, there remain a few differences between men and women. Females who lucid dream and/or meditate are not generally anxious; male lucid dreamers who are not meditators often are (question sixteen).

Based on her work, which includes many studies that have not been discussed here, Gackenbach has concluded that on a psychological level, the lucid woman does not perceive herself as having economic, religious, or occupational problems. She is practical-minded, forthright, and in touch with her emotions. She is willing to experiment, welcoming new experiences. She also takes good care of herself by not drinking, by eating well, and by exercising on a regular basis. The lucid male, on the other hand, is a more perplexing individual. He seems to be a seeker, often searching for religious meaning, who may have difficulty with smoking, other aspects of his health, and group relationships. Despite his problems, however, the lucid male is emotionally stable, conscientious, and is often a meditator. It may be that in men, it is the religious "seeker," the man who is questioning the nature of his faith, who experiences lucidity. His troubles may also be a reflection of the toll strict masculine roles can take on such men. Because of the women's movement, which has fought for a relaxing of strict male and female roles, women, to a greater degree than ever before, feel free to take on new experiences and to redefine themselves and their roles. But many men continue to be limited by society's accepted definition of the masculine character. A man who pursues his internal life, in spite of these constrictions, may suffer for that choice.

It seems clear that in many respects, lucid dreamers are "in tune" with their inner selves; they rely on some internal sense to interpret and maneuver in waking and dreamed spaces, and they welcome experiences that challenge or enlarge their sense of who they are. Lucid dreamers are modern-day explorers who, like explorers of past centuries, are out to conquer new worlds.

Chapter 10

The Evolving Soul

MOVING TOWARD PURE CONSCIOUSNESS

If the theory that lucid dreaming is only one step along a continuum of human consciousness is correct, at least two important questions follow: What comes after lucid dreaming, and why should we care? As we have discussed earlier, one of the stages of consciousness that is related to lucid dreaming is dream witnessing, a characteristic of pure consciousness. We have described briefly what pure consciousness or transcendence is, but in this chapter we will explore the state more deeply, explaining its relationship to lucidity and why these states are important to the future of humankind.

We'll begin with an extraordinary story from college student Mark Block, who three years ago was in a serious automobile accident near his home in Fort Dodge, Iowa. The accident left him in a coma and on a respirator. So damaging were his injuries (broken neck, severe head injury, various lung and soft tissue

damage) that doctors were unsure if he would live, let alone surface from the coma, be able to breathe on his own, or ever walk
again. Block relates in an article he wrote for *Lucidity Letter* that
during his coma, the deepest state of "sleep" or unconsciousness,
he was aware of himself. (Remember that thoughts have been
found to exist in all levels of sleep, not just in REM.) He explains
his initial awareness during the coma:

> Having no remembrance of that night and the events which were to
> follow, I awoke within myself seemingly suspended in the midst of a
> dark void to encounter the most shocking combination of pain and
> confusion. I felt lost within a nightmare as I struggled to awaken and
> free myself from the grasp of this horrifying dream. It was as though
> my eyelids had been sewn shut. I struggled to open my eyes but could
> not. I was aware of the radiant glow of the lights external to my body
> as they passed through my eyelids far above me.

Unable to awaken himself, he felt as if he were being pulled by
a "current" deeper into himself:

> As the pain continued to grow and overcome my confusion and I
> realized the futility of my struggle to awaken, I sought to escape the
> pain by seeking shelter deep within my body. No longer did I resist
> the pull of the current and ceased my struggle, allowing the current to
> carry me away . . . to safety.

Block felt as though his "inner" self was being pushed to safety
while his body endured the pain for him. He found himself moving through a series of mental "shelters," or "cellars," in an attempt to escape the pain:

> I would wait and gather strength until the pain caught up with me,
> forcing me to go deeper to elude it. This journey downward was like
> that of a soldier in a war retreating from the chaos of the front lines
> to avoid the torrents of bombshells raining down upon him threaten-
> ing his life, and seeking shelter within one foxhole and then another
> progressively getting farther from danger and closer to safety.

With this the quality of his consciousness began to change:

I felt a gentle current overcome me with its flow as it carried me away within its security, No longer did I resist its pull and I wondered to where I was drifting. No longer did I feel the urgency to breathe and realized that it was not necessary. No longer did I feel the panic to awaken or struggle to resist the flow. No longer did I experience the pain and uncontrollable nightmares and feelings that came with them. No longer did I sense movement of my physical body around me, and the uncontrollable gagging and choking noises I had previously identified as being my own had ceased.

In this expanded field of consciousness, Block began seeking an explanation for his condition:

I could not explain how I could be lost in a dream yet awake and talking to myself, I did not understand why I was unable to awaken from the grasp of this dream. When would I awaken? I found no justifiable answer to my questions and soon came to the worst of all possible explanations. Was I dead?

At this point he sought his last and final shelter:

Somehow I "knew" that here I would remain and had reached the end of my journey. This last refuge became a fortress different than those before it. The pain which I desperately sought to elude was never able to penetrate the walls of this refuge as it had been able to before. I left all contacts with my physical body far behind, and above me, and [they] never caught up with me. Here I left all physical needs and drives behind, leaving only my inner "self," the core of my "being," now separated from the external world far above and outside the new world of my "self."

Block's previous feelings of fear, confusion, and pain gave way to feelings of peace, tranquility, and safety:

There were no sounds to be heard, yet I could "hear" the many feelings that emanated within my refuge. I became "aware" of the absolute darkness yet was never blinded by it nor did it hinder my vision. There was nothing to see, yet I could "see" like never before. Everything became so "real" as my senses heightened to an acuteness like never before. Here I remained "alone" but was never lonely, as something, someone, somehow instilled me with safety and well-being. I grew content with the feelings of peace and tranquility that surrounded me. "Warmth" radiated within my refuge and here I had no answers to my questions. [In fact] I had no questions at all.

Block's description of his state of mind—perhaps state of being would be a more accurate description—echoes that of people who have experienced pure consciousness. One excellent description of the state of mind he experienced can be found in *The Book of Wen-Tse*:

He who penetrates the great universal harmony keeps himself withdrawn. . . . He moves in this immeasurable harmony as if he had never left the ground of the creation of beings. This is called the great penetration. . . . He moves toward the perfect void. . . . He takes his way where there is no door. He hears what has no sound. He sees what has no form. He does not cling to time.

The mind is turned completely inward; there is no duality, nothing to see or hear, yet one's awareness is expansive in nature. Likewise, the "warmth" Block speaks of in his refuge is echoed by the Maharishi Mahesh Yogi:

One experience . . . occurs very frequently. It is of being completely enveloped in an indescribable, soft, divine gentleness. It embraces me outside and is lively within me. I feel I am that indescribable thing, so enormously wonderful, beyond intellectual description, so complete, so lively with pure love. . . . I feel infinitely protected and cared for.

Both of these experiences are considered descriptions of pure consciousness.

But Block's story does not end here.

As I waited here and gathered strength, the storm began to pass and soon I had the feeling it was time to go. Something, someone, somewhere, who had instilled me with a sense of well-being, stood behind me reassuring me of my safety. As I left my dark corner towards the hatch door securing my refuge, I stopped to gather the courage to open the door. As I did so, I looked far ahead of me towards the front lines from which I had previously escaped. The first few steps were very awakening and shocking as I felt the sting of the pain which I had previously eluded.

Block opened his eyes five days after the accident, and the "reassurance and security that I had learned to feel within my refuge went with me. . . . Although I did not know what was awaiting me, I knew from this that I could face it."

In the weeks that followed, Block drifted in and out of consciousness. He was repeatedly told that he would be a quadriplegic and require a wheelchair for the rest of his life. Doctors remained convinced of their prognosis even after Block's surgery to fuse his neck. They were wrong. Two weeks after the surgery, a nurse noticed that one of Block's toes was moving. She thought it was a muscle spasm and ignored it. But when another nurse saw the toe move, she called in the attending physician, who was astonished to find that Block could move the toe on command. Five months after the accident, Block writes, "after prayers and hard work," he walked out of Iowa Methodist Medical Center with only a cane for support. Block attributes his miraculous recovery to the experience of pure consciousness:

Now conscious, I was filled with a great feeling of "aliveness," as I continually expressed to those around me the true joy of life that I felt. . . . Doctors, nurses and friends were skeptical to believe the genuineness of my feelings as they labeled [me] "confused," "denial" and "unrealistic" optimism for being alive. . . . As they waited for my spirit to subside and for me to "come to grips" with my problem, my spirit grew. They could not understand how I could feel "alive" and yet be without the use of my body. . . . [And so] I began the struggle to repair my damaged body. Deep within me, my refuge acted as the source which supplied my body with energy of life, providing it with the necessary warmth to draw upon. My refuge now acted as a well which supplied my body with the necessary nutrients for me, draining off to other areas of my body as *I directed its flow*. I slowly felt my body come "alive," little by little, part by part, each night as I focused upon a different area of my body. Equally anxious to go to therapy the next day, I was also anxious to return to the silence of my room to focus on my body.

Block's experience is one of the most dramatic and moving accounts of the "reality" and potential of pure consciousness. It clearly illustrates the transpersonal aspect of this state of consciousness, for which, as we have repeatedly pointed out, dream lucidity may be a precursor.

Let's look more closely at the relationship between lucidity and pure consciousness (witnessing) in sleep. Just as each human lives through a life cycle, beginning with birth and moving on through childhood to adulthood with accompanying changes in thought, so too do people experience various stages of self-reflective consciousness in sleep. Alan Moffitt and his associates at Carleton University in Canada have charted a nine-point scale measuring self-reflectiveness in sleep, which begins with the "unawareness" of ordinary dreaming and culminates in lucidity, with the dreamer reflecting on the fact that he or she is dreaming. But the evolution of self-reflective consciousness does not end with lucidity. One can move further along the continuum to a quieter, uninvolved state of awareness that is experienced as having no boundaries. According to MIU's Charles Alexander this stage, known as witnessing, most often emerges spontaneously. It can, however, be conceptualized as part of a continuum.

An associate professor of physics at a large southeastern university (he prefers to remain nameless) has been practicing TM since 1971, and in a conversation with Gackenbach he outlined five basic stages in the movement from lucidity to witnessing. In order to understand these stages one must think of the progression, at least in part, as the dreamer shifts from being an "actor" in the dream to being the "observer" of it. In brief, the stages go like this:

Stage 1. Initially in lucid dreaming, the actor is dominant. The only role the observer plays is to recognize, however briefly, that the self is dreaming. Despite this recognition, the feeling is still that the dream is "out there" and that the self is "in here." As the dreamer becomes more familiar with lucidity, it may occur to him/her that he/she can manipulate the dream. In this form of lucid dreaming one is, the professor believes, "trying to manipulate the dream in some way, so there is a greater degree of wakefulness inside, but still one is tied into the figures of the dream. It's a matter of accent. . . . It's more that you're an object in the dream and less that you are a witness to that dream."

Stage 2. At some point it may occur to the dreamer that what is "out there" is actually "inside." At this point two paths seem open to the dreamer: The dreamer may either become actively engaged in the dream events, while also recognizing that it is the self as well as the dream ego that is involved, or shift his/her attention to the "inside" I, allowing the "outside" I—the dream scene—to fade. It is easy during these preliminary stages to flip back and forth between observing the dream with a quiet detachment and being actively lucid. When lucid, one is still aware of the dream while being caught up in its activity. Frequent lucid dreamer George Gillespie explains, "There is little in lucidity itself that will disrupt the production of dream images and sense effects. But because I know I am dreaming, I can proceed to do these actions or nonactions that disrupt the dreaming process. My interaction with the dream keeps it going normally. If I become passive, by stopping to watch what happens, or just to try to think of something, the activity in the dream environment diminishes or stops altogether."

Stage 3. Lucid dreams in this stage tend to be short. The professor describes a dream as a thought that arises that you take note of and then let go of. "The action of the dream," he says, "is not dominant. It does not grip you so that you are identified with it as opposed to the first step in which the focus was more on the active [participation]. In this case it's just a state of inner awareness that's really dominant. Awareness is there very strongly. The dream is a little dust flying about so to speak." This is, he says, analogous to when "I'm just sitting while awake and doing nothing and thoughts pop up, like an involuntary knee jerk. I'm not caught up in that, so [consequently] the dreams do not have much significance. . . . I never tried to hold onto them. The state of awareness is more satisfying. Since you don't get caught up [in the dreams] there isn't much intensity to them." Gillespie explains that the meditator in sleep "knows that he is not to interact with or be tempted by anything that may happen phenomenally. He is not to desire or anticipate anything."

Stage 4. In this stage an "inner wakefulness" dominates. "You don't have dreams, or in any case you don't remember having dreams," says the professor. You are absorbed not in dreams but in the witness. This sort of sleep awareness can be so continuous that one may go for months without recalling a dream and even lose awareness of the passage of time. "When all waking and dream imagery and all mental content are eliminated," Gillespie explains, "there is dreamless sleep. Each night I, the dreamer, move into dreamless sleep. Here I desire no desire and see no dream. There is only an ocean of objectless consciousness. The inner Self still sees, because the Self is imperishable, but there is nothing distinct from it to see. Likewise there is no second thing from the Self for the Self to smell, taste, speak, hear, think, touch, or discern. The Self is conscious of nothing within or without. This is the home base from which the Self moves out into the dream and waking image and thought, the home to which the Self, like a tired bird, returns from waking and dream experience to rest."

At this point, it becomes extremely difficult to distinguish or describe further stages, but the physicist continues to make a distinction.

Stage 5. Once the dreamer has moved into this transcendental state, or pure consciousness, the "dream" will characteristically take symbolic forms not generally found in nonlucid or lucid dreams of an earlier stage. They will be much more abstract and have no sensory aspects to them, no mental images, no emotional feelings, no sense of body or space. There is a quality of unboundedness to them. "One experiences oneself to be a part of a tremendous composite of relationships," the professor explains. These are not social or conceptual or intellectual relationships, only "a web of relationships. I am aware of the relationship between entities without the entities being there." He says there is "a sense of motion yet there are no relative things to gauge motion by; it's just expansiveness. There are no objects to measure it. The expansiveness is one of light—like the light of awareness."

We should add a note here: The vocabulary for expressing this kind of experience is limited compared with the vocabulary found in, say, psychology or sociology. The scientists and nonscientists who are exploring higher states of consciousness are still evolving a descriptive language. Consequently, their explanations of such states often use words that come close to accurate description but inevitably fall short of it. When, for example, the professor used the phrase "light of awareness" it was, he says, because of all the things he "could refer to in the sensory or mental worlds, that word would be it." But, he explains, it is not like light in a room; it's "visual but not visual, more like light in an ocean; an intimate experience of the light." Perhaps one day there will be a word for that sort of light.

Frequent lucid dreamer George Gillespie has referred to this vision as the "fullness of light." And Mircea Eliáde details in *The Two and the One* the role of "the light" in many of today's spiritual traditions. "Considered as a whole," he writes, "the different experiences and appraisals of the interior Light advanced in Indian and in Indo-Tibetan Buddhism can be integrated into a perfectly consistent system. Experience of the Light signifies primarily a meeting with ultimate reality."

The professor further describes the experience as an "expansive ocean of awareness and a sense of motion. . . . It's like attention moving within this expansiveness. There is nothing relative; it's simply the ocean moving in the ocean; it's simply awareness moving in awareness. . . . There is a sense of movement which is ecstatic. It's like flying. . . . I've had a lot of dream experiences of flying. . . . You take off by the bootstraps and it's exhilarating and all that, but it's like a normal dream in the sense that you see yourself flying. . . . In this case it's pure flight without the body there. . . . The exhilarating feeling of flying is there . . . more like flight within this ocean of awareness. That is extremely ecstatic. . . . The 'dream' is within awareness not within a grosser mental image."

Control in the dream state of pure consciousness is a moot point. "The body does not exist," the professor explains. "There is no awareness of the body, no awareness of anything sensory."

But is the professor's continuum true for other people?

Another perspective on the relationship of dream lucidity to dream witnessing comes from Anja Savolainen of Helsinki, Finland. After several negative experiences with dream lucidity she actively pursued nonlucid dreams, which finally evolved into witnessing dreams. "I now believe that the state of consciousness of lucid dreamers is totally different from [that of] nonlucid ones, not higher, not lower, just different," she explains. "I totally disagree with those who insist that lucidity is the next step after nonlucidity and a necessary step before so-called witnessing. It can be for some or even for most, but there are other types of dreamers for whom the developmental sequence is just the opposite: from lucidity to nonlucidity and from there to witnessing or to whatever their next stages are. Lucidity and nonlucidity cannot be put on a single continuum in any simple way."

In order to explore this question, Gackenbach, along with Robert Cranson and Charles Alexander of MIU, collected sleep experiences from five groups of TM meditators and four groups of controls. They were looking for distinctive characteristics of lucid dreams versus both witnessing dreams and witnessing during nondreaming sleep. The researchers described each state in the following way:

• A lucid dream is a dream in which you are actively thinking about the fact that you are dreaming.

• A witnessing dream is a dream in which you experience a quiet, peaceful, inner awareness or wakefulness completely separate from the dream.

• Witnessing in deep sleep is a dreamless sleep in which you experience a quiet, peaceful, inner state of awareness or wakefulness.

Here are examples from the TM meditators of the three states of awareness:

Lucid dreaming: "During a dream I will become aware of the dream as separate, then aware that I am dreaming. Then I begin to manipulate the story and the characters to create whatever situation I desire. At times, in unpleasant situations, I'll think as the dreamer, 'I don't have to put up with this,' and I change the dream or at least 'back out' of the involvement."

Witnessing dreaming: "Sometimes, whatever the content of the dream is, I feel an inner tranquillity of awareness that is removed from the dream. Sometimes I may even be caught up in the dream, but the inner awareness of peace remains."

Witnessing deep sleep: "It is a feeling of infinite expansion and bliss and nothing else. Then I become aware that I exist but there is no individual personality. Gradually I become aware that I am an individual, but there are no details of who, where, what, when, etc. Eventually, these details fill in and I might awaken."

The researchers found that the meditators reported experiencing all three phenomena more frequently than did the nonmeditating controls. But both meditators and nonmeditators reported more lucid dreams than witnessing dreams or witnessing in deep sleep, a finding that supports the theory that lucid dreams are easier to access no matter what one's training or personal skills and may therefore be a precursor to the other experiences.

In order to examine the differences among these three forms of sleeping consciousness, Gackenbach, Cranson, and Alexander turned to a group of highly advanced meditators who, the researchers believed, were best equipped (because of their training) to discern the subtle differences between states of mind in sleep. Indeed, the results of the study showed that the sixty-six males, who can best be described as TM monks because they have devoted their lives to the practice of meditation, were able to remember and describe far more experiences of sleep consciousness than the nonmeditating college students in Gackenbach's previous studies.

From the meditators' descriptions of their dreams, which included 55 lucid dreams, 41 witnessing ones, and 47 cases of witnessing in deep sleep, Gackenbach, Cranson, and Alexander found a number of important differences among these states of sleeping consciousness. For one thing, feelings of separateness were much more common in witnessing dreams than in lucid ones: The subjects felt more separate or outside of the dream when they were witnessing. As one meditator put it, "There is me *and* the dream, two different realities." Another difference involved positive emotions. Although lucid dreams were reported as being positive, witnessing in dreams and in dreamless sleep were felt to be even more so. The feeling in the latter two states is reminiscent of the idea of "bliss" in the Eastern religions, and, in fact, the term "bliss" was most often used to describe the witnessing state but virtually never used to describe lucidity. On the other hand, dream control was much more frequent during lucid dreaming than during witnessing dreams. In lucidity, the "will," or volitional capacity of the individual ego, can act on thoughts and desires, while in pure consciousness one is content and feels no desire to enter into the dream.

The same is true of witnessing while awake. A homemaker and mother who practices TM found that one of her first experiences of witnessing while awake occurred as she was yelling at her two children who were being singularly uncooperative about going to bed. She was amazed to realize that although she was yelling, she felt a calm, quiet awareness within her. Although that awareness "pondered" why she was yelling, it had no control over the action but rather remained a quiet onlooker.

More than half the lucid dreams in the Gackenbach, Cranson, and Alexander study were reported to have been triggered by a mental event such as a bizarre element. Witnessing dreams or sleep were virtually never triggered by a thought; the awareness was simply present. The TM monks also reported that witnessing in dreams seems to be associated with lucid dreaming. It is, says one of the meditators, "a clearer experience of [lucid dreaming]. The sense of self is more full and transcends the dream completely. It is large Self." Almost 20 percent of the meditators mentioned the relationship between lucidity and witnessing without being asked about it, a fact that supports the idea that there is indeed a developmental continuum in night consciousness, with lucidity emerging first, followed by witnessing in dreams, and finally witnessing in dreamless sleep. This continuum fits in nicely with the Vedic belief that pure consciousness provides the foundation for the development of stable higher states of consciousness or enlightenment. "According to the Maharishi," Alexander explains, "the first stable higher stage of consciousness, termed 'cosmic consciousness,' is defined as the maintenance of pure consciousness throughout the twenty-four-hour cycle of waking, dreaming, and deep sleep."

But experiencing pure consciousness, or the void, as it is sometimes called, is not the only transpersonal aspect of lucidity. For many, especially those on a spiritual path, lucidity is a doorway to ecstasy.

THE PATH OF ECSTASY

In *Lucid Dreaming: Dawning of the Clear Light*, Scott Sparrow suggests that lucid dreaming may be viewed as a "visual representation of the meditative process." The practice of meditation, he writes,

> has as its ultimate goal the reunion of the conscious self with those aspects which lie unrecognized in the recesses of the unconscious, and which offer completion to the individual. Yet, before this can happen, the meditator must confront his preconceptions and fears which act as a barrier between himself and the elements of completion. Often these obstacles are very subtle, manifesting only as confusion or an incomprehensible emotional state which arises in the meditation process. The lack of concreteness in these awakening patterns makes a successful reconciliation a vague and difficult endeavor. The dream provides us, however, with a vivid pictorial representation of the encounter which we face. In addition, the dream allows the individual to view the results of his responses toward the obstacle.

Sparrow suggests that the self-reflecting consciousness available in lucid dreaming interacts with the unconscious needs of the individual, thus speeding up the process of integration. Not only does this have beneficial effects in waking life, but it also serves to accelerate the meditative process, often culminating in a "break-through experience of light and fulfillment." Sparrow illustrates his thinking with one of his own lucid dreams:

> As I am facing my desired direction, light comes from behind me. I see his shadow creep past me as if the light were behind him. As I turn in fear, I say, 'Lord, have mercy!' Instead of the devil, a beautiful woman clothed in white is here. Light surrounds her. She walks up to me, reaches down and touches my forehead. The dream is over. I am aware that light is building within me. A bright warmth fills my vision. Then I awaken.

Psychotherapist Kenneth Kelzer also talks about the devotional intensity of lucid dreams. In a lucid dream that he entitled the "Gift of the Magi," Kelzer describes his role as one of the three wise men in search of the baby Jesus. As he and the other wise men are traveling, "I enter a state of deep meditation and see so clearly that my ability to see the star at all is based on my inner attunement. Without this fine, delicate, inner tuning of conscious-ness I would not even see the star nor care that Christ had been born, much less find him."

In the dream, when Kelzer reaches the Christ child he feels a tremendous rush of emotion so strong that he begins to sob; all his emotions about the journey and the meaning of finding the child pour through him. When he sees the Christ child, he kneels before him "entranced by the dazzling, beautiful light that ema-nates continuously from his whole body and especially from his loving eyes that simply look back at me, so calm and steady," Kelzer relates. "I feel as if I could kneel here forever."

If a dream can be said to change someone's life, this one changed Kelzer's. It has been years since he had the dream, but to this day whenever he thinks of it he feels inspired and uplifted.

Like Kelzer, Daryl Hewitt, who holds the record for the longest lucid dream ever recorded in a sleep lab (one hour), also pursues spiritual experiences in his lucid dreams. He became interested in doing so out of boredom; he was simply running out of things to do in his lucid dreams and longed for some greater depth and meaning in them. He decided to begin working with meditation while lucid dreaming. Here is an example of one such effort:

> I . . . try to meditate, sitting on the grass, but he keeps interrupting me. I remember Stephen's [LaBerge's] admonition to me to not always ignore dream characters, and minutes later he seems to dissipate into me. I go on flying and exploring on the ground for awhile, concentrating much of the time on keeping my mind free of thoughts, to simply perceive the dreamworld around me as deeply as possible. I ask for some help, saying, "Highest Father-Mother, help me to get the most from this," and just relax, floating in the sky. Shortly thereafter I experience potent flashes of awareness of extreme clarity— what seem to be glimpses of higher reality, in some way deeply personal and familiar. One of these flashes is accompanied by an image from afar of an Eastern spiritual master I admire. I feel convinced that these glimpses are indeed flashes of a higher reality, and can honestly say it is one of the most intensely spiritual experiences of my life.

Hewitt's experience, like those of Sparrow and Kelzer, highlights the euphoria that often accompanies more spiritual lucid dreams. Kelzer, in fact, has even described the "jolt of energy" that sometimes shoots through his body upon becoming lucid, a jolt that he likens to the release of *kundalini* energy as described by Hindu Yogis. According to Hindu belief, *kundalini* energy is the spiritual energy that is within all of us and can be released through serious meditative practice.

Are the ecstatic lucid-dreaming experiences of Hewitt, Sparrow, and Kelzer related to the experiences of pure consciousness or the void described earlier? Or are ecstatic and void experiences significantly different types of spiritual awakenings? One lucid dreamer who has explored both phenomena is George Gillespie. As an American Baptist missionary in India in 1975, Gillespie had his first lucid dream. Despite his religious training, however, it did not occur to him to consider these sleep experiences in a religious manner. In fact, it was not until 1981 that Gillespie had his first ecstatic lucid dream.

> I dreamed that I was in front of my childhood home. I wanted to show some people a high jump. When I jumped high in front of the house, I realized I was dreaming. I was far above the people. I descended. It became a fall. I remembered that I can fall in a dream without fear. I fell, not expecting to land on the ground. I just stopped below. Then I was flying again. I remembered to close my eyes and eliminate the visual environment. I did not remember to do any more. I remained floating with body awareness. I saw a bright light to my left. I remembered that a bright light does not need to mean that I am waking up. I was then surrounded by light. I seemed to float in the light and began to contemplate prayerfully what I was doing and might see. I called, "Father," spontaneously, meaning God. I remained some time in this attitude and then woke up.

Gillespie, who is currently a doctoral candidate in Sanskrit at the University of Pennsylvania, had also studied the sacred Hindu teachings called the Upanishads and was eager to explore the state of "dreamless sleep" that they described. "Dreamless sleep, according to the Upanishads," he explains, "is the state in which the delusion of both waking and dreaming is eliminated. In dreamless sleep the experiencer desires no desire and sees no dream. He knows nothing within or without, for there is no second thing for him to experience. Dreamless sleep is the state of nonduality, the experience of Brahma, ultimate reality."

Gillespie began trying to attain this state by systematically removing the content of his dreams while lucid. Of his first attempt he writes:

> I closed my [dream] eyes. It became dark. I remained very much aware of sitting on a chair with my feet on the floor and leaning on the table. I wanted to remove these perceptions also. I pushed the table away, then raised my feet off the floor. I was hesitant to push the chair from under me. I willed the chair away. I remained with my legs raised and became unaware of the chair. I was first floating, then spinning, very much aware of my body. Charlotte came along and thought we should leave. So I got out of the chair.

Eventually, after many attempts, Gillespie was able to eliminate his awareness of all objects including his dream body. "I reached the point where nothing was left except my own consciousness in darkness, though I have no memory of maintaining that state," he explains. "I was satisfied that I had reached the point of dream-less sleep. He practiced remaining passive and developing this state of being and reports, "If I concentrate on the darkness, I tend to lose my contact with the ground and I float up. This may lead to flying, tossing about, or the sensation of projection. In this context I also have seen patterns of light, including versions of lattices, and have felt buzzing, vibrations, extreme joy, religious feelings, and other unworldly effects." Gillespie explains that one of the signals that the dreamer is becoming free of dream entan-glements and thus is moving toward transcendence or liberation is the ability to fly. "Flying, like the related sensations of floating, levitation, and projection, though giving partial freedom from the dream environment, is often as much a hindrance as it is a help in attempts to completely eliminate dreaming, for it focuses atten-tion on body awareness, which is then extremely difficult to elim-inate."

Despite these experiences, Gillespie is wary of instilling lucid dreaming with any sort of mystical meaning. "All the extraordi-nary phenomena that have accompanied my lucid dreaming," he says, "even the religious feelings and awareness of God, no matter how self-validating they appear to be, can be explained in terms of dreaming. I feel that any belief that there is ontological or theological meaning in even 'an experience of God' is a matter of faith, not of self-evidence."

Gillespie did eventually reconcile lucid dreaming with his faith, accepting his experiences to be what they appeared to be—experiences of God. "I recognize that this faith is based on the insight of my intuitive self and not my rational self, for I will always be able to explain it away," he says. "Because of my devotional experiences in the light, because of my belief that phe-nomena described in mystical literature are explainable in terms of dreaming, particularly lucid dreaming, and because I see a relationship between meditation and lucid dreaming, my interest in lucid dreams has become largely religious. I had not intended that it become so. But now I use my lucid dreams for times of worship—prayer, praise, and singing."

What is the connection between ecstatic lucid dreams and witnessing ones? Some clues come from the work of Roland Fisher, a retired psychiatrist. In his article in the American Association for the Advancement of Science's publication *Science,* Fisher suggests that transpersonal states run along a continuum with ecstatic, or rapturous, mystical experiences being the most highly aroused of states and void experiences the least aroused of states. An ecstatic experience, he argues, results when a section of the midbrain called the reticular formation is electrically stimulated to capacity and then rebounds or shuts down, resulting in an experience of the void. In other words, you can only have so much stimulation, so much ecstasy, before your mind goes to "sleep," so to speak, and you experience the void. This unusual experiential flip can be illustrated by a sleep experience of Hewitt's:

> In 1985 I began experimenting with meditation in lucid dreams in an effort to discover this depth. These experiments brought profound results. On a half dozen occasions I succeeded in remembering my intention to sit down in the dynamic atmosphere of the lucid dream, and managed to be undistracted by dream imagery long enough to practice deep, rhythmic breathing. In each case awareness seemed to expand into an egg-shaped sphere which encompassed my dream body, with a corresponding dramatic intensification of consciousness. As this happened, colors flowed like pools of neon light in my inner vision, as they sometimes do in meditation and before falling asleep. The state intensified until the dream imagery, through half-shut eyes, took on a diaphanous character and finally disappeared. I became a point of consciousness contentedly floating in an intense yellow-orange field of light.

Psychologist Harry Hunt agrees with Fisher that ecstatic experiences may culminate in the void. He likens the flipping of perception to a child learning to talk. Initially, he says, the child is caught up in the sounds of words and how to make them, but eventually such concerns habituate and the child's focus is on the meaning of the words. Likewise, when a child initially learns to ride a bike he or she is caught up with the feel of the cycle and sensations associated with balancing. Eventually, the child "gets it" and enjoys the thrill of a fast ride down a steep hill. In Eastern religious practice, the goal, if one can call it that, is to reach the void, to experience the oneness, the all, the unity, the nothing. That is why yogis and other teachers have generally told their students not to pay too much attention to ecstatic experiences or the special powers, such as precognition or visions, that may accompany the journey. Those experiences are merely steps along the path.

Hunt and Fisher theorize that the rebound effect may work both ways, that is, once you reach the void, you may reexperience ecstasy. But this experience of ecstasy will be different from other ecstatic experiences: It will be more profound and more deeply felt than the initial ecstasy that precedes knowledge of the void. Once we experience the void, the experience "opens up" again, but it is of such a profoundly different quality that equating it to an experience with sensory, emotional, or intellectual content would be inappropriate.

SEEKING THE HIGHEST

Although scientists know relatively little about how lucid dreaming contributes to the development of pure consciousness or if its role is essential for the appearance of higher states of consciousness, there is some interesting research that has begun to probe this most mystic of territories. At the California Institute of Integral Studies, for instance, Fariba Bogzaran conducted a study in which she asked volunteers, all of whom had had lucid dreams, to seek the "highest" while lucid. Each of the seventy-six subjects was asked to describe "desiring to seek the highest" in his or her own words before going to sleep. Questions tended to be phrased in two ways: active—"I want to find God"; and passive—"Allow me to experience the divine." Bogzaran found that those who phrased their requests in the active voice tended to actively seek the divine in their dreams; for those who posed a passive request, "things just happened." Furthermore, in Bogzaran's judgment, in the experiences of those who had a passive framing, the dream "seemed to be more profound." Their experiences were more powerful and enriching. One dreamer said, "I felt a renewed feeling of awe . . . respect for the splendor of the universe."

Bogzaran also evaluated the effect that the active or passive approach had on the images in the dreams. She found that though most of the subjects had impersonal (mathematical symbols and the like) rather than personal (religious figures) experiences of the divine, the effect was especially pronounced for those who phrased the task in a passive fashion. Bogzaran also discovered that seeking the divine in lucid dreams doesn't always result in positive dreams. This is illustrated in a lucid dream of Gackenbach's in which she tried to "seek my God" while working on her dissertation. After realizing that she was dreaming and recalling what she wanted to do, she had the following dream:

> I was sitting cross-legged in front of a square mirror in a void and looking at myself, and I thought, "Yep, that's me. I look okay." Then I started to let my image take different shapes, like wavy mirrors in a circus. Then I saw a yellow glint in my right eye and I got afraid and I was afraid I'd turn into something evil, so I decided to stop letting it happen. So then I was sitting on a stool in the cabin in the living room —fully aware that I was dreaming. The suggestion was gone but I sensed I was supposed to ask something but couldn't figure out what, so I thought I'll float/fly to the ceiling. But I had a bit of a problem flying. . . . I got to the ceiling and went through to a gray void again and panicked again.

Gackenbach's experience also illustrates Sparrow's contention that such a dream may sometimes occur as a kind of backlash to "storming the gates of heaven," of seeking too much too quickly. It is an experience he himself has had. His journal entry dated September 9, 1974, reads: "Something aches within me for change, for transformation. If I only knew what to give up, what to do. I feel that I too easily grow satisfied with my world and myself. The world of Light recedes in the light of my indifference. I want to meet my obstacles; and I pray for the strength to meet them. . . ."

The same night that Sparrow made this entry in his diary, he had the following lucid dream:

> I am standing in the hallway outside my room. It is night and hence dark where I stand. Dad comes in the front door. I tell him that I am there so as not to frighten him or provoke an attack. I am afraid for no apparent reason.
>
> I look outside through the door and see a dark figure which appears to be a large animal. I point at it in fear. The animal, which is a huge black panther, comes through the doorway. I reach out to it with both hands, extremely afraid. Placing my hands on its head, I say, "You're only a dream." But I am half pleading in my statement and cannot dispel my fear.
>
> I pray for Jesus' presence and protection. But the fear is still with me as I awaken.

Sparrow also recounts a dream in which Jesus suddenly materializes. Sparrow is so excited, he runs to embrace him. At this point, Jesus abruptly disappears. Sparrow explains that it was his desire "to incorporate or grasp the in-flowing Spirit into a limited understanding" that ended the dream. In desiring to embrace Christ, Sparrow was in effect offering himself as a "sacrifice to a greater vision, a deeper love." In order to be able to do so successfully, however, one's desire must be "a well-established 'ideal' within the dreamer's mind prior to the mystical dream. Without an idea to serve as a pattern, the experience lacks direction and can perhaps be confusing or harmful." Note that in the second part of Gackenbach's "seeking my God" dream, she forgot what she was supposed to be seeking.

Preparation and direction—the practice of meditation restructures the mind, guiding it toward new forms of conscious awareness including lucid dreams. Both meditation and lucid dreaming can lead to the experience of pure consciousnesss. But aside from the personal pleasure and the psychological and physical benefits that accompany this state of mind, what, one may ask, is there to be gained from it?

THE CASE FOR PEACE

In our culture, people believe good works form the basis for a better world. We band together in all sorts of ways to help each other and those in need elsewhere. Charities give food to the poor both at home and abroad. Volunteer organizations direct the distribution of clothing and supplies to the needy. Churches host bazaars to raise money for their outreach programs. The government provides subsidies and job training programs for the underprivileged. We work in food kitchens, man drug hot lines, and donate money to the United Way. We believe, as William Blake put it, that "he who would do another good must do so in minute particulars."

To some extent this view of how to make the world better comes from the Judeo-Christian ethics of the Europeans who settled this country (after the Native Americans, of course), and there is no doubt that society is made better by most, if not all, of our efforts. But is this all we can do? The ancient religious teachings of the East—and indeed the more mystical teachings of our Western religions—suggest that the answer to this question is no.

In a recent book called *The Maharishi Effect*, sociologists Elaine and Arthur Aron discuss the work of TM meditators to change the world, not only through "good works," but through the power of their minds. "If a large enough group of people . . . were all drawing on the calm, coherence, and wisdom deep within the silent human mind," they write, "then those qualities would prevail in the environment and the right changes, whatever they were, would come about." Although meditators may appear to be doing nothing but sitting quietly, they are, contend the Arons, positively affecting the human climate in which we all exist. They do so through pure consciousness, which, TMers claim, alters the "field" of human consciousness.

The idea here is that consciousness can be likened to a field—the gravitational field, say, or the electromagnetic field. The earth and moon's gravitational fields interact all the time, a sort of invisible dance in which one partner's movement influences the other's. The tidal cycle of the oceans is but one example of this dance. It is possible that consciousness also functions in a wave pattern, or to use the Arons' analogy, perhaps an individual's consciousness is like a cork floating in a pail of water with myriad other corks. Touch one and make it bob and the motion it creates in the water moves all the other corks.

That consciousness may function in this way is a concept familiar to both physicists and mystics.

In their book *Margins of Reality: The Role of Consciousness in the Physical World*, Robert F. Jahn, dean emeritus of the School of Engineering and Applied Science at Princeton University, and Brenda J. Dunne, manager of the Princeton Engineering Anomalies Research Laboratory, set forth a detailed model of how the human mind can affect the world around it. Their studies have tested subjects (quite ordinary people, on the whole, who claimed no particular psychic powers) to see if they can influence the otherwise random pattern of balls released from a machine and to "send" messages to another test subject often living hundreds, if not thousands, of miles away. Jahn and Dunne discovered that their subjects were capable of successfully "willing" the balls into a pattern or sending and receiving messages over thousands of miles, *and* they found that the ability was quite commonplace.

To explain these remarkable findings, Jahn and Dunne suggest that perhaps a wave function is at work. A "resonance" somehow develops between the two participants that enables knowledge to be passed from one to the other without benefit of the postal system, the telephone, or any other mechanical channel. Perhaps consciousness shares some properties of atomic particles. Perhaps thoughts are capable of "tunneling"—a quantum mechanical magic act in which electrons jump across a space without actually traveling through it. Like electrons, our minds may not always be contained locally in either space or time, but capable of being omnipresent.

"Our atomic model predicts that an individual consciousness immersed in a given environmental situation establishes a set of characteristic experiences . . . ," the authors explain. "A second individual, exposed to the same situation, develops a different set of experiences. . . . However, if these two consciousnesses are strongly interacting, their experiential wave functions become intertwined in some resonant process, and their common environmental container is also modified by their mutual influence upon it."

In related research, TM researchers have been investigating the potential of accessing pure consciousness to influence other people's consciousness, to, in other words, affect the field. Since 1974 they have been conducting studies that provide evidence that pure consciousness is not a passive state that has no measurable effects except on the meditator but is, in fact, an active one with ripples that touch the shores of all minds.

We turn to two of those scientists—David Orme-Johnson and Michael Dillbeck—for a brief explanation of how the process works:

> Maharishi predicted a number of years ago that when as few as 1% of the population of a society practiced the TM program, a measurable improvement, such as a decrease in crime rate, would occur in the quality of life of that society. This effect has been observed in a number of different studies conducted in populations of various sizes. For example, in one study . . . the crime rate trend in 48 different cities was analyzed over a 12-year period. The 24 experimental cities, defined by having 1% of the population practicing the TM program, showed a significant decrease in crime rate trend as compared to 24 control cities randomly selected from matched cities with similar economic, educational, and other demographic characteristics. This decrease in crime rate trend in the "one percent" cities has been shown to be independent of such factors as police coverage, unemployment, prior crime trend, difference in age composition, and ethnic background.

TM researchers applied similar controls to another study, this one designed to see if pure consciousness could affect an area of extreme social stress. Orme-Johnson and Charles Alexander traveled to Israel in early August 1983. By August 19, 200 advanced meditators from Israel and surrounding areas had been enlisted. This was, the researchers calculated, the number of meditators that would be required to successfully influence the country's field of consciousness. For several weeks they conducted regular meditation sessions and kept track of a complex variety of social variables to chart what effect they might be having. The researchers also noted when the number of meditators dropped below the 200 mark. After factoring in the controls that would highlight any areas of uncertainty, Orme-Johnson and Alexander, working with a group of Israeli scientists, began analyzing their data. They found that during the times when 200 people were at "work," social cohesion was higher and discord (the number of deaths related to the war, for instance) lower than when there were fewer than 200 meditators.

This and other studies indicate that the Maharishi effect may indeed be worthy of more investigation. But even the best of TM studies often meet with great resistance from other researchers. The Israel study, for instance, recently appeared in the prestigious *Journal of Conflict Resolution*. The editor of the journal explained in a preface to the study that though he personally could not "believe" the extraordinary findings, he could not suppress the study because the quality of the work was impeccable.

What does all this have to do with lucid dreaming? You'll recall from chapter 8 that brain coherence peaks during meditation, especially during times of transcendence to pure consciousness and theoretically during lucid dreaming. Some evidence suggests that it is highest of all during witnessing dreaming. A 1979 study conducted by Orme-Johnson shows how this peak in coherence reflects the effects of meditation on the field of consciousness. He wanted to see if three meditators in Iowa could feel the effects of twenty-five hundred advanced meditators sitting some 1,170 miles away in Amherst, Massachusetts. He and his associates placed each of the three Iowa meditators in soundproof rooms. The meditators were unaware of the purpose of the experiment and did not know anything about the specifics of the twenty-five hundred meditators' schedule in Amherst. While the Amherst group meditated, the three subjects were asked to meditate also. They were also asked to meditate three times when the Amherst group was not meditating, and then another three times after the Amherst meeting was over. The results, which were published in the *International Journal of Neuroscience*, showed that although EEG coherence did not increase in the three Iowa meditators, "their brains all reflected a pattern of functioning that was very similar to each other's." It was as if one cork bobbed (2500 meditators in Amherst) and the others (three Iowan meditators) moved with it. No bobbing of the cork was evidenced when the three Iowans meditated at times when the Amherst group was not meditating.

A similar effect was reported some years later in the same journal. A team of Mexican scientists asked pairs of individuals who had never met before to "feel each others' presence" while in a room together. Before they engaged in this task and also while doing it, the scientists measured EEG coherence levels in both their brains. The resulting polygraphs revealed that although the two individuals exhibited different patterns of coherence initially, during the experiment both showed almost identical patterning. Furthermore, each person's graph showed two lines with peaks and valleys that looked almost identical. Although there was no talking or touching during these sessions, some subjects reported feeling physical sensations, and others said they had active images and thoughts about their partners. Furthermore, the subject whose brain was highest in coherence most influenced the session.

Obviously, many more studies need to explore this facet of the human mind. But if the findings described above can be repeated and expanded, if we find that empathizing with one another and experiencing pure consciousness can be shown to effect a change in the field of consciousness, then we will indeed be on the threshold of a new understanding of the human mind. One day we may be able to say more about the importance of lucid dreaming and pure consciousness than that they are altered states of awareness that broaden our vision, make us feel better, and give us added insight into ourselves and reality. We may be able to say that by meditating and working with our lucid dreams we can change the quality not only of our own lives but also the lives of those with whom we share the world. It will be a day worth waiting for.

Resources

The **Association for the Study of Dreams** is an international, multidisciplinary organization dedicated to the pure and applied investigation of dreams and dreaming. Its goal is to promote an awareness and appreciation of dreams in both professional and public arenas; to encourage research into the nature, function, and significance of dreaming; to advance the application of the study of dreams; and to provide a forum for the eclectic and interdisciplinary exchange of ideas and information. ASD publishes a newsletter and holds an annual conference. Information about ASD can be obtained by writing the association at Box 1600, Vienna, Virginia 22180.

The **Lucidity Association** publishes the semiannual journal *Lucidity Letter* from which some of the information for this book was drawn. The association is devoted to education about and research into the lucid dream and related states of consciousness, and holds an annual symposium, the proceedings of which are published in its journal. An important component of *Lucidity Letter* is the publication of case material. These first-hand experiences of consciousness in sleep are both interesting to the general reader as well as invaluable for the scientist and theoretician interested in the phenomenon. Thus readers who have had an interesting experience with consciousness in sleep are encouraged to submit an article for possible publication in *Lucidity Letter*. Information about the Lucidity Association's activities and publications can be obtained by writing to *Lucidity Letter*, 8703 109th Street, Edmonton, Alberta, Canada T6G2L5. Dr. Gackenbach can be contacted through the Lucidity Association.

Bibliography

GENERAL READING BOOKS AND ARTICLES—DREAMS

Cartwright, R. D. (1978). *A primer on sleep and dreaming*. Reading, MA.: Addison-Wesley Publishing Company.

Cohen, D. B. (1979). *Sleep and dreaming: Origins, nature, and functions*. Oxford: Pergamon Press.

de Saint-Denys, H. (1982). *Dreams and how to guide them*. (N. Fry, Trans.). London: Duckworth. (Original work published 1867.)

Delaney, G. M. V. (1979/1989). *Living your dreams*. San Francisco, CA: Harper & Row.

Dement, W. C. (1972). *Some must watch while some must sleep*. New York: W. W. Norton.

Faraday, A. (1974). *The dream game*. New York: Harper & Row.

Freud, S. (1953). *The interpretation of dreams: The complete psychological works of Sigmund Freud*. London: Hogarth Press.

Garfield, P. (1974). *Creative dreaming*. New York: Ballantine Books.

Garfield, P. (1979). *Pathway to ecstasy*. New York: Holt, Rinehart & Winston.

Garfield, P. (1984). *Your child's dream*. New York: Ballantine Books.

206

Garfield, P. (1988). *Women's bodies, women's dreams*. New York: Ballantine Books.

Gendlin, E. T. (1986). *Let your body interpret your dreams*. Wilmette, IL: Chiron Publications.

Globus, G. (1987). *Dream life, wake life*. New York: SUNY Press.

Green, C. (1968a). *Lucid dreams*. London: Hamish.

Hartmann, E. (1984). *The Nightmare: The Psychology and Biology of Terrifying Dreams*. New York: Basic Books.

Hobson, J. A. (1988). *The dreaming brain*. New York: Basic Books.

Holroyd, S. (1976). *Dream worlds*. London: Danbury Press.

Jones, R. M. (1970). *The new psychology of dreaming*. New York: Penguin Books.

Jung, C. (1979). *Dreams*. Princeton: Princeton University Press.

Kelzer, K. (1987). *The sun and the shadow: My experiment with lucid dreaming*. Virginia Beach, VA: A.R.E. Press.

Koch-Sheras, P. R., Hollier, E. A., & Jones, B. (1983). *Dream on: A dream interpretation and exploration guide for women*. Englewood Cliffs, NJ: Prentice-Hall.

Kohr, E. R., & Johnson, K. (1983). *Visualization: The uses of imagery in the health professions*. Homewood, IL: Dow Jones–Irwin.

LaBerge, S. (1985). *Lucid dreaming*. New York: Ballantine.

LaBerge, S., & Gackenbach, J. (1987). Lucid dream experiment. *Omni*, April.

Long, M. E. (1987). What is this thing called sleep? *National Geographic*, 172, 787–821.

Rossi, E. (1972). *Dreams and the growth of personality: Expanding awareness in psychotherapy*. New York: Braunner/Mazel.

Sparrow, G. S. (1976a). *Lucid dreaming: Dawning of the clear light*. Virginia Beach, VA: A.R.E. Press.

Tart, C. T. (1969). *Altered states of consciousness*. New York: John Wiley & Sons.

Tedlock, B. (1987). *Dreaming: Anthropological and psychological perspectives*. New York: Cambridge University Press.

Trowbridge, B. (1988). Dreams as initiations: An interview with Scott Sparrow. *Dream Network Bulletin, 7*, 6–7.

Ullman, M., Krippner, S., & Vaughn, A. (1973). *Dream telepathy*. London: Turnstone.

Ullman, M., & Zimmerman, N. (1979). *Working with dreams*. Los Angeles: Jeremy P. Tarcher.

von Franz, M. L. (1987). *On dreams and death: A Jungian interpretation*. (E. X. Kennedy & V. Brooks, Trans.). Boston & London: Shambhala.

Watkins, M. M. (1976). *Waking dreams*. New York: Gordon and Breach.

Woods, R. L., & Greenhouse, H. B. (1974). *The new world of dreams.* New York: Macmillan Publishing Co.

GENERAL READING BOOKS AND ARTICLES— MEDITATION AND MISCELLANEOUS

Benson, H. (1976). *The relaxation response.* New York: Avon.

Chang, G. C. C. (1977). *Teachings of Tibetan yoga.* Secaucus, NJ: Citadell Press.

Chopra, D. (1989). *Quantum healing.* New York: Bantam.

Denniston, D. (1986). *The TM book: How to enjoy the rest of your life.* Fairfield, IA: Fairfield Press.

Eliade, M. (1962). *The two and the one.* (J. M. Cohen, Trans.). Chicago: University of Chicago Press.

Evans-Wentz, W. Y. (1958). *Tibetan yoga and secret doctrines.* New York: Oxford University Press.

Evans-Wentz, W. Y. (1960). *The Tibetan book of the dead.* New York: Oxford University Press.

Gelman, D., & Hager, M. (1988). Body and soul. *Newsweek,* 88–97.

Goldberg, P. (1976). *The TM program: The way to fulfillment.* New York: Holt, Rinehart & Winston.

Goleman, D. (1988). *The meditative mind.* Los Angeles: Jeremy P. Tarcher.

Jahn, R. G., Dunne, B. J. (1987). *Margins of reality.* New York: Harcourt Brace Jovanovich.

Levy, J. (1985). Right brain, left brain: Fact and fiction. *Psychology Today,* 38–44.

Locke, S., & Colligan, D. (1986). *The healer within.* New York: E. P. Dutton.

Lockhart, R. A. (1977). Cancer in myth and dreams: An exploration into the archetypal relation between dreams and disease. *Spring,* 1–26.

Maharishi Mahesh Yogi, (1969). *Maharishi Mahesh Yogi on the Bhagavad-Gita: A new translation and commentary, chapters 1–6.* Baltimore: Penguin.

Reps, P. (no date). *Zen flesh, Zen bones.* New York: Doubleday Anchor.

Roth, R. (1987). *Maharishi Mahesh Yogi's Transcendental Meditation.* New York: Donald Fine.

Sheik, A. A. (Ed.) (1984). *Imagination and healing.* Farmington, NY: Baywood.

Siegel, B. (1987). *Love, medicine, and miracles.* New York: Harper & Row.

Simonton, O. C., Matthews-Simonton, S., & Creighton, J. L. (1981). *Getting well again.* New York: Bantam Books.

Wilber, K. (1979). *No boundary: Eastern and Western approaches to personal growth.* Boston & London: New Science Library Shambhala.

Wilber, K. (1987). The spectrum model. In D. Anthony, B. Ecker, & K. Wilber (Eds.), *Spiritual choices*. New York: Paragon.

Yatri. (1988). *Unknown man*. New York: Simon & Schuster.

RESEARCH BIBLIOGRAPHY

Achterberg, J. (1984). Imagery and medicine: Psychophysiological speculations. *Journal of Mental Imagery, 8,* 1–14.

Albert, I. B., & McNeece. (1974). The reported sleep characteristics of meditators and nonmeditators. *Bulletin of the Psychonomic Society, 3,* 73–74.

Alexander, C. N. (1987). Dream lucidity and dream witnessing: A developmental model based on the practice of Transcendental Meditation. *Lucidity Letter, 6*(2), 113–124.

Alexander, C. N. (1988). A conceptual and phenomenological analysis of pure consciousness during sleep. *Lucidity Letter, 7*(2), 39–43.

Alexander, C. N., Boyer, R., & Alexander, V. (1987). Higher states of consciousness in the Vedic psychology of Maharishi Mahesh Yogi: A theoretical introduction and research review. *Modern Science and Vedic Science, 1*(1), 89–126.

Alexander, C. N., Boyer, R., & Orme-Johnson, D. (1985). Distinguishing between transcendental consciousness and lucidity. *Lucidity Letter, 4*(2), 68–85.

Alexander, C. N., Davies, J. L., Dixon, C. A., Dillbeck, M. C., Oetzel, R. M., Muehlman, J. M., & Orme-Johnson, D. W. (in press). Higher stages of consciousness beyond formal operations: The Vedic psychology of human development. In C. N. Alexander & E. J. Langer (Eds.), *Higher stages of human development: Adult growth beyond formal operations*. New York: Oxford University Press.

Antrobus, J. (1987). Cortical hemisphere asymmetry and sleep mentation. *Psychological Review, 94*(3), 359–368.

Armitage, R., Hoffmann, R., Loewy, D., & Moffitt, A. (1988). Interhemispheric EEG during REM and NREM sleep. *Sleep Research, 17.*

Armitage, R., Hoffmann, R., & Moffitt, A. (1987). The continuity of rhythmic EEG synchronicity across sleep and wakefulness. *Sleep Research, 16,* 5.

Armitage, R., Hoffmann, R., & Moffitt, A. (in press). Interhemispheric EEG activity in sleep and wakefulness: Individual differences in the basic rest-activity cycle (BRAC). In J. Antrobus (Ed.), *The mind in sleep* (Vol. 2.).

Armitage, R., Stelmack, R., Miles, J., Robertson, A., & Campbell, K. (1988). Asymmetrical auditory-evoked potentials during sleep. *Sleep Research, 17.*

Armstrong-Hickey, D. (1988). A validation of lucid dreaming in school-age children. *Lucidity Letter, 7*(2), 35–38.

Aserinsky, E., & Kleitman, N. (1953). Regularly occurring periods of eye motility and concomitant phenomena, during sleep. *Science, 118,* 273–274.

Bagby, R. M., Taylor, G. J., & Ryan, D. (1986). Toronto alexithymia scale: Relationship with personality and psychopathology measures. *Psychotherapy and Psychosomatics, 45,* 207–215.

Banquet, J. P. (1972). EEG and meditation. *Electroencephalography and Clinical Neurophysiology, 33,* 454.

Banquet, J. P. (1983). Inter- and intra-hemispheric relationships of the EEG activity during sleep in man. *Electroencephalography and Clinical Neurophysiology, 55,* 51–59.

Banquet, J. P., & Sailhan, M. (1976). Quantified EEG spectral analysis of sleep and Transcendental Meditation. In D. W. Orme-Johnson & J. T. Farrow (Eds.), *Scientific research on the Transcendental Meditation program: Collected papers* (Vol. 1, pp. 182–186). Rheinweiler, West Germany: MERU Press.

Banquet, J. P., Sailhan, M., Carette, F., Hazout, S., & Lucien, M. (1976). EEG analysis of spontaneous and induced states of consciousness. In D. W. Orme-Johnson & J. T. Farrow (Eds.), *Scientific research on the Transcendental Meditation program: Collected papers* (Vol. 1, pp. 165–172). Rheinweiler, West Germany: MERU Press.

Barber. (1984). Changing "unchangeable" bodily process by (hypnotic) suggestions: A new look at hypnosis, cognitions, imagining, and the mind-body problem. In A. A. Sheikh (Ed.), *Imagination and healing* (pp. 69–120). Farmingdale, NY: Baywood.

Barcaro, U., Denoth, F., Murri, L., Navona, & Stefanini, A. (1986). Changes in the interhemispheric correlation during sleep in normal subjects. *Electroencephalography and Clinical Neurophysiology, 63,* 112–118.

Barrett, D. (1987). Flying dreams and lucidity: An empirical study of their relationship. *Lucidity Letter, 6*(2), 33–37.

Beaumont, J. G., Mayes, A. R., & Rugg, M. D. (1978). Asymmetry in EEG alpha coherence and power: Effects of task and sex. *Electroencephalography and Clinical Neurophysiology, 45,* 393–401.

Becker, M., & Herter, G. (1973). Effect of meditation upon SREM. *Sleep Research, 2,* 90.

Belicki, K. (1987). Recalling dreams: An examination of daily variation and individual differences. In J. I. Gackenbach (Ed.), *Sleep and dreams: A sourcebook* (pp. 187–206). New York: Garland.

Bersford, M., Jedrczak, A., Toomey, M., & Clements, G. (in press). EEG coherence, age-related psychological variables, and the Transcendental Meditation and TM-Sidhi program. In R. A. Chalmers, G. Clements, H. Schenkluhn & M. Weinless (Eds.), *Scientific research on the Transcendental Meditation and TM-Sidhi programme: Collected papers* (Vol. 3). Vlodrop, the Netherlands: MIU Press.

Blackmore, S. (1982). More sex differences in lucid dreaming frequency. *Lucidity Letter, 1*(2), 9.

Blackmore, S. (1988a). Lucid dreams and OBEs. *Lucidity Letter, 7*(1), 35–43.

Blackmore, S. (1988b). A theory of lucid dreams and OBEs. In J. I. Gackenbach and S. L. LaBerge (Eds.), *Conscious mind, sleeping brain: Perspectives on lucid dreaming.* New York: Plenum.

Block, M. (1989). Code Blue: New beginnings. *Lucidity Letter, 8*(1).

Bogzaran, Fariba (1987). The creative process: Paintings inspired from the lucid dream. *Lucidity Letter, 6*(2).

Boivin, D., Cote, J., Lapiene, G., & Montplaisir, J. (1987). Interhemispheric coherence during sleep before and after anterior callosotomy in human. *Sleep Research, 16,* 6.

Brown, D. P. (1987). The transformation of consciousness in meditation. *Institute of Noetic Sciences: Exceptional Abilities,* 1–45.

Brown, D. P. (1988). The transformation of consciousness in meditation. *Noetic Sciences Review, 6,* 15–16.

Brylowski, A. (1986). H-reflex in lucid dreams. *Lucidity Letter, 5*(1), 116–118.

Brylowski, A. (1987a). Dreaming (& waking) lucidity and healing, a proposal: Can lucid dreaming effect immunocompetence? *Lucidity Letter, 6*(1).

Brylowski, A. (1987b). Potential effects of lucid dreaming on immunocompetence. *Lucidity Letter, 6*(2).

Busby, K., & DeKoninck, J. (1980). Short-term effects of strategies for self-regulation on personality dimensions and dream content. *Perceptual and Motor Skills, 50,* 751–765.

Busk, J., & Galbraith, G. C. (1975). EEG correlates of visual-motor practice in man. *Electroencephalography Clinical Neurophysiology, 38,* 415–422.

Buss, A. H. (1980). *Self-consciousness and social anxiety.* San Francisco: Freeman.

Cartwright, R. (1986). Affect and dream work from an information-processing point of view. *Journal of Mind and Body: Special Issue: Cognition and Dream Research, 7*(2,3), 411–428.

Clerc, O. (1983). Natural induction of lucid dreams. *Lucidity Letter, 2*(1), 38.

Crick, F., & Mitchison, G. (1983). The function of dream sleep. *Nature,* *304,* 111–114.

Dane, J. (1983) *An empirical evaluation of two techniques for lucid dream induction.* Unpublished doctoral dissertation, Georgia State University.

Dane, J. P., Craig, E., & Schatzman, M. (1987). Ethical issues for applications of lucid dreaming. *Lucidity Letter,* 6(2).

Davidson, R. J., & Goleman, D. J. (1977). The role of attention in meditation and hypnosis: A psychobiological perspective on transformations of consciousness. *International Journal of Clinical and Experimental Hypnosis,* *25,* 291–308.

Derogatis, L. R. (1986). The psychosocial adjustment to illness scale (PAIS). *Journal of Psychosomatic Research,* *30*(1), 77–91.

Descartes, R. (1947). The difficulty of distinguishing between waking and sleeping. In R. L. Woods (Ed.), *The world of dreams: An anthology.* New York: Random House.

Dillbeck, M. C., & Bronson, E. C. (1981). Short-term longitudinal effects of the Transcendental Meditation technique on EEG power and coherence. *International Journal of Neuroscience,* *14,* 147–151.

Dillbeck, M. C., & Orme-Johnson, D. W. (1987). Physiological differences between Transcendental Meditation and rest. *American Psychologist,* 879–881.

Dillbeck, M. C., Orme-Johnson, D. W., & Wallace, R. K. (1981). Frontal EEG coherence, H-reflex recovery, concept learning, and the TM-Sidhi program. *International Journal of Neuroscience,* *15,* 151–157.

Dillbeck, M. C., & Vesely, S. A. (1986). Participation in the Transcendental Meditation program and frontal EEG coherence during concept learning. *International Journal of Neuroscience,* *29,* 45–55.

Dorian, B., & Garfienkle, P. E. (1987). Stress, immunity and illness—a review. *Psychological Medicine,* *17,* 393–407.

Dorus, E., Dorus, W., & Rechtschaffen, A. (1971). The incidence of novelty in dreams. *Archives of General Psychiatry,* *25,* 364–368.

Druckman, D., & Swets, J. A. (Eds.) (1988). *Enhancing human performance: Issues, theories, and techniques.* Washington, DC: National Academy Press.

Dubs, G. (1988). Trends in research. *The Common Boundary,* 6, 21–23.

Dumermuth, G., Lange, B., Lehmann, D., Meier, C. A., Dinkelmann, R., & Molinari, L. (1983). Spectral analysis of all-night sleep EEG in healthy adults. *European Neurology,* *22,* 322–339.

Dumermuth, G., & Lehmann, D. (1981). EEG power and coherence during non-REM and REM phases in humans in all-night sleep analyses. *European Neurology,* *20,* 429–434.

Faber, P. A., Saayman, G. S., & Touyz, S. W. (1978). Meditation and archetypal content of nocturnal dreams. *Journal of Analytical Psychology, 23,* 1–21.

Farrow, J. T., & Herbert, J. R. (1982). Breath suspension during the Transcendental Meditation technique. *Psychosomatic Medicine, 44*(2), 133–153.

Fellows, P. (1988). Working within the lucid dream. In J. I. Gackenbach and S. L. LaBerge (Eds.), *Conscious mind, sleeping brain: Perspectives on lucid dreaming.* New York: Plenum.

Fenigstein, A., Scheier, M. F., & Buss, A. H. (1975). Public and private self-consciousness: Assessment and theory. *Journal of Consulting and Clinical Psychology, 43*(4), 522–527.

Fenwick, P., Schatzman, M., Worsley A., Adams, J., Stone, S., & Baker, A. (1984). Lucid dreaming: Correspondence between dreamed and actual events in one subject during REM sleep. *Biological Psychology, 18,* 243–252.

Finke, R. (1980). Levels of equivalence in imagery and perception. *Psychological Review, 87*(2), 113–133.

Finke, R. (1986). Mental imagery and the visual system. *Scientific American, 254*(3), 88–95.

Flor-Henry, P. (1987). The influence of laterality in psychopathology. In M. Hamilton (Ed.) *Psychiatry in the 80's, 5,* 1–4.

Flor-Henry, P., & Koles, Z. J. (1982). EEG characteristics in normal subjects: A comparison of men and women and of dextrals and sinistrals. *Research Communications in Psychology, Psychiatry, and Behavior, 7,* 21–38.

Flor-Henry, P., Koles, Z. J., & Lind, J. (1987). Statistical EEG investigation of the endogenous psychoses: Power and coherence. In R. Takahashi, P. Flor-Henry, J. Gruzelier, and S. Niwa (Eds.), *Cerebral dynamics, laterality and psychopathology.* New York: Elsevier Science Publishers.

Flor-Henry, P., Koles, Z. J., & Reddon, J. R. (1987). Age and sex related EEG configurations in normal subjects. In A. Glass (Ed.), *Individual differences in hemispheric specialization.* New York: Plenum.

Ford, M. R., Goethe, J. W., & Dekker, D. K. (1986). EEG coherence and power in the discrimination of psychiatric disorders and medication effects. *Biological Psychiatry, 21,* 1175–1188.

Foulkes, D. (1982). *Children's dreams: Longitudinal studies.* New York: John Wiley & Sons.

Foulkes, D. (1985a). *Dreaming: A cognitive-psychological analysis.* Hillsdale, NJ: Lawrence Erlbaum Associates.

Foulkes, D. (1985b). Dreaming: Lucid and non. *Lucidity Letter, 4*(1), 118.

Freeman, W. J. (1983). The physiological basis of mental images. *Biological Psychiatry, 18,* 1107–1125.

French, C. C., & Beaumont, J. G. (1984). A critical review of EEG coherence studies of hemisphere function. *International Journal of Psychophysiology, 1,* 241–254.

Fuson, J. W. (1976). *The effect of the Transcendental Meditation program on sleeping and dreaming patterns.* Unpublished doctoral dissertation, Yale Medical School, New Haven, CT.

Gackenbach, J. I. (1978). *A personality and cognitive style analysis of lucid dreaming.* Unpublished doctoral dissertation, Virginia Commonwealth University.

Gackenbach, J. I. (1980). Lucid dreaming project. *A.R.E. Journal, 15,* 253–260.

Gackenbach, J. I. (1981a). Lucid dreaming: Individual differences in personal characteristics. *Sleep Research, 10,* 145.

Gackenbach, J. I. (1981b). Sex differences in lucid dreaming incidence. *Lucidity Letter, 1*(1), 2.

Gackenbach, J. I. (1985a). Eye movement direction and the lucid dreaming ability. *Lucidity Letter, 4*(1), 124.

Gackenbach, J. I. (1985b). Sex differences in lucid dreaming self-reported frequency: A second look. *Lucidity Letter, 4*(1), 127.

Gackenbach, J. I. (1985–86). A survey of considerations for inducing conscious awareness of dreaming while dreaming. *Imagination, Cognition, and Personality, 5,* 41–55.

Gackenbach, J. I. (Ed.) (1986). *Sleep and dreams: A sourcebook.* New York: Garland.

Gackenbach, J. I. (1987). Manifest content analysis of sleep-laboratory-collected lucid and nonlucid dreams. *Lucidity Letter, 6*(2).

Gackenbach, J. I. (1988a). From ordinary to lucid dreaming: Research and politics of dreaming in North America. *Lucidity Letter, 7*(1), 19–25.

Gackenbach, J. I. (1988b, July). *Is lucid dreaming naturally female?* Paper presented at a symposium, Women's Bodies, Women's Dreams, at the annual meeting of the Association for the Study of Dreams, Santa Cruz, CA.

Gackenbach, J. I. (1988c). Personality differences between individuals varying in lucid dreaming frequency. *Journal of Communication Therapy, 4,* 49–64.

Gackenbach, J. I. (1988d). The psychological content of lucid dreams. In J. I. Gackenbach and S. LaBerge (Eds.), *Conscious mind, sleeping brain: Perspectives on lucid dreaming.* New York: Plenum.

Gackenbach, J. I. (in press-a). A developmental model of consciousness in sleep. In J. I. Gackenbach and A. A. Sheikh (Eds.), *Dream images: A call to mental arms.* Farmington, NY: Baywood.

Gackenbach, J. I. (in press-b). Interhemispheric EEG coherence in REM sleep and meditation: The lucid dreaming connection. In J. Antrobus

(Ed.), *The mind in sleep (Vol. 2)*. Hillsdale, NJ: Lawrence Erlbaum Associates.

Gackenbach, J. I., Cranson, R., & Alexander, C. (1986). Lucid dreaming, witnessing dreaming, and the Transcendental Meditation technique: A developmental relationship. *Lucidity Letter, 5*(2), 34–40.

Gackenbach, J. I., Cranson, R., & Alexander, C. N. (1989). *Consciousness during sleep*. Unpublished manuscript.

Gackenbach, J. I., Curren, R., & Cutler, G. (1983). Presleep determinants and postsleep results of lucid versus vivid dreams. *Lucidity Letter, 2*(2), 52.

Gackenbach, J. I., Curren, R., LaBerge, S., Davidson, D., & Maxwell, P. (1983). Intelligence, creativity, and personality differences between individuals who vary in self-reported lucid dreaming frequency. *Lucidity Letter, 2*(2), 52.

Gackenbach, J. I., & Hammons, S. (1984). Lucid dreaming ability and verbal creativity. *Dreamworks, 3*(3), 219–223.

Gackenbach, J. I., Heilman, N., Boyt, S., & LaBerge, S. (1985). The relationship between field independence and lucid dreaming ability. *Journal of Mental Imagery, 9*(1), 9–20.

Gackenbach, J. I., & Hunt, H. (in press). Lucid dreaming as a transpersonal (meditational) state: A potential distinction from dream-work methods. *Journal of Mental Imagery*.

Gackenbach, J. I., & LaBerge, S. P. (1986). An overview of lucid dreaming. In A. A. Sheikh (Ed.), *International review of mental imagery* (pp. 57–89). New York: Human Sciences Press.

Gackenbach, J. I., & Moorecroft, W. (1987). Psychological content of "consciousness" during sleep in a TM subject. *Lucidity Letter, 6*(1), 29–36.

Gackenbach, J. I., Moorecroft, W., Alexander, C. N., & LaBerge, S. (1987). Physiological correlates of "consciousness" during sleep in a single TM practitioner. *Sleep Research, 16*, 230.

Gackenbach, J. I., & Schillig, B. (1983). Lucid dreams: The content of conscious awareness of dreaming during the dream. *Journal of Mental Imagery, 7*(2), 1–14.

Gackenbach, J. I., Snyder, T. J., McKelvey, K., McWilliams, C., George, R., & Rodenelli, B. (1981). Lucid dreaming: Individual differences in perception. *Sleep Research, 10*, 146.

Gackenbach, J. I., Snyder, T. J., Rokes, L., & Sachau, D. (1986). Lucid dreaming frequency in relationship to vestibular sensitivity as measured by caloric stimulation. In R. Haskel (Ed.), *Cognition and Dream Research: The Journal of Mind and Behavior* (special issue), *7*(2, 3), 277–298.

Gackenbach, J. I., & Tart, C. (1988). A discussion between Charles Tart and *Lucidity Letter* Editor, Jayne Gackenbach, examining similarities between dream lucidity, witnessing, and self-remembering. *Lucidity Letter*, 7(2), 59–66.

Gackenbach, J. I., Walling, J., & LaBerge, S. (1984). The lucid dreaming ability and parasympathetic functioning. *Lucidity Letter*, 3(4), 101.

Garfield, P. (1988a). Clinical applications of lucid dreaming: Introductory comments. In J. I. Gackenbach and S. LaBerge (Eds.), *Conscious mind, sleeping brain: Perspectives on lucid dreaming*. New York: Plenum.

Garfield, P. (1988b). Creative lucid dreams. In J. I. Gackenbach and S. LaBerge (Eds.), *Conscious mind, sleeping brain: Perspectives on lucid dreaming*. New York: Plenum.

Gillespie, G. (1985a). Can we distinguish between lucid dreams and dreaming-awareness dreams? *Lucidity Letter*, 3(2, 3), 95–96.

Gillespie, G. (1985b). Comments on "Dream lucidity and near-death experience—A personal report." *Lucidity Letter*, 4(2), 21–23.

Gillespie, G. (1985c). Lucid dreaming and mysticism: A personal observation. *Lucidity Letter*, 2(3), 64.

Gillespie, G. (1985d). Memory and reason in lucid dreams: A personal observation. *Lucidity Letter*, 2(4), 76–78.

Gillespie, G. (1985e). The phenomenon of light in lucid dreams: Personal observations. *Lucidity Letter*, 3(4), 99–100.

Gillespie, G. (1985f). Problems related to experimentation while dreaming lucidly. *Lucidity Letter*, 3(2, 3), 87–88.

Gillespie, G. (1985g). Statistical description of my lucid dreams. *Lucidity Letter*, 3(4), 104–111.

Gillespie, G. (1986). Ordinary dreams, lucid dreams and mystical experiences. *Lucidity Letter*, 5(1), 27–30.

Gillespie, G. (1987a). Distinguishing between phenomenon and interpretation: When does lucid dreaming become transpersonal experience? *Lucidity Letter*, 6(2), 125–130.

Gillespie, G. (1987b). Dream light: Categories of visual experience during lucid dreaming. *Lucidity Letter*, 6(1), 73–79.

Gillespie, G. (1988a). Lucid dreams in Tibetan Buddhism. In J. I. Gackenbach and S. LaBerge (Eds.), *Conscious mind, sleeping brain: Perspectives on lucid dreaming*. New York: Plenum.

Gillespie, G. (1988b). When does lucid dreaming become transpersonal experience? *Psychiatry Journal of the University of Ottawa*, 13, 107–110.

Gillespie, G. (1988c). Without a guru: An account of my lucid dreaming. In J. I. Gackenbach and S. LaBerge (Eds.), *Conscious mind, sleeping brain: Perspectives on lucid dreaming*. New York: Plenum.

Goldstein, L., Staltzfus, N., & Gardocki, J. (1972). Changes in interhemispheric amplitude relations in EEG during sleep. *Physiological Behavior, 8,* 811–815.

Gottschalk, L. A., Stone, W. N., Gleser, G. C., & Iacono, J. M. (1966). Anxiety levels in dreams: Relation to changes in plasma-free fatty acids. *Science, 153,* 654–657.

Gray, K. (1988). From the beginning through feast or famine. *Lucidity Letter, 7*(2), 97–100.

Greer, S. (1983). Cancer and the mind. *British Journal of Psychiatry, 143,* 535–543.

Grinberg-Zylberbaum, J., & Ramos, J. (1987). Patterns of interhemispheric correlation during human communication. *International Journal of Neuroscience, 36,* 41–53.

Grindel, O. M. (1985). Intercentral relations in the cerebral cortex revealed by EEG coherence during recovery of consciousness and speech after protracted coma. *Zhurnal Vysshei Nervnoi Deyatel'nosti. 35*(1), 60–67. (References in *Psychological Abstracts*)

Hall, C. S., Domhoff, G. W., Blick, K., & Weesner, K. E. (1982). The dreams of college men and women in 1950 and 1980: A comparison of dream contents and sex differences. *Sleep, 5,* 188–194.

Hall, C. S., & Van de Castle, R. L. (1966). *The content analysis of dreams.* New York: Appleton-Century-Crofts.

Hall, N. R. (1984). Cancer and imagery. In A. A. Sheikh (Ed.), *Imagination and healing.* Farmington, NY: Baywood.

Halliday, G. (1988). Lucid dreaming: Using nightmares and sleep-wake confusion. In J. I. Gackenbach and S. LaBerge (Eds.), *Conscious mind, sleeping brain: Perspectives on lucid dreaming.* New York: Plenum.

Haraldsson, Enlendur (1982). Near-death, out-of-body and lucid experiences: Additional comments. *Lucidity Letter, 1*(3), 18.

Haskell, R. E. (1985a). Dreaming, cognition, and physical illness: Part I. *Journal of Medical Humanities and Bioethics, 6,* 46–56.

Haskell, R. E. (1985b). Dreaming, cognition, and physical illness: Part II. *Journal of Medical Humanities and Bioethics, 6,* 109–122.

Haynes, C. T., Hebert, J. R., Reber, W., & Orme-Johnson, D. W. (1977). The psychophysiology of advanced participants in the Transcendental Meditation program: Correlations of EEG coherence, creativity, H-reflex recovery, and experience of transcendental consciousness. In D. W. Orme-Johnson & J. T. Farrow (Eds.), *Scientific research on the Transcendental Meditation program: Collected papers* (Vol. 1, pp. 208–212). Rheinweiler, West Germany: MERU Press.

Hearne, K. M. T. (1978). *Lucid dreams: An electrophysiological and psychological study.* Unpublished doctoral dissertation, University of Liverpool.

Hearne, K. M. T. (1982). Keith Hearne's work on lucid dreaming. *Lucidity Letter, 1*(3), 15–17.

Hewitt, D. E. (1988). Induction of ecstatic lucid dreams. *Lucidity Letter, 7*(1), 64–66.

Hobson, J. A., & McCarley, R. W. (1977). The brain as a dream state generator: An activation-synthesis hypothesis of the dream process. *American Journal of Psychiatry, 134,* 1335–1348.

Holmes, D. (1984). Meditation and somatic arousal reduction: A review of experimental evidence. *American Psychologist, 39*(1), 1–10.

Hunt, H. T. (1982). Forms of dreaming. *Perceptual and Motor Skills, 54,* 559–633.

Hunt, H. T. (1984). A cognitive psychology of mystical and altered-state experience. *Perceptual and Motor Skills, 58,* 467–513.

Hunt, H. T. (1985). Dream lucidity and near-death experience: A lucidity-meditation analysis. *Lucidity Letter, 4*(2), 17–20.

Hunt, H. T. (1986). Toward a cognitive psychology of dreams. In J. I. Gackenbach (Ed.), *Sleep and dreams: A sourcebook.* New York: Garland.

Hunt, H. T. (1987). Lucidity as a meditative state. *Lucidity Letter, 6*(2), 105–112.

Hunt, H. T. (1988). The multiplicity of dreams. *Lucidity Letter, 7*(2), 5–14.

Hunt, H. T. (1989). *The multiplicity of dreams: A cognitive psychological perspective.* New Haven, CT: Yale University Press.

Hunt, H. T., & McLeod, B. (in press). Lucid dreaming as a meditative state: Some evidence from long-term meditators in relation to the cognitive-psychological bases of transpersonal phenomena. In J. I. Gackenbach & A. A. Sheikh (Eds.), *Dream images: A call to mental arms.* New York: Baywood.

Hunt, H. T., & Ogilvie, R. (1988). Lucid dreams in their natural series: Phenomenological and psychophysiological findings in relation to meditative states. In J. I. Gackenbach and S. L. LaBerge (Eds.), *Conscious mind, sleeping brain: Perspectives on lucid dreaming.* New York: Plenum.

Irwin, H. J. (1988). Out-of-body experiences and dream lucidity: Empirical perspectives. In J. I. Gackenbach and S. LaBerge (Eds.), *Conscious mind, sleeping brain: Perspectives on lucid dreaming.* New York: Plenum.

Jahn, R. G., & Dunne, B. J. (1987). *Margins of reality: The role of consciousness in the physical world.* New York: Harcourt Brace Jovanovich.

Jedrczak, A. (1984). The Transcendental Meditation and TM-Sidhi programme and field independence. *Perceptual and Motor Skills.*

Kelzer, K. (1988). East meets West, Buddhism meets Christianity: The lucid dream as a path for union. *Lucidity Letter, 7*(2), 22–27.

Kesterson, J. (1985). *Respiratory control during Transcendental Meditation*. Doctoral dissertation, Department of Neuroscience of Human Consciousness, Maharishi International University, Fairfield, IA.

Klippstein, H. (1988). Hypnotherapy: A natural method of learning lucid dreaming. *Lucidity Letter, 7*(2), 79–88.

Koles, Z. J., & Flor-Henry, P. (1986). *EEG correlates of male-female differences in verbally and spatially based cognitive tasks*. Abstract for the 12th C.M.B.E.C./1st Pan Pacific Symposium, Vancouver, Canada.

Koles, Z. J., & Flor-Henry, P. (1987). The effect of brain function on coherence patterns in the bipolar EEG. *International Journal of Psychophysiology, 5*, 63–71.

Kruck, J. S., & Sheikh, A. A. (1986). Alexithymia: A critical review. *International Review of Mental Imagery* (Vol. 2). New York: Human Sciences Press.

LaBerge, S. (1980). *Lucid dreaming: An exploratory study of consciousness during sleep*. Unpublished doctoral dissertation, Stanford University, Stanford, CA.

LaBerge, S. (1986). Healing through lucid dreaming. *Lucidity Letter, 5*(2).

LaBerge, S. (1987a). Induction of lucid dreaming by luminous stimulation. *Lucidity Letter, 6*(2).

LaBerge, S. (1987b). Varieties of experience from light-induced lucid dreams. *Lucidity Letter, 6*(2).

LaBerge, S. (1988a). Induction of lucid dreams including the use of the dreamlight. *Lucidity Letter, 7*(2), 15–21.

LaBerge, S. (1988b). Lucid dreaming in western literature. In J. I. Gackenbach and S. LaBerge (Eds.), *Conscious mind, sleeping brain: Perspectives on lucid dreaming*. New York: Plenum.

LaBerge, S. (1988c). The psychophysiology of lucid dreaming. In J. I. Gackenbach and S. LaBerge (Eds.), *Conscious mind, sleeping brain: Perspectives on lucid dreaming*. New York: Plenum.

LaBerge, S., & Brylowski, A. (1987). EEG and other physiological findings. *Lucidity Letter, 6*(2).

LaBerge, S., & Dement, W. (1982). Voluntary control of respiration during REM sleep. *Sleep Research, 11*, 107.

LaBerge, S., & Gackenbach, J. I. (1986). Lucid dreaming. In B. B. Wolman & M. Ullman (Eds.), *Handbook of altered states of consciousness* (pp. 159–198). New York: Van Nostrand Reinhold.

LaBerge, S., Greenleaf, W., & Kediskerski, B. (1983). Physiological responses to dreamed sexual activity during lucid REM sleep. *Psychophysiology, 20*, 454–455.

LaBerge, S., Levitan, L., & Dement, W. (1986). Lucid dreaming: Physiological correlates of consciousness during REM sleep. *Journal of Mind and Behavior, 7*, 251–258.

LaBerge, S., Nagel, L., Dement, W., & Zarcone, V. (1981). Lucid dreaming verified by volitional communication during REM sleep. *Perceptual and Motor Skills, 52,* 727–732.

Levine, P. H. (1976). The coherence spectral array (COSPAR) and its application to the study of spatial ordering in the EEG. In J. I. Martin (Ed.), *Proceedings of the San Diego Biomedical Symposium,* Vol. 15. New York: Academic Press.

Levine, P. H., Herbert, R., Haynes, C. T., & Strobel, U. (1977). EEG coherence during the Transcendental Meditation technique. In D. W. Orme-Johnson & J. T. Farrow (Eds.), *Scientific research on the Transcendental Meditation program: Collected papers* (Vol. 1). Rheinweiler, West Germany: MERU Press.

Levitan, H. (1976–77). The significance of certain catastrophic dreams. *Psychotherapy and Psychosomatics, 27,* 1–7.

Levitan, H. (1980). Traumatic events in the dreams of psychosomatic patients. *Psychotherapy and Psychosomatics, 33,* 226–232.

Livanov, M. N., Gavrilova, N. A., & Aslanov, A. S. (1974). Intercorrelations between different cortical regions of human brain during mental activity. *Neuropsychologica, 2,* 281–289.

Magallon, L. L. (1987). Awake in the dark: Imageless lucid dreaming. *Lucidity Letter, 6*(1), 86–90.

Malamud, J. R. (1979). *The development of a training method for the cultivation of "lucid" awareness in fantasy, dreams, and waking life.* Unpublished dissertation available from University Microfilms International, Ann Arbor, MI.

Malamud, J. R. (1988). Learning to become fully lucid: A program for inner growth. In J. I. Gackenbach and S. LaBerge (Eds.), *Conscious mind, sleeping brain: Perspectives on lucid dreaming.* New York: Plenum.

Manseau, C., & Broughton, R. (1984). Bilaterally synchronous ultradian EEG rhythms in awake adult humans. *Psychophysiology, 21,* 265–273.

Marcot, B. G. (1987). A journal of attempts to induce and work with lucid dreams: Can you kill yourself while lucid? *Lucidity Letter, 6*(1).

Martin, J. B., Pihl, R. O., Young, S. N., Ervin, F. R., & Tourjman, S. V. (1986). Prediction of alexithymic characteristics from physiological, personality, and subjective measures. *Psychotherapy and Psychosomatics, 45,* 133–140.

Miskiman, D. E. (1972). The effect of the Transcendental Meditation program on compensatory paradoxical sleep. In D. W. Orme-Johnson & J. T. Farrow (Eds.), *Scientific research on the Transcendental Meditation program: Collected papers* (Vol. 1). Rheinweiler, West Germany: MERU Press.

Mitchell, G. P., & Lundy, R. M. (1986). The effects of relaxation and imagery inductions on responses to suggestions. *International Journal of Clinical & Experimental Hypnosis, 34*(2), 98–109.

Moffitt, A., & Hoffman, R. On the single-mindedness and isolation of dream psychophysiology. In J. I. Gackenbach (Ed.), *Sleep and dreams: A sourcebook* (pp. 145–176). New York: Garland.

Moffitt, A., Purcell, S., Hoffman, R., Pigeau, R., & Wells, R. (1986). Dream psychology: Operating in the dark. *Lucidity Letter, 5*(1), 180–196. (A version of this paper also appears in Gackenbach, J. I., & LaBerge, S. (Eds.), *Conscious mind, sleeping brain,* 1988.)

Mullen, B., & Suls, J. (1982). "Know thyself": Stressful life events and the ameliorative effects of private self-consciousness. *Journal of Experimental Social Psychology, 18,* 43–55.

Murphy, M., & Donovan, S. (1983). A bibliography of meditation theory and research: 1931–1983. *The Journal of Transpersonal Psychology, 15,* 181–228.

Murphy, M., & Donovan, S. (1988). *The physical and psychological effects of meditation.* San Rafael, CA: Esalen Institute.

Neilsen, T. (1986). Kinesthetic imagery as a duality of lucid awareness: Descriptive and experimental case studies. *Lucidity Letter, 5*(1), 147–159.

O'Connor, K. P., & Shaw, J. C. (1978). Field dependence, laterality and the EEG. *Biological Psychology, 6,* 93–109.

O'Connor, K. P., & Shaw, J. C. (1982). Comment on Zoccolotti's "Field dependence, laterality and the EEG: A reanalysis of O'Connor and Shaw." *Biological Psychology, 15,* 209–213.

Ogilvie, R. D. (1982). Is dream lucidity work another Reich's orgone box. *Lucidity Letter, 1*(2), 6.

Ogilvie, R. D., Hunt, H. T., Sawicki, C., & McGowan, K. (1978). Searching for lucid dreams. *Sleep Research, 7,* 165.

Ogilvie, R. D., Hunt, H. T., Tyson, P. D., Lucescu, M. L., & Jenkins, D. B. (1982). Lucid dreaming and alpha activity: A preliminary report. *Perceptual and Motor Skills, 55,* 795–808.

Ogilvie, R. D., Vieira, K. P., & Small, R. J. (1988). EEG activity during signaled lucid dreams. *Lucidity Letter, 7,*(1), 57–58.

Orme-Johnson, D. W. (1987). Maharishi's program to create world peace: Theory and research. *Modern Science and Vedic Science, 1,* 207–265.

Orme-Johnson, D. W., Clements, G., Haynes, C. T., & Badaoui, K. (1977). Higher states of consciousness: EEG coherence, creativity and experience of the Sidhis. In D. W. Orme-Johnson & J. T. Farrow (Eds.), *Scientific research on the Transcendental Meditation program: Collected papers* (Vol. 1). Rheinweiler, West Germany: MERU Press.

Orme-Johnson, D. W., Dillbeck, M. C., Wallace, R. K., & Landrith, G. S. (1982). Intersubject EEG coherence: Is consciousness a field? *International Journal of Neuroscience, 16,* 203–209.

Orme-Johnson, D. W., & Granieri, B. (1977). The effects of the Age of Enlightenment Governor Training Courses on field independence, creativity, intelligence, and behavioral flexibility. In D. W. Orme-Johnson & J. T. Farrow (Eds.), *Scientific research on the Transcendental Meditation program: Collected papers* (Vol. 1). Rheinweiler, West Germany: MERU Press.

Orme-Johnson, D. W., & Haynes, C. T. (1981). EEG phase coherence, pure consciousness, creativity, and TM-Sidhi experiences. *Neuroscience, 13,* 211–217.

Orme-Johnson, D. W., Wallace, R. K., Dillbeck, M., Alexander, C. N., & Ball, O. E. (in press). The functional organization of the brain and the Maharishi technology of the unified field as indicated by changes in EEG coherence and its cognitive correlates: A proposed model of higher states of consciousness. In R. Chalmers, G. Clements, H. Schenkluhn, & M. Weinless (Eds.), *Scientific research on the Transcendental Meditation and TM-Sidhi programme: Collected papers* (Vol. 4). Vlodrop, the Netherlands: MIU Press.

Pagano & Weanenberg (1983). Meditation in search of a unique effect. In Davidson, Scheat, & Shipiro (Eds.), *Consciousness and self regulation: Advances.*

Pivik, R. T. (1978). Tonic states and phasic events in relation to sleep mentation. In A. M. Arkin, J. S. Antrobus, & S. J. Ellman (Eds.), *The mind in sleep: Psychology and psychophysiology.* Hillsdale, NJ: Erlbaum.

Posner, M. I., & Friedrich, F. J. (1986). Attention and the control of cognition. In S. L. Friedman, K. L. Klivington, & R. W. Peterson (Eds.), *The brain, cognition, and education.* New York: Academic Press.

Possey, L. The rediscovery of the mind. *Advances, 5,* 70–73.

Price, R. (1987). Dream content within the partially lucid REM period: A single-subject content analysis. *Lucidity Letter, 6*(2).

Price, R., & Cohen, D. (1988). Lucid dream induction: An empirical evaluation. In J. I. Gackenbach and S. LaBerge (Eds.), *Conscious mind, sleeping brain: Perspectives on lucid dreaming.* New York: Plenum.

Prichep, L. S. (1987). Neurometric quantitative EEG features of depressive disorders. In R. Takahashi, P. Flor-Henry, J. Gruzelier & S. Niwa (Eds.), *Cerebral dynamics, laterality and psychopathology* (pp. 55–69). New York: Elsevier Science Publishers.

Qualls, P. J. (1982–83). The physiological measurement of imagery: An overview. *Imagination, Cognition, and Personality, 2,* 89–101.

Rechtschaffen, A. (1978). The single-mindedness and isolation of dreams. *Sleep, 1,* 97–109.

Reed, H. (1977). Meditation and lucid dreaming: A statistical relationship. *Sundance Community Dream Journal, 2,* 237–238.

Reed, H. (1978). Improved dream recall associated with meditation. *Journal of Clinical Psychology, 34,* 150–156.

Rogo, D. S. (1985). Out-of-body experiences as lucid dreams: A critique. *Lucidity Letter, 4*(2), 43–46.

Schatzman, M., Worsley, A., & Fenwick, P. (1988). Correspondence during lucid dreams between dreamed and actual events. In J. I. Gackenbach and S. LaBerge (Eds.), *Conscious mind, sleeping brain: Perspectives on lucid dreaming.* New York: Plenum.

Schneider, D. (1973). Conversion of massive anxiety into a heart attack. *American Journal of Psychotherapy, 27,* 360–378.

Shapiro, D. H. (1982). Overview: Clinical and physiological comparison of meditation with other self-control strategies. *American Journal of Psychiatry, 139,* 267–274.

Sheikh, A. A. (Ed.) (1983). *Imagery: Current theory, research, and application.* New York: John Wiley & Sons.

Sheikh, A. A., Richardson, A., & Moleski, L. M. (1979). Psychosomatics and mental imagery: A brief review. In A. A. Sheikh & J. T. Shaffer (Eds.), *The potential of fantasy and imagination.* New York: Brandon House.

Shopenhauer, A. (1947). Dream versus reality. In R. L. Woods (Ed.), *The world of dream: An anthology.* New York: Random House.

Silverman, S. (1985). Psychoanalytic observations on vulnerability to physical disease. *Journal of the American Academy of Psychoanalysis, 13,* 295–315.

Smith, R. (in press). The meaning of dreams: A current warning theory. In J. I. Gackenbach & A. A. Sheikh (Eds.), *Dream images: A call to mental arms.* Farmington, New York: Baywood.

Snyder, T. J., & Gackenbach, J. I. (1981). Lucid dreaming and cerebral organization. *Sleep Research, 10,* 154.

Snyder, T. J., & Gackenbach, J. I. (1988). Individual differences associated with lucid dreaming. In J. I. Gackenbach and S. LaBerge (Eds.), *Conscious mind, sleeping brain: Perspectives on lucid dreaming.* New York; Plenum.

Snyder, T. J., & Gackenbach, J. I. (in press). Vestibular contributions to the neurocognition of lucid dreaming. In J. I. Gackenbach & A. A. Sheikh (Eds.), *Dream images: A call to mental arms.* Farmington, NY: Baywood.

Sparrow, G. S. (1976). Effects of meditation on dreams. *Sundance Community Dream Journal. 1*(1), 48–49.

Sparrow, G. S. (1983). An exploration into the inducibility of greater reflectiveness and "lucidity" in nocturnal dream reports. *Lucidity Letter*, 2(4), 75.

Sparrow, G. S. (1988). Letter from Scott Sparrow. *Lucidity Letter*, 7(1), 6–9.

Stoffregen, T. A., & Riccio, G. E. (1988). An ecological theory of orientation and the vestibular system. *Psychological Review*, 95, 3–14.

Stuss, D. T., & Benson, D. F. (1986). *The frontal lobes*. New York: Raven Press.

Suinn, R. M. (1983). Imagery and sports. In A. A. Sheikh (Ed.), *Imagery: Current theory, research, and application*. New York: John Wiley & Sons.

Suls, J., & Fletcher, B. (1985). Self-attention, life stress, and illness: A prospective study. *Psychosomatic Medicine*, 47(5), 469–481.

Sun, F., et al. (1984). An analysis of EEG power spectrum and coherence during quiet state in qigong. *Acta Psychologica Sinica*, 16(4), 422–427.

Takigawa, M. (1987). Directed coherence and EEG prints in schizophrenia. In R. Takahashi, P. Flor-Henry, J. Gruzelier & S. Niwa (Eds.), *Cerebral dynamics, laterality and psychopathology*. New York: Elsevier Science Publishers.

Taneli, B., & Krahne, W. (1987). EEG changes of Transcendental Meditation practitioners. *Advances in Biological Psychiatry*, 16, 41–71.

Tart, C. T. (1979). From spontaneous event to lucidity: A review of attempts to consciously control nocturnal dreaming. In B. B. Wolman (Ed.), *Handbook of dreams: Research, theories, and applications* (pp. 226–268). New York: Van Nostrand Reinhold. (Also in *Conscious mind, sleeping brain*, New York: Plenum.)

Tart, C. T. (1984). Terminology in lucid dream research. *Lucidity Letter*, 3(1), 82.

Tart, C. T. (1987). The world simulation process in waking and dreaming: A systems analysis of structure. *Journal of Mental Imagery*, 11, 145–158.

Thatcher, R. W., Krause, P. J., & Hrybyk, M. (1986). Cortico-cortical associations and EEG coherence: A two-compartmental model. *Electroencephalography and Clinical Neurophysiology*, 64, 123–143.

Tholey, P. (1983a). Cognitive abilities of dream figures in lucid dreams. *Lucidity Letter*, 2(4), 71.

Tholey, P. (1983b). Techniques for inducing and manipulating lucid dreams. *Perceptual and Motor Skills*, 57, 79–90.

Tholey, P. (1988). Psychotherapeutic application of lucid dreaming. In J. I. Gackenbach & S. LaBerge (Eds.). *Conscious mind, sleeping brain: Perspectives on lucid dreaming*. New York: Plenum.

Wallace, R. K. (1976). The physiological effects of Transcendental Meditation: A proposed fourth major state of consciousness. *Scientific research on the Transcendental Meditation program: Collected papers* (Vol. 1). Rheinweiler, West Germany: MERU Press.

Wallace, R. K. (1986). *The Maharishi technology of the unified field: The neurophysiology of enlightenment*. Fairfield, IA: Maharishi International University Press.

Wallace, R. K., & Benson, H. (1976). The physiology of meditation. In D. W. Orme-Johnson & J. T. Farrow (Eds.), *Scientific research on the Transcendental Meditation program: Collected papers* (Vol. 1). Rheinweiler, West Germany: MERU Press.

Wallace, R. K., Fagan, J. B., & Pasco, D. S. (1988). Vedic psychology. *Modern Science and Vedic Science, 2,* 3–59.

Walters, M., & Dentan, R. (1985). Are lucid dreams universal? Two unequivocal cases of lucid dreaming among Han Chinese university students in Beijing, 1985. *Lucidity Letter, 4*(1), 128.

Warnes, H., & Finkelstein, A. (1971). Dreams that precede a psychosomatic illness. *Canadian Psychiatric Association Journal, 16,* 317–325.

Wescott, M. (1977). Hemispheric symmetry of the EEG during the Transcendental Meditation technique. In D. W. Orme-Johnson & J. T. Farrow (Eds.), *Scientific research on the Transcendental Meditation program: Collected papers* (Vol. 1). Rheinweiler, West Germany: MERU Press.

West, M. A. (1980). Meditation and the EEG. *Psychological Medicine, 10,* 369–375.

West, M. A. (1982). Meditation and self-awareness: Physiological and phenomenological approaches. In G. Underwood (Ed.), *Aspects of consciousness: Vol. 3: Awareness and self-awareness*. New York: Academic Press.

Witkin, H. A., Dyk, R. B., Faterson, H. F., Goodenough, D. R., & Darp, S. (1974). *Psychological differentiation: Studies of development*. New York: John Wiley & Sons.

Witkin, H. A., Lewis, H. B., Hertzman, M., Machover, K., Meissner, P. B., & Wapner, S. (1954). *Personality through perception*. New York: Harper & Brothers.

Wolf, F. A. (1984). *Star wave*. New York: Macmillan.

Wolf, F. A. (1987a). Interview with physicist Fred Alan Wolf on the physics of lucid dreaming. *Lucidity Letter, 6*(1).

Wolf, F. A. (1987b). The physics of dream consciousness: Is the lucid dream a parallel universe? *Lucidity Letter, 6*(2).

Wolman, B. B., & Ullman, M. (Eds.) (1986). *Handbook of states of consciousness*. New York: Van Nostrand Reinhold.

Wolman, B. B., Ullman, M., & Webb, W. B. (Eds.) (1979). *Handbook of dreams: Research, theories and applications.* New York: Van Nostrand Reinhold Company.

Worsley, A. (1982). Alan Worsley's work on lucid dreaming. *Lucidity Letter, 1*(4), 21–22.

Worsley, A. (1983). Objective vs. subjective approaches to investigating dream lucidity: A case for the subjective. *Lucidity Letter, 2*(2), 55.

Worsley, A. (1988a). Lucid dreaming: Ethical issues. *Lucidity Letter, 7*(1), 4–5.

Worsley, A. (1988b). Personal experiences in lucid dreaming. In J. I. Gackenbach and S. LaBerge (Eds.), *Conscious mind, sleeping brain: Perspectives on lucid dreaming.* New York: Plenum.

Wren-Lewis, J. (1985). Dream lucidity and near-death experience: A personal report. *Lucidity Letter, 4*(2), 4–11.

Yates, J. (1985). The content of awareness is a model of the world. *Psychological Review, 92,* 249–284.

Ziegler, A. (1962). A cardiac infarction and a dream as synchronous events. *Journal of Analytic Psychology, 7,* 141–148.

Zoccolotti, P. (1982). Field dependence, laterality and the EEG: A reanalysis of O'Connor and Shaw (1978). *Biological Psychology, 15,* 203–207.

Index

Notes

P7, 15,